ADVANCE PRAISE FOR *MANAGING MICROAGGRESSIONS*

"In this fantastic resource, Dr. Williams provides clear examples of how to identify, prevent, and respond to microagressions in therapy (and daily life). Managing Microaggressions: Addressing Everyday Racism in Therapeutic Spaces will be required reading for all therapist trainees I supervise, and I believe that clinicians at any career stage will benefit from Dr. Williams' wisdom."

—**CJ Seitz-Brown**, PhD, Assistant Clinical Professor,
University of Maryland, College Park

"This book is an important reference for instructors, clinicians, and researchers regarding microaggressions, and brings needed clarity to common misconceptions on the topic. Dr. Williams has used her extensive expertise and knowledge of microaggressions to provide practical vignettes, clinical dialogues, and discussion prompts that will enrich practice and teaching."

—**Matthew D. Skinta**, PhD, ABPP, Department of Psychology,
Roosevelt University

ABCT Clinical Practice Series

Series Editor

Susan W. White, PhD, ABPP, Professor and Doddridge Saxon Chair in Clinical Psychology, University of Alabama

Associate Editors

Lara J. Farrell, PhD, Associate Professor, School of Applied Psychology, Griffith University and Menzies Health Institute of Queensland, Australia

Matthew A. Jarrett, PhD, Associate Professor, Department of Psychology, University of Alabama

Jordana Muroff, PhD, LICSW, Associate Professor, Clinical Practice, Boston University School of Social Work

Marisol Perez, PhD, Associate Professor and Associate Chair, Department of Psychology, Arizona State University

Titles in the Series

Managing Microaggressions

*Addressing Everyday Racism in
Therapeutic Spaces*

MONNICA T. WILLIAMS

OXFORD
UNIVERSITY PRESS

Oxford University Press is a department of the University of Oxford. It furthers
the University's objective of excellence in research, scholarship, and education
by publishing worldwide. Oxford is a registered trade mark of Oxford University
Press in the UK and certain other countries.

Published in the United States of America by Oxford University Press
198 Madison Avenue, New York, NY 10016, United States of America.

Library of Congress Cataloging-in-Publication Data
Names: Williams, Monnica T., author.
Title: Managing microaggressions : addressing everyday racism in therapeutic spaces /
Monnica T. Williams.
Description: New York : Oxford University Press, 2020. |
Series: Abct clinical practice series |
Includes bibliographical references and index.
Identifiers: LCCN 2020003920 (print) | LCCN 2020003921 (ebook) |
ISBN 9780190875237 (paperback) | ISBN 9780190875251 (epub) | ISBN 9780190875268
Subjects: LCSH: Microaggressions. | Race. | Prejudices. |
Discrimination—Psychological aspects. | Behavioral assessment.
Classification: LCC BF575.P9 W55 2020 (print) | LCC BF575.P9 (ebook) |
DDC 303.3/85—dc23
LC record available at https://lccn.loc.gov/2020003920
LC ebook record available at https://lccn.loc.gov/2020003921

9 8 7 6 5 4 3 2 1

Printed by Marquis, Canada

CONTENTS

Mental health clinicians desperately want to help their clients, and they recognize the importance of implementing evidence-based treatments toward achieving this goal. In the past several years, the field of mental health care has seen tremendous advances in our understanding of pathology and its underlying mechanisms, as well as proliferation and refinement of scientifically informed treatment approaches. Coinciding with these advances is a heightened focus on accountability in clinical practice. Clinicians are expected to apply evidence-based approaches and to do so effectively, efficiently, and in a patient-centered, individualized way. This is no small order. For a multitude of reasons, including but not limited to client diversity, complex psychopathology (e.g., comorbidity), and barriers to care that are not under the clinician's control (e.g., adverse life circumstances that limit the client's ability to participate), delivery of evidence-based approaches can be challenging.

This series, which represents a collaborative effort between the Association for Behavioral and Cognitive Therapies (ABCT) and the Oxford University Press, is intended to serve as an easy-to-use, highly practical collection of resources for clinicians and trainees. The ABCT Clinical Practice Series is designed to help clinicians effectively master and implement evidence-based treatment approaches. In practical terms, the series represents the "brass tacks" of implementation, including basic how-to guidance and advice on troubleshooting common issues in clinical practice and application. As such, the series is best viewed as a complement to other series on evidence-based protocols, such as the Treatments That Work series and the Programs That Work series. These represent seminal bridges between research and practice, and they have been instrumental in the dissemination of empirically supported intervention protocols and programs. The ABCT Clinical Practice Series, rather than focusing on specific diagnoses and their treatment, targets the practical application of therapeutic and assessment approaches. In other words, the emphasis is on the *how-to* aspects of mental health delivery.

It is my hope that clinicians and trainees find these books useful in refining their clinical skills, as enhanced comfort as well as competence in delivery of evidence-based approaches should ultimately lead to improved client outcomes. Given the emphasis on application in this series, there is relatively less emphasis on review of the underlying research base. Readers who wish to delve more deeply into the theoretical or empirical basis supporting specific approaches are encouraged to go to the original source publications cited in each chapter. When relevant, suggestions for further reading are provided.

In this timely volume, Dr. Monnica Williams brings to light the reality of racial microaggressions in the therapeutic context. We live in a time of considerable confusion and controversy about race, culture, equality, and interpersonal sensitivity and aggression. Unfortunately, therapy is not immune from these issues, and to act as though it is can be harmful to our clients.

In addition to defining the scope of microaggressions and explaining how their experience is both common and harmful, Dr. Williams provides insightful commentary about how to try to prevent them from occurring and how to manage them when they do occur. Useful resources for assessing the impact of microaggressions and for conducting culturally sensitive intakes are provided. This volume is likely to be helpful to trainees as well as seasoned clinicians who wish to provide a respectful and safe therapeutic environment for diverse clients.

Susan W. White, PhD, ABPP
Series Editor

ACKNOWLEDGMENTS

I thank Terence Ching, Jamilah George, Destiny Printz, Imani Faber, and Matthew Jahn for assistance with therapist dialogue examples. I thank Sonya Faber and Matthew Skinta for helping with proofreading. I thank Chad Wetterneck for his support and providing examples of microaggressions. I thank Sophia Gran-Ruiz for help with figures and proofing. I also thank my University of Connecticut undergraduate research assistants—Jade Gallo, Joel Lopez, Michael Cruz, and Hayley Rowe—for their assistance and support in this project.

Monnica T. Williams, PhD, is the Canada Research Chair for Mental Health Disparities at the University of Ottawa, where she conducts psychological research, mentors students, and teaches courses in multicultural psychology and psychopathology. She completed her undergraduate work at the Massachusetts Institute of Technology and the University of California at Los Angeles, and she received her doctoral degree from the University of Virginia. She was an Assistant Professor at the University of Pennsylvania School of Medicine in the Department of Psychiatry for more than 4 years, where she worked with Dr. Edna Foa at the Center for the Treatment and Study of Anxiety, before her move to the University of Louisville in 2011, where she served as the Director for the Center for Mental Health Disparities. She also worked at the University of Connecticut for 3 years, where she had joint appointments in the Departments of Psychological Science and Psychiatry. She has published more than 100 peer-reviewed articles and book chapters, focused on anxiety-related disorders and cultural differences. She is an associate editor of the journals *Behavior Therapist* and *New Ideas in Psychology*, and she serves on the editorial board of several scientific journals. She has been awarded federal, local, and foundation grants to conduct psychological research. She is a licensed psychologist in the United States and Canada. She is the Clinical Director of the Behavioral Wellness Clinic in Tolland, Connecticut. She treats adults with anxiety disorders and provides clinical instruction to trainees. In the community, she conducts trainings and lectures for local organizations and treatment providers. She was president-elect of the Delaware Valley Association of Black Psychologists, co-founded the International OCD Foundation's Diversity Advisory Board, and serves on the board of directors for the Chacruna Institute for Psychedelic Plant Medicines.

Understanding Racial Microaggressions

It has been more than 50 years since the passage of the Civil Rights Act of 1964 in the US, outlawing discrimination based on race, color, religion, sex, or national origin; nonetheless, ethnic and racial disparities in access and use of mental health care stubbornly persist. These disparities have several causes, including differing cultural attitudes about mental illness, lack of access to appropriate services, and lack of culture-specific therapies. However, mental health disparities are also caused by clinician behaviors that have unintended negative consequences (Penner, Blair, Albrecht, & Dovidio, 2014). When clinicians lack needed skills and knowledge to effectively interact with those who are ethnoracially different, clients of color may be left feeling misunderstood, invalidated, or even traumatized. As a result, people of color may worry about what will happen in therapy or fail to return for treatment after just a single session.

Racial microaggressions have been described as "brief, everyday exchanges that send denigrating messages to people of color because they belong to a racial minority group" (Sue et al., 2007, p. 273), although additional types of microaggressions have since been described, such as lesbian, gay, bisexual, transgender, and queer (LGBTQ); gender; religious; and other microaggressions. Microaggressions are probably the most common reason for dissatisfaction among clients with stigmatized identities, indeed a troubling cause for poor retention and inadequate treatment outcomes. In addition, microaggressions have been linked to numerous mental health problems. However, many clinicians are completely unaware of the presence of microaggressions occurring all around them or that they may even commit themselves. Microaggressions are common, automatic, and often unintentional. For these reasons, all clinicians can benefit from a better understanding of microaggressions to improve their clinical work and to help clients navigate the racial microaggressions they may be experiencing from multiple sources in their daily lives.

UNDERSTANDING STIGMATIZED RACIAL AND ETHNIC IDENTITIES

There are many important ways that people may exhibit diversity. Recognition and appreciation of diverse identities have focused on categories such as race/ethnicity, culture, gender/sex, sexual orientation, socioeconomic status, age, disability, and religion. Included within each of these identities are varying degrees of social stigma or privilege. Stigmatized identities are more likely to be met with disfavor and ostracization, whereas privileged identities garner favor and respect. As a result, discrimination on the basis of these identities is common and, as noted previously, often prohibited by law. Almost all of the identities listed previously are ascribed and not acquired, meaning that people have very little control at an individual level as to which of these identities they possess. This holds true for privileged identities as well (i.e., able-bodied status, cisgender identity, etc.), which are also rarely chosen. Although some degree of change is possible, for the most part people are born with these identities or socialized into them from an early age, and therefore no one should be stigmatized or privileged on the basis of such identities alone.

Race and ethnicity are among the most highly stigmatized identities in our culture and as such are powerful determinants of many basic attributes, such as where one lives, where one goes to school, how much money one makes, who one will marry, and whether one will become incarcerated. Western culture places a high value on being nondiscriminatory; nonetheless, individuals do react to others based on their presumed racial and ethnic identity. No doubt, most clinicians would consider themselves unprejudiced and even committed to the well-being of people from all ethnoracial groups. However, to truly appreciate the struggles of people of color in America (and many other Western nations as well), a wide lens is needed to understand the hierarchical system that unfairly advantages some at the expense of others. Historically, nearly all of our country's institutions, policies, procedures, laws, and statutes were, by design, crafted to advantage White people at the expense of people of color. These underpinnings continue to propagate inequality in everyday life. The expression of this system is termed *structural racism* because it does not require the actions of any one biased person to perpetrate discrimination against people of color. But rather than acknowledge the biased systems that produce these differences, society develops *legitimizing myths* to explain away disadvantage in a manner that blames the disempowered group. The resulting mischaracterizations about people in the disempowered group are termed *pathological stereotypes* (Williams, Gooden, & Davis, 2012). These stereotypes perpetuate the notion that out-groups lack desirable characteristics, which in turn provides justification for ongoing discriminatory treatment by the empowered group.

For example, when slavery was legal in the United States, the slave trade was legitimized with myths that Black Americans were docile, happy, simple, and childlike to rationalize their ongoing control by slave owners. After the Civil

War, the legitimizing myths changed, with Black Americans stereotyped as hostile and violent to justify terror organizations such as the Ku Klux Klan to keep them "under control," in conjunction with lynching and mass incarceration. When the civil rights movement started, resistance to removing inequalities was legitimized with myths that Black Americans were demanding, wanting things they did not deserve, and pushing too hard for too much (Hyers, 2006). Interestingly, the pathological stereotype of Black people having lower intelligence briefly waned during that time because it was more useful to portray Blacks as clever and crafty in order to motivate White resistance against efforts to change entrenched social systems. So pathological stereotypes arise from legitimizing myths that support the interests of the dominant group, and these may change with the shifting interests and concerns of a society (Sidanius, Pratto, & Devereux, 1992).

Can Terminology Be a Microaggression: People of Color or Ethnic Minority?

Many terms have been used to label various racial and ethnic groups broadly. The word "minority" is often used to describe non-White groups, but this term is problematic because it contains an implicit justification for marginalization of these groups. In a society in which we ascribe to "majority rule" (one might even argue this is one of our democratic values), the term suggests that "minority" needs, concerns, and place in society are less important due to being numerically fewer. It is important to understand that numerical minority status is not the cause of power imbalances between groups; rather, inequities are due to oppression and inequitable access to resources. In addition, the term minority is misleading because people of color are a numerical majority worldwide ("global majority"). Furthermore, according to the US Census Bureau, White Americans will be a numerical minority by 2045; thus, the term "ethnic minorities" as commonly used will over time become technically incorrect or meaningless.

Although I may occasionally use the term "minority" or "ethnoracial minority," I prefer the term "people of color," which should not to be confused with the outdated term "colored people." Whereas the word "minority" has negative connotations surrounding disempowerment, the word "color" is often considered positive and bright. I think we should all embrace a more diverse and "colorful" society, which is another reason this terminology may be preferred.

It is important to note that these terms are used and understood differently in different cultures. For example, in Canada, there are two distinct categorization for people of color: indigenous people and visible (racialized) minorities. Indigenous groups used to be called "Indians" or, more recently, "Aboriginals" (but this term is falling out of favor), and "racialized minorities" includes all other non-Whites. In Germany, the term "colored" has been used, but it is falling out of favor, and there is currently a great deal of uncertainty regarding how to refer to people such as a Black German (e.g., Afro-deutscher). Germans recommend asking people how they would like to be identified.

What Is Whiteness?

To best understand issues related to race and racism, it is important to understand Whiteness as well. The concept of Whiteness was imported from Spain and Portugal in the 1600s during the slavery era. Whiteness was defined as way to contrast one's identity as different from slaves. This was devised to create a deliberate hierarchy, to define who was privileged and who was property or a second-class citizen (Wood, 2015). The concept of race continues to define people in this way, socially although not legally anymore, albeit with stubbornly disparate outcomes (Salter, Adams, & Perez, 2018).

I have been asked by well-intentioned White Americans if it is appropriate to be proud of having a White racial identity. In the course of studying race and culture, it becomes evident that the concept of race is a destructive thing because it categorizes people into castes based on their appearance and presumed ancestry. Ethnicity and culture are good things because they are built by a group for the well-being of that group, whereas race is defined by the dominant culture and imposed upon nondominant groups. This is why we sometimes refer to certain groups as "racialized." This is akin to words such as "marginalized" or "stigmatized"—generally a negative thing.

Whiteness can be defined as an unfairly privileged exclusionary category, based on physical features—most notably a lack of melanin. So, although one can be proud of one's German heritage, American culture, or African American ethnicity, one should not be proud of one's Whiteness. Whiteness is forced group membership that originated by oppressing people of color. It leads to unjust benefits at the expense of others, which is antisocial and unethical. In this way, it causes psychological damage to White people just as it damages non-Whites.

People may then ask why it is okay to be proud of being Black. This is because pride in Blackness represents pride in the accomplishments and resilience of a racialized people group in the face of continual oppression. It is healthy for Black people to celebrate these small victories to maintain their self-esteem, despite pervasive social messages of inferiority. Furthermore, most Black Americans were forcefully deprived of their original diverse African identities and had no choice but to forge a new ethnic identity as a single group (African Americans).

Generally, Americans who identify as Black can be of any skin shade and ethnicity, even if mostly of European ancestry. This is not the case with Whiteness, which, as noted previously, is an exclusionary category. The term "White" is in fact a euphemism because White people have a range of skin shades. White people do not have actually white skin unless they have an extreme medical melanin deficiency (e.g., albinism). So, rejecting the construction of Whiteness has nothing to do with whether or not a person likes their actual skin color. A person can like light-colored skin and still dislike Whiteness.

DEFINING MICROAGGRESSIONS

The term *microaggression* was first used to describe the more common types of racial maltreatment experienced by African Americans (Pierce, 1970), but many racial and ethnic groups are subject to frequent microaggressions as well, including Asian Americans (Lin, 2010; Ong, Burrow, Fuller-Rowell, Ja, & Sue, 2013), Hispanic Americans (Huynh, 2012; Yosso, Smith, Ceja, & Solórzano, 2009), Native Americans/American Indians (Jones & Galliher, 2015; Walls, Gonzalez, Gladney, & Onello, 2015), and others. Arab Americans also experience microaggressions, but because individuals of Middle Eastern descent are not officially recognized as a minority group, research is sparse and many instances of discrimination are not documented (Awad, 2010). Although, as noted previously, there are other types of microaggressions, the focus of this book is on microaggressions connected to the target's presumed racial and ethnic group, and so use of the term microaggressions herein should be taken to mean ethnoracial microaggressions, unless otherwise indicated. This is because microaggressions against people in groups that are stigmatized differently have a unique history that changes the nature of the construct in ways requiring a different understanding than how it is described here. However, some of the concepts presented may apply to these other groups as well.

Pierce (1970, 1974) explains microaggressions as emotionally damaging "offensive mechanisms," a type of opposite or analogue to the Freudian concept of defensive mechanisms that, like microaggressions, often occur outside conscious awareness. Furthermore, Pierce (1970) likens the delivery of microaggressions to an offensive maneuver one might observe in the sport of football, and as such he urges people of color to have ready defenses to counter these attacks. Therefore, the term *offender* is used to refer to those who commit microaggression, in homage to Piece and also in recognition of the fact that microaggressions are by nature offensive because they are a form of racism (Kanter et al., 2017), making offender an apt description. Some people prefer terms such as "deliverer" or "perpetrator." I find the term deliverer awkward and believe it also understates the harms done. I also prefer not to use the word perpetrator because it may imply conscious malevolence on the part the offender, although microaggressions are not always unintentional.

Some have argued that microaggressions are best defined as the target's subjective feeling about an interaction. Although the subjective experience is certainly of paramount importance, the foundational perspective of this book is that microaggressions can be well defined and are not simply a subjective experience (Williams, 2020a). As such, an offender directs a microaggression at a specific person or group of people, but it may or may not land on a victim causing harm (e.g., the target may not perceive the microaggression). Thus, the term *target* is used to refer to the intended recipient of the microaggression, although the term *victim* is appropriate if the target is harmed by the microaggression. In addition, observers may also witness a microaggression and be harmed by it, even if it was not aimed at the observers. For example, a non-Hispanic White person might hear someone repeat a pathological stereotype about Hispanic Americans. And let's suppose that non-Hispanic White observer is married to a Puerto Rican woman who has suffered greatly due to such stereotypes. The hearer may feel distress that a person he loves is being mischaracterized in such a thoughtless manner. So even people from privileged groups can be harmed by microaggressions if they care deeply about people of color.

THE CONNECTION BETWEEN RACIAL MICROAGGRESSIONS AND RACISM

It may be tempting to consider microaggressions as simple cultural missteps or racial faux pas, but in fact microaggressions are a form of oppression that reinforces traditional power differentials between groups, whether or not this was the conscious intention of the offender. As such, there is an underlying connection between the message embedded in the microaggression and its relationship to pathological stereotypes about the target that mirror existing power structures. Therefore, one can predict that microaggressions will indeed reinforce unfair pathological stereotypes about people of color (Sue et al., 2007). Because these stereotypes are pervasive, any person can commit a microaggression.

Some have wondered if the commission of microaggressions is related to racially biased attitudes on the part of the offender. Research on this topic to date seems to indicate this to be the case. In my own lab, we collected data from White students about racial prejudice using several validated measures, which included color-blind, symbolic, and modern racist attitudes (Kanter et al., 2017). We also collected data on affinity toward out-group members (allophilia), which we expected to be negatively correlated to racism. Finally, because it has been noted that some measures of racism may be confounded with political views, we administered a racial feelings thermometer, a more pure measure of racial bias, where White participants are simply asked to indicate their attitudes toward Blacks on a scale ranging from 0° (extremely unfavorable) to 100° (extremely favorable). Even after controlling for social desirability, the likelihood of students engaging in microaggressions across several common contexts was robustly correlated with all five of our measures of racial prejudice. Specifically, White students who reported that they were more likely to commit microaggressions were more likely to endorse the color-blind, symbolic, and modern racist attitudes, and they held significantly less favorable feelings and attitudes toward Black people. These data were obtained from a sample of students at the University of Louisville in Kentucky; we have since collected data from students in Seattle and New England with similar findings (Parigoris et al., 2018).

The aforementioned study provided some important empirical support for something that diversity researchers knew all along—that microaggressive acts are linked to racist beliefs and underlying feelings of hostility that are not simply the subjective impressions of the target. However, even if we had found no correlation between racism and microaggressions, subjective perceptions of targets are still important, and if targets agree that microaggressions are offensive, this still constitutes an important problem that needs to be addressed.

Readers may wonder if this means that all people who commit microaggressions are racists. In common discourse, we generally think of a "racist" as perhaps someone who gets sadistic pleasure out of abusing people of color. We may think of skinheads, neo-Nazis, or White supremacists running around at night with tiki torches, chanting threats or wearing white robes. However, in contrast to what the term means colloquially, we use the term racist rather differently in academic contexts. There are many types of "racists" (e.g., old-fashioned racists vs. aversive racists) and also many racist ways people can act (e.g., explicit or implicit) while still eschewing racism in general. Furthermore, individuals may hold such biases toward all people of color or only those from certain ethnoracial groups. People of color may have biases toward those from different minority groups, their own group, or even themselves (internalized racism). In addition, people can knowingly or unknowingly comply with structural racism and be perpetrating racism indirectly. So if we examine the many different ways racism is perpetuated and the degree of individual compliance with these norms, just about everyone could be considered a racist to some extent.

Racism is everywhere, and given the biased messages about people of color that we are subjected to in the media and life in general, it would be difficult to be completely unaffected. As a result, almost everyone has some ethnic and racial biases. Correspondingly, people can commit racist acts without being reprehensible human beings. Good people unknowingly do racists things all the time, myself included. Like everyone else, I have committed my own share of microaggressions against people who are different, propagated pathological stereotypes, and judged people based on their appearance even when I tried not to do so. My students have sometimes pointed out unintentional racist things I have said or done, and I appreciate it. Although it is embarrassing and hurtful at times to be called out, it is much more functional to apologize, learn, and grow than to get angry and defensive.

STEREOTYPES OF SOME COMMON ETHNIC AND RACIAL GROUPS

As previously discussed, microaggressions are a form of racism, linked to pathological stereotypes that are the product of legitimizing myths. In order to be able to identify a microaggression, one must have an awareness of how various groups are stereotyped. It can be uncomfortable to acknowledge these stereotypes, knowing that they are largely untrue and cause hurt to others. Some people may even deny knowledge of pathological stereotypes to avoid appearing racist to others (or even themselves). However, if we shy away from learning about these problems, it impedes our ability to overcome them. Forrest-Bank and Jenson (2015) studied microaggressions among Asian, Hispanic, Black, and White American young adults ($N = 409$). Although microaggressions were experienced at similar rates among the different non-White groups, there were a number of significant differences in types of microaggressions based on ethnoracial group, and these were in alignment with pathological stereotypes. So I now review some of the most common North American ethnic and racial groups and the types of false stereotypes and subsequent microaggressions they typically experience. It is worth noting, however, that nearly all societies have some system whereby groups are advantaged or disadvantaged based on skin color or ethnicity, so what is presented here may have relevance to people in other societies as well.

African Americans

African Americans are defined as those with ancestry from any of the darker skinned (Black) racial groups indigenous to Africa. Because the economy of the United States was driven in part by African slave labor for more than a century, racism in America is a deeply entrenched system of oppression, rooted in the institutionalized subjugation of disempowered groups, creating castes of people based on heritage and appearance. These classifications determined who could enjoy the rights and privileges of citizenship outlined in the Constitution and who were considered slaves or some other form of second-class citizen. This system of classification persists today, with those having any discernable African ancestry classified as "Black" and those who appear wholly European in ancestry classified as "White." In general, White people prefer not to interact with people of color, with Black people being the most highly stigmatized among all ethnoracial groups (Cox, Navarro-Rivera, & Jones, 2016). As a result of historical and current ostracization, Black people in America have developed their own culture around their African heritage, shared history, and the experience of being stigmatized in America. This group of people is referred to as African American, which is an ethnic specifier that includes most Black people in the United States but not all. It used to be that Black people in the United States were almost always descended from enslaved Africans who had survived the trans-Atlantic slave trade. However, as the number of African and Caribbean Black people immigrating to the United States has increased, so have the chances that someone who identifies as Black or African American is a first- or second-generation immigrant. Such people may include those with Caribbean heritage (e.g., Jamaican American) and recent immigrants (e.g., South African comedian and commentator Trevor Noah). So not all Black people are African American (ethnic group), but all African Americans are considered Black (racial group). Pervasive negative stereotypes about Black people include notions such as being antagonistic, lazy, poor, unintelligent, criminal, and sexually predatory/deviant, which function to explain educational disparities, deny job opportunities, and deprive Black Americans of their liberty. Black women may also be stereotyped as mammies or caretakers. These stereotypes can contribute to feelings of stigma and shame in African Americans. As a result, Black American immigrants may be reluctant to identify with the African American label. However, Black people in America suffer from microaggressions related to these themes, no matter where they are from.

Asian Americans

Asian Americans are composed of very heterogeneous subgroups—including Chinese, Filipino, Japanese, Korean, Cambodian, Vietnamese, Pakistani, and Indian Americans. Taken as a whole, they are one of the fastest growing racial groups in America. Traditionally, Indians and other South Asians were categorized separately, but in the 2010 census they were grouped in one combined category along with those having East Asian heritage. In addition, many researchers have studied these populations together because of similar cultural views in comparison to those of their Western counterparts. However, there remain very distinct differences among the various subgroups that make combining them into a single group problematic. Also, there are different stereotypes ascribed to these different people groups, which will result in some different types of microaggressions being levied against them.

A century ago, East Asian Americans were unfairly perceived in negative terms, not unlike those ascribed to African Americans historically. They were considered unassimilable members of the human race, denied the right to become US citizens, and segregated to ethnic enclaves. But a change in the US immigration law in 1965 that gave preference to well-educated and highly skilled applicants gave rise to a new wave of Asian immigrants that forced a change in the stereotype. The new immigrants came to be considered "model minorities"—perceived to be studious, productive, quiet, agreeable, hard-working, enlightened, and good at math and science (Lee, Wong, & Alvarez, 2009). But even positive stereotypes can be damaging: Stereotypes of being technically competent and quiet make Asians less likely to be promoted into management and leadership positions and less likely to be identified as in need of special services or financial assistance. They also experience negative stereotypes such as having poor interpersonal skills, poor English, and being passive.

In the United States, South and Southeast Asian Americans are also likely to be stereotyped as intelligent, but not to the same extent as East Asians. They may be unfairly cast as convenience store owners, cab drivers, or motel operators who are uneducated, greedy, or living in crowded homes. Alternatively, they are stereotyped as snobbish, upwardly mobile doctors and computer engineers, who speak poor English. Sometimes they are stereotyped as terrorists as well. As a result, microaggressions may include these themes.

Hispanic Americans

The US Census Bureau defines Hispanic or Latino as "a person of Cuban, Mexican, Puerto Rican, South or Central American, or other Spanish culture or

origin regardless of race" (Ennis, Ríos-Vargas, & Albert, 2011, p. 1) and states that
Hispanics or Latinos can be of any race or ancestry. Generically, this definition
of Hispanic or Latino is intended for people from Central and South America
and the Caribbean, although sometimes it includes those who are Spanish or
Portuguese. *Latino* can refer to males or females, whereas *Latina* refers to only
females, and *Latinx* is now often used as a new gender-inclusive term. Because
of the technical distinctions involved in defining "race" versus "ethnicity," there is
confusion among the general population about the designation of Hispanic identity, even among those who identify as Hispanic. When forced to choose a racial
category that does not include Hispanic, 47% of Hispanic Americans identify as
White, whereas over 40% do not identify with any race (Ríos, Romero, & Ramírez,
2014). So perhaps the Census Bureau might want to reconsider its categories for
"race" in the future. Pathological stereotypes about Hispanics include being aggressive, lazy, criminal, intellectually inferior, traditional, foreign born, and un-
documented. Also, it should not be assumed that all Hispanic Americans speak
Spanish; although most do, approximately one-third do not. Hispanic Americans
who do not speak Spanish are often subject to disparaging remarks by other
Hispanics for losing touch with their culture, leading to feelings of guilt, shame,
and defensiveness. Therefore, assuming a Hispanic person speaks Spanish when
they do not can be particularly hurtful to targets.

Native Americans

Native Americans, also known as American Indians or Indigenous Americans,
are the original people of the United States. Native Americans were very much
impacted by European colonization of the Americas, which began in 1492, and
their population declined precipitously due to introduction of deadly diseases,
warfare, and slavery. After the founding of the United States, many Native
American groups were subjected to genocide, relocation, and one-sided treaties,
and they continue to suffer from discriminatory government policies. Many
Native Americans were forced to assimilate into White culture through adopting
English, converting to Christianity, and attending special boarding schools
away from their families. Those who could pass for White had the advantage of
White privilege, and today, after generations of racial whitening, many Native
Americans are visually indistinguishable from White Americans. There are currently more than 5 million Native Americans in the United States and more than
500 federally recognized tribes, with approximately half associated with Indian
reservations. Approximately 22% of the country's 5.2 million Native Americans
live on tribal lands, often under poor living conditions. Native American identity
has historically been based on culture and not just biology. Stereotypes about
Native Americans include being noble savages, bloodthirsty savages, teary-eyed
environmentalists, alcoholics, nonexistent people, and having an oversimplified
homogeneous (pan-Indian) culture. Perhaps no other group is as vulnerable
to unchecked racism because it remains socially acceptable to use derogatory

epitaphs and stereotypical depictions of Native Americans as sports team names and mascots.

Indigenous Canadians, also known as Aboriginal Canadians, are the original inhabitants within the boundaries of present-day Canada. They comprise the First Nations, Inuit, and Métis, although Indian is a term still commonly used for legal purposes in Canada for First Nations people. Many bands are the same as American Indian tribes but happen to live north of the US border, whereas others are indigenous to arctic regions. Currently, there are 1.6 million Indigenous Canadians, and 56% live in urban areas. For First Nations peoples, rules regarding who has "Indian status" are complicated, dictated by federal law, and, until recently, subject to revocation. Historically, any First Nation person who obtained a university degree, became a professional, served in the armed forces, or any First Nation woman who married a non-status man would lose their Indian status and become an "enfranchised" full Canadian citizen. When this occurred, they lost ties to their ancestry and communities and were unable to pass Indian status and rights to their children. The Métis and Inuit do not have federally recognized Indian status. Inuit, who are arctic bands, are sometimes referred to as "Eskimos," which has pejorative connotations in Canada.

The media tends to portray Indigenous Canadians as what has been described as angry warriors, pathetic victims, or noble environmentalists (Harding, 2005). They are often stereotyped as alcoholics and savages unfit to raise children, which may be a reason for the widespread problem of coerced sterilization for Indigenous women and increased intrusions of child protective services into the lives of Indigenous families. As late as 1996, Indigenous children were required to attend boarding schools, which were frequently abusive, to erase their culture in an attempt at forced assimilation. Microaggressions are a pervasive problem reported by Indigenous Canadians today; these include ostracization and "othering" (Canel-Çınarbaş & Yohani, 2018; Clark, Kleiman, Spanierman, Isaac, & Poolokasingham, 2014). *Othering* means any action by which a person or group becomes mentally classified as "not one of us." Indigenous Canadian experiences with racial microaggressions include expectations of primitiveness, exoticization, jealous accusations, and elimination or misrepresentation of their contributions from history, which results in living with daily cultural and social isolation (Clark et al., 2014).

Middle East and North African Americans

In 2014, the Census Bureau announced that it would consider a new category for populations from the Middle East and North Africa (MENA). The population of Middle Eastern Americans is at least 10 million, which includes 3.7 million Arab Americans and 6.5 million Jewish Americans. Arab Americans experience a great deal of prejudice in the United States, but there is little research on this topic because MENA Americans were previously classified as White on the census, which has limited study of this problem (Awad, 2010). Among Arab Americans, the majority are Lebanese in heritage, but this also includes many other groups as well, such as Egyptian and Syrian Americans. Arab Americans are a group that is largely misunderstood and much maligned in the media. Arab women may be stereotyped as silent, burka-clad, and submissive or as exotic belly-dancing harem girls. They may also be stereotyped as terrorists, fanatical Islamists, or wealthy billionaires. Arab Americans are often assumed to be Muslims, although only approximately one-fourth of Arab Americans are Muslim, with more than half identifying as Christian and the remainder belonging to another religion or no religion. They may feel embarrassed about their ancestors and homeland due to negative stereotypes (Suleiman, 1988), and many have experienced discrimination and acts of outright racism.

Biracial and Multiracial Americans

As US society has become increasingly diverse, the number of people who identify as biracial and multiracial has increased, and indeed this appears to the fastest growing ethnoracial grouping with more than 9 million individuals, according to the US census (Parker, Horowitz, Morin, & Lopez, 2015). Most Americans of mixed race ancestry (61%) self-identify with just one group culturally and socially, although they are generally proud of their mixed race ancestry. The largest of these subgroups is White in combination with some other race (Black, Asian, Native American, or other). Multiracial Americans may experience microaggressions from multiple sources, including questions from strangers about their heritage, microaggressive statements from their own family members, and pressure from friends who question their allegiance to one group or another (Nadal, Sriken, Davidoff, Wong, & McLean, 2013). White–Black biracial adults are much more likely than adults with a biracial White and other backgrounds to say they have been treated badly by a family member (Parker et al., 2015). Johnston and Nadal (2010) proposed a taxonomy of microaggressions experienced by multiracial individuals that includes five categories: exclusion or isolation, exoticization or objectification, assumption of monoracial or mistaken identity, denial of multiracial reality, and pathologizing of identity and experiences. Multiracial individuals report experiencing microaggressions just as frequently as monoracial people of color, and these microaggressions appear to be equally distressing (Nadal et al., 2013; Williams, Printz, & DeLapp, 2018).

TYPES AND CLASSIFICATIONS OF MICROAGGRESSIONS

In proposing categorizations of microaggressions, Sue et al. (2007) described three classes: microassaults, microinsults, and microinvalidations. The main difference between these is that microassaults are considered intentional behaviors, whereas microinsults and microinvalidations are not consciously intended to be harmful. Regarding latter two, microinsults denigrate the target for simply being a person of color, and microinvalidations are hurtful because they invalidate the thoughts, feelings, or experiences of the target as a person of color.

It has been argued that microassaults do not capture the true definition of microaggressions because they are intentionally meant to cause harm, whereas the others are not (Lilienfeld, 2017; Wong, Derthick, David, Saw, & Okazaki, 2014). However, all microaggressions are meant to cause harm, either by the individual or by society at large, and this is what makes them all forms of aggression. A microaggression can be unintentional at the individual level but still advance the larger intentions of dominant culture and thus be intended by the group even though not by the individual. It generally cannot be known how much of a given microaggression was intentional (the offender wanted to harm the target purely because he or she was a person of color) versus quasi-intentional (the offender came up with a reason other than race to aggress, although it was actually motivated by racial hostility) versus "good intentions" (the offender meant to be helpful but was actually being patronizing). Inferences about harmful intent are not particularly useful because even people who are overtly racist in their behaviors may claim to have good intentions. In all cases, whether intentional, quasi-intentional, or unintended by the individual, the microaggression is racially offensive, conveniently explained away as valid, and frustrating to victims. Therefore, microaggressions cannot be defined purely in terms of conscious intentionality.

However, research on the types of behaviors and statements deemed personally likely by potential offenders has borne out that microassaults do appear to represent a discrete category of microaggressions, characterized by verbal aggression and hostility. Examples of microassaults include statements such as "Black people should work harder to fit in to our society" and "A lot of minorities are too sensitive" or using the N-word in a song over the objections of others (Parigoris et al., 2018).

MICROAGGRESSIVE BEHAVIORS

Sue et al. (2007) proposed nine categories of racial microaggressive situations, described as (a) assumptions that a person of color is not a true American, (b) assumptions of lesser intelligence, (c) statements that convey color-blindness or denial of the importance of race, (d) assumptions of criminality or dangerousness, (e) denial of individual racism, (f) promotion of the myth of meritocracy, (g) assumptions that one's cultural background and communication styles are pathological, (h) being treated as a second-class citizen, and (i) having to endure environmental messages of being unwelcome or devalued. Since that time, numerous researchers have examined these categorizations, finding generally similar groupings based on qualitative and factor analytic studies.

Our own lab's examination of our data combined with a review of the current literature arrived at 16 final groupings. Focus group participants were recruited from one private and two public predominately White institutions of higher learning located in Kentucky and Seattle, Washington. Study eligibility criteria were self-identification as Black, African American, biracial (with Black), or Continental African. Next, I describe each of the categories and provide a sample statement from focus group participants to help readers understand the potential impact of these experiences on people of color.

1. *Not a True Citizen*: First described by Sue et al. (2007) as "alien in own land," this form of microaggression reinforces notions that people of color are not legitimate citizens nor a meaningful part of the larger society. It is typically leveled against those who appear Asian or Hispanic, those who may speak with an accent, or people who have a non-Anglo name; however, any person of color may be a target for this microaggression. Microaggressive statements in this category may include "Where are you from?" or "Where is your family from?" Although showing interest in a person's background is not necessarily a microaggression, such questions are often asked in order to help the offender determine the race of the target. This type of microaggression can serve as a form of "othering"—a means of reinforcing notions that non-Whites are not real Americans and not a meaningful part of the social tapestry. It communicates lack of belonging and exclusion. Repeatedly making a person feel alienated can be psychologically damaging.

   My head is shaved, actually. I hear a lot of things. It's really annoying . . . "Oh, do you shave your head for a religious thing? Or like an African ritual or something? . . . Oh, where are you from? Are you from, like, Africa?" — Female respondent

2. *Racial Categorization and Sameness*: This describes the situation in which individuals are compelled to disclose their racial group to others, often leading to the expression of pathological stereotypes based on that identity (see also the next category). Microaggressions of forced racial categorization may be experienced by people of color as being squeezed into a one-size-fits-all box that overlooks complexity of a person's identity. Individuals who do not have stereotypical features connected to a major racial group are often targeted for this sort of microaggression. Although offenders may defend this behavior as "simple curiosity," it is generally done for the purpose of establishing the unspoken social hierarchy. People who have multiple ethnic identities—that is, those who consider themselves mixed or biracial—are frequently targets, and such individuals may feel pressure to choose one group over another (Williams, Printz, et al., 2018).

   Sometimes my friends are like, "You're so White," or something like that. And I mean, I'm half-White. But I'm just like annoyed with it. I know I'm mixed, I understand that I am Black and White. I don't have to act a certain way. —Female respondent

This category also includes the assumption that all people from a particular group are all alike in various ways. Targets may find such comments to be frustrating or annoying because of the underlying assumptions that everyone from a specific ethnic group can relate to the same experiences (Nadal, Vigilia Escobar, Prado, David, & Haynes, 2012). This results in the harmful ascription of stereotypes that may disconnect an individual from their actual heritage or lived experience, incorrectly ascribe attributes to one's heritage or experience, or force unwanted attributes or group responsibility to an individual. Intersectionality due to characteristics such as gender, sexual identity, or religion may also be overlooked.

3. *Assumptions About Intelligence, Competence, or Status*: Similar to the category termed "ascription of intelligence" by Sue et al. (2007), this is when a person indicates that they have made an assumption about another's intelligence, competence, knowledge, or social status based on racial stereotypes. It can include statements that may indicate surprise about a person's achievements—for example, saying to a Hispanic person, "I would have never guessed you were a valedictorian"—or it could include just a look of disbelief on one's face at hearing some information that is counter stereotypical about that person's aptitude based on their group membership. Many African Americans in our focus groups reported they encountered disbelief when they demonstrated academic excellence or expressed professional career ambitions. However, reverse assumptions are often made about people of Asian heritage, with others assuming they are smart, studious, and good at math and science (Poolokasingham et al., 2014).

We were deciding where we wanted to go to college, and [the school counselors] were supposed to help us. I went in there, and I was like, "Oh, here are the places I want to apply to and I'm interested in." And she's like, "I think you should look at community colleges." I'm like, "What are you talking about?" I had a 3.7 GPA—What do you mean I should look at community colleges?! I was like, "Well, I'm not really interested in community college, this is my list I've already decided." She was like, "No, let's look at this," and it was some random college I had never heard of like in the middle of nowhere. I got really upset. I went home, I cried. —Female respondent

4. *False Color-Blindness/Invalidating Racial or Ethnic Identity*: As described by Sue et al. (2007), "color-blindness" is the idea that an individual's racial or ethnic identity should not be recognized or acknowledged. When people say this, they often mean that they are not racially biased, but it is often said as a way to avoid discussing race because racial

discussions feel uncomfortable to the offender. This sort of statement can function to silence targets when they want to talk about race, making them feel invalidated. Furthermore, it can seem disingenuous to targets because they know their race is apparent despite what others may say. People of color typically welcome the idea that they could be treated equally by others rather than being racialized, but false color-blindness communicates just the opposite. For people of color especially, race, ethnicity, and culture are important parts of one's identity, and these should be considered in positive terms rather than something that needs to be avoided. Membership in various groups is critical to defining identity, and so it deserves to be recognized, even if it may be a source of pain or challenge.

I told my roommate that I was going to a Black Lives Matter event, and he said, "No bro, it's all lives matter." And I was like, "Ah, come on man. Where are all of the All Lives Matter events? Who is doing the All Lives Matter protests?" —Male respondent

5. *Criminality or Dangerousness*: This is based in stereotypes that people of color are dangerous and likely to commit crimes or cause bodily harm to others (Sue et al., 2007). It could also include concerns about being treated badly by people of color (i.e., verbal aggressions), leading to emotional harm. This category is very strongly represented in the literature, especially as it applies to Black, Hispanic, and Native Americans. People with darker skin of any race and males are more likely to be feared and stereotyped in this way, which sometimes involves profiling and harassment by law enforcement (Smith, Allen, & Danley, 2007). For example, when people of color are seen in predominately White spaces, police may be called to investigate a person who "doesn't seem to belong" in a given area (e.g., a college campus, affluent neighborhood, or coffee shop), and law enforcement disproportionally stop, frisk, pull over, question, and search people of color with alarming regularity. Examples of microaggressions in this category include people locking their doors when a dark-skinned person walks by or a person not entering an elevator when a Black male is inside.

I was coming down the stairs, and this really tall White guy was going up [the stairs] and I was in his way. He flinched! I'm 5'3", I'm not going to injure you. —Female respondent

6. *Denial of Individual Racism*: This is when a person attempts to make a case that they are not biased. It can take the form of attacking the other person (e.g., "You just see racism everywhere!"), or it may be more defensive (e.g., "I am not a racist!"). It may include talking about anti-racist things the offender has done, describing friends of color, or

describing their own stigmatized identities. Although described at length by Sue et al. (2007), very little research has been done on these types of microaggressions. Minikel-Lacocque (2013) describes this as "the contested microaggression." When employed as a response to criticism, it can be invalidating to people of color who are trying to draw attention to a problematic behavior. This is typically done to deflect perceived scrutiny and shut down conversations about where the offender may have committed an act of racism (Sue et al., 2007). Sometimes as a way to ward off criticism or manage White guilt, individuals may give to charities that help African children, vote for people of color, or even adopt internationally. However, these behaviors impose a danger of acting out a White savior complex, which only reinforces the harmful stereotype that people of color need Whites to save them.

When I bring it up to them, about something, they kinda say, "Well, it's not anything offensive." Well some of them think of themselves as being Black, like some girls I know really have this identity crisis, where they just think they can relate so much to our culture that they are like. . . . They want to be Black, like they date the Black boys and stuff like that, so they feel like the comments they make don't matter, because they feel like they already are within our culture. But they don't understand like, if you understood what it meant to be us, you wouldn't make comments like that towards us. — Female respondent

7. *Myth of Meritocracy/Race Is Irrelevant for Success*: This is when a person makes statements about success being rooted in personal efforts, which typically include denial of White privilege and placing blame on struggling people of color for the negative impact of racism. This includes denying the existence of ongoing systemic racism or harmful discriminatory behavior, specifically in regard to personal achievement or barriers to achievement. Such individuals embrace the myth of meritocracy and the notion that determinants of success are rooted in personal efforts alone. It refutes that White privilege is an unearned benefit resulting in tangible differences in outcomes at a personal or societal level (Sue et al., 2007). These sorts of statements are extremely invalidating to people of color who have struggled to succeed but have been hindered by individual or structural racism.

I've had a mixed girlfriend of mine sit there and say . . . "Black people are just blaming the system, and they just need to take advantage of, you know, the opportunities they have." And it's like, well really, how many opportunities do we have? Can you sit up here and put on a list of how many opportunities we as African Americans have compared to all the opportunities that Whites have, or you know, Asian Americans or Mexican Americans? Because if you sat up there and compared the list, our list is going to be pretty short.

You know, can you explain to me why it is that we have [so many] African American men in prisons, a lot of African American women in prisons who still haven't gone through trial, and it's two years later that they've been sitting in jail. I know friends who have seen their friends sitting in jail awaiting trial for two years. —Female respondent

8. *Reverse Racism Hostility*: This microaggression includes expressions of jealousy or hostility surrounding the notion that people of color get unfair advantages and benefits due to their race, often coupled with the assertion that Whites are being treated unjustly and are suffering as a result. Often embedded in this sentiment is the idea that people of color are undeserving of success. This category is represented by Smith et al.'s (2007) description of White resentment and hostility about affirmative action. It has been elucidated in a measure of White bias—for example, "Latinos receive lots of unearned benefits just for being minorities" (Mekawi & Todd, 2018). This type of microaggression also occurs cross-culturally, with Clark et al. (2014) describing the theme of withstanding jealous accusations in relation to indigenous people in Canada.

Then he said that Black on White crime is also very prevalent and that we should stop killing them because of their race, and that I have Black privilege. At that point . . . I didn't want to know what he meant by that. If there is Black privilege, I haven't seen it. I would like some. —Male respondent

9. *Pathologizing Minority Culture or Appearance*: This is when people criticize others based on real or perceived cultural differences in appearance, traditions, behaviors, or preferences (Sue et al., 2007). This may occur when others make remarks about cultural practices or traditions as if they are odd, abnormal, or irregular. Nadal et al. (2012) describe a situation in which a woman was asked to speak her native Filipino language and then was told it "sounded like a bunch of drunk chicken." It can also be present in the environment, such as pictures for charities that only show impoverished children of color and no White children, implying that only children of color are poor. Pathologizing comments may take the form of a backhanded compliment, such as when a person says, "You know, you're not that Black. You seem pretty White to me." Embedded in this sentiment is the idea that Whiteness is preferred, and consequently there is something negative or shameful about a non-White identity. Hence, these microaggressions may include statements that advance pronouncements of apparent Whiteness and White culture as superior.

I went to a predominantly White school and lived in a predominantly White town in western Kentucky and one of my really close friends told me, "You would be the perfect girlfriend if you were White." —Female respondent

10. *Second-Class Citizen/Ignored*: This microaggression captures situations in which people of color are treated with less respect, consideration, or care than is normally expected or customary. This category is meant to include both the experience of being treated as a "second-class citizen" (e.g., the preferential treatment of White individuals; Sue et al., 2007) and the experience of being ignored, unseen, or invisible. Much has been written about this type of microaggression because it seems to be common across racial groups. Examples include people refusing to learn a non-Anglo-sounding name, getting worse service at dining establishments, being passed over for promotions at work, having one's comments ignored at meetings, and having one's contributions not considered as valuable as those of a White person. For example, despite being one of the most visible women in the world, Michelle Obama is rarely recognized when not in the limelight, such as when grocery shopping or jogging. She said, "Oftentimes I think African-American women are invisible . . . We are discounted and we are not relevant to some people's frame of reference" (Ryan, 2016).

With all the shootings that have been happening in the Black community, I kind of felt a certain way when I didn't hear anything from my school that there was some kind of support for us—to just acknowledge that there are people that are here that can be affected, but with the Orlando shootings there was a different response. There were emails, there were ceremonies,. . . . The first thing I said to myself was like, "They're not allowed to probably bring politics and other things into schools. That's why they didn't send an email." But then there was such an overwhelmingly, overwhelming response to the Orlando shootings, I was like, "That's not the case." —Female respondent

11. *Tokenism*: This is when a person of color is included simply to promote the illusion of inclusivity and not for the qualities or talents of the individual. An example is hiring one person of color in an academic department so that others do not think the rest of the faculty are racists. Another example is the placement of one person of color on a committee to make it appear as if diverse concerns are being addressed. In both cases, the unique perspectives and knowledge of the tokenized person are not valued—only what they may represent to others. Niemann (1999) provides the following example from a graduate student of color:

I had not yet even been hired, and already I was stigmatized and tokenized by the perception that the department was forced to hire me. The reality was that the department faculty did not take the time and effort to widely solicit ocher candidates for the position. I was the one paying the price for their reliance on convenience . . . the department faculty felt a sense of benevolence for having offered me the tenure track position. . . They were incredulous that I would consider postponing working with them to work with the ethnic studies program for one year. —Female respondent

In a more blatant example, one is reminded of an embarrassing attempt by the University of Wisconsin–Madison to promote the appearance of diversity by using an altered photograph to adorn the front of its 2001–2002 undergraduate application booklet. The picture was of a cheering crowd at a university football game, and the image of a Black student had been added to the sea of White faces. When the alteration was discovered, the university had to reprint more than 100,000 application booklets. Ironically, the photoshopped individual was a prominent African American student activist who had never attended a University of Wisconsin football game and was deeply involved in efforts to promote campus diversity (Durhams, 2013).

12. *Attempting to Connect Using Stereotypes*: This occurs when a person tries to communicate or connect with another person through use of stereotyped ethnic speech or behavior, believing that it will help them be accepted or understood (Harwood, Huntt, Mendenhall, & Lewis, 2012). Endo (2015) describes situations in which Asian Americans were asked to teach their friends Vietnamese words or asked what to order in a Korean restaurant. This category can also include racist jokes and epitaphs used as terms of endearment for people of color. These types of microaggressions may be more frequently committed by people who think they are accepted by members of a non-White ethnic group and therefore have license to take liberties that would be clearly offensive when done by "outsiders." For example, many Black students have complained that their White friends think it is ok to use the N-word.

> *He just came up to me, and he was like so "Wassup?" And he's like talking with his hands and doing all these [gestures]. Just like "wassup," like trying to talk to me but using like things that he thinks like—I guess to connect with me . . . I don't know what it was, but it was just weird and made me feel uncomfortable. Um, so I just asked him. I was like, "What, like, what are you trying to say? What are you doing?" And basically I just had to end the conversation. . . . Why try to use like this hip cool language to try to connect when we could have had like a conversation just as well?* —Female respondent

13. *Exoticization and Eroticization*: This is when a person of color is treated according to sexualized stereotypes or attention to differences that are characterized as exotic in some way. These types of microaggressions were not described in Sue et al.'s (2007) original taxonomy but are represented in most of the validated measures of microaggressions and many qualitative studies (e.g., Nadal, 2011; Torres-Harding, Andrade, & Romero Diaz, 2012). For example, women of color are often fetishized and viewed as sexual objects or part of an exotic fantasy. Asian men

are frequently demasculinized, whereas Black men are viewed as hypersexual. Black women often share how they are exoticized when they wear their hair in curly styles, and they describe how many White women violate their personal space by touching it, as shown in Figure 1.1.

I've actually been to a few frat parties, and I stopped going because every time I go they'll be like, "Hey, the Black girl's here!" They'll be like, "Hey, can you twerk on me or something?" And I always get that, and I'm just like, ugh. And it's really sad, because like White women will come up to me and ask, "Can you teach me how to twerk?" —Female respondent

14. *Avoidance and Distancing*: This is when people of color are avoided or measures are taken to prevent physical contact or close proximity— for example, when a cashier at a store puts change for people of color on the counter instead of in their hands. People of color have often described situations in which other people will not sit next to them on public transportation or in class. This includes the exclusion of members of targeted groups through physical distancing that prevents them from participating in shared activities, such as parties or other social events (Poolokasingham et al., 2014). It also applies to situations

Figure 1.1 Many Black women are made to feel uncomfortable when others try to touch their hair.

in class in which groups are picked and the person(s) of color is selected last, which can be a lasting source of low self-esteem. It can even include avoiding close or emotionally intimate relationships with people of color or difficult discussions about race.

We were alternating group leaders to lead discussions about a paper we read for the week. And it was kind of like this random thing, so I was excited when it was my turn to be the group leader because I was interested in the subject. I had spent hours thinking of, you know, thoughtful questions to talk about, and then nobody showed up to my group. . . . There was like five different group leaders, and so everyone kind of dispersed to the other four groups and no one showed up to my group, and I was just in tears because this has happened my whole life. Like no one has ever wanted to hear what I had to say. —Female respondent

15. *Environmental Exclusion*: As noted by Sue et al. (2007), someone's racial identity can be unintentionally minimized or made insignificant through the omission of decorations, depictions, or literature that represent their racial group. For example, it can describe situations in which representations of people of color are not present in the classroom or workplace and people color are not depicted as leaders or innovators. Common examples include buildings and classrooms named after White men only, an absence of people of color from textbooks, and art that only depicts White people. Native Americans report that they are often omitted and ignored because there is a general misperception that they no longer exist. Examples in mental health include trainings that only focus on issues common to White families or the experiences of White therapists, descriptions of mental health disorders with symptoms most common to White people, or generalizing the results of research studies as universally applicable even though the studies did not include people of color.

[In medical school] we're learning about what happens to White people when they get sick for instance. So, a White person is pale when they get anemia. Well, how do you tell if a Black person is anemic? I mean there is a way to tell, but they don't ever talk about that. So I think that it is mostly geared towards White people, treating White people and not people of color. —Female respondent

16. *Environmental Attacks*: This category is intended to describe situations in which decorations or depictions pose a known affront or insult to a person's cultural group, history, or heritage (e.g., buildings named after slave owners, Confederate monuments, and Columbus Day). This category is intended to capture particularly hurtful and often frightening depictions (Desai & Abeita, 2017; Murty & Vyas, 2017) that

have been an ongoing source of consternation, public attention, and institutional resistance (Crowe, 2018). For example, many Black people report feeling afraid and uncomfortable when others display Confederate flags, although people doing so deny they are a symbol of racism and note they are simply honoring their heritage. Native Americans are often depicted in hurtful and degrading ways as sports mascots. Stereotypical caricatures of people of color have been used to advertise household products and eating establishments. Such denigrating depictions appear even in classic Disney films, including *Peter Pan* (e.g., Indian Chief), *Dumbo* (e.g., Jim Crow), and *Moana* (e.g., demi-god Maui). These or other potentially offensive characters may be used in the form of dolls, toys, or storybooks that therapists use with children and families.

If you were to see a swastika or any other symbol of somebody who went through a similar situation they would immediately take it down, but anything that has to do with pertaining to the Black struggle, what we went through, they don't really seem to acknowledge it. Just like they arrested that lady, I think it was in South Carolina, when she went up and took that [Confederate] flag down and she got arrested for it. That really makes me mad. —Female respondent

ARE MICROAGGRESSIONS ALWAYS OFFENSIVE?

Because microaggressions are common, many people are so used to them that they do not regard them as offensive or even notice them. In fact, there has been some question as to whether or not most people of color find microaggressions objectionable at all (Lilienfeld, 2017). To answer this question, we conducted our own study of microaggressions. My research team developed several racially charged scenarios along with a series of microaggressive behaviors that people might commit in these situations. The scenarios were created based on the reports of the Black students who participated in focus groups about their experiences on various campuses at different predominately White institutions. Participants had been provided with the definition of microaggressions from Sue et al. (2007) and asked to discuss incidents in their lives consistent with that definition, but they were not recruited on the basis of prior knowledge of the microaggression construct.

Their experiences spanned a range of statements, actions, omissions, and environmental assaults, and these were not unlike experiences reported by students of color who participated in similar focus groups at other institutions (Harwood et al., 2012). This aided us in the development of eight scenarios involving cross-racial individual or group interactions. For example, Scenario 1 was the following:

A friend of yours has wanted you to meet a friend, saying they think you will like the person. You meet this person one-on-one. He turns out to be a tall, fit-looking Black man who says he is a law student. He seems very smart and he has a very sophisticated vocabulary. You like his personality.

Participants were also provided with a picture of the purported individual to aid in visualizing the encounter.

The eight scenarios included (a) having a conversation with a Black law student at a get-together, (b) meeting a young Black female with African-style dress and braided hair, (c) a discussion about White privilege at a diversity training, (d) a study session talking about racial current events and political issues, (e) a lost Black man asking for directions in the respondent's neighborhood, (f) doing karaoke with friends and a song with the N-word comes up, (g) watching the news about police brutality with diverse friends at a sports bar, and (h) talking to a racially ambiguous lab mate about a science project.

After each scenario, White participants were provided a series of potential actions or statements one might make in that situation, including those that would be considered microaggressive (e.g., "Did you get into school through a minority scholarship?") and not microaggressive (e.g., invite the Black student to a future social engagement such as a lecture, group lunch, or party). Respondents were asked to report how likely they would be to think or say each response (or something similar) on a 5-point scale. To explore the degree to which the items would be experienced as microaggressive, Black students were given the same scenarios and items and asked to rate how racist they would experience each item on a similar scale.

Out of 51 items that we predicted Black people would deem microaggressions, 96% were in fact considered potentially or definitely racially objectionable by 30% or more of the Black students. Although not all the Black participants found all the items to be racist, a behavior does not have to be offensive to everyone or even most people in order to be problematic. For the purposes of that study, we considered any comment or behavior that was objectionable by 30% or more of Black participants to be problematic and best avoided for the sake of maintaining a harmonious, functional environment. (This is, of course, assuming there is no important need to commit the offensive behavior.) We found that most White students found the microaggressions objectionable as well. In a related study, we found a very strong correlation between the Black student scores on what they considered racist and whether or not the White students would say or do the microaggression ($r = .93$, $p < .001$), with White students denying they would commit most microaggressions (Michaels, Gallagher, Crawford, Kanter, & Williams, 2018). That tells us there is some degree of agreement between Black and White students as to what microaggressions are. This also shows us that it is not particularly difficult to identify microaggressions by consensus, and many or most people of color (and White people) do interpret them negatively.

Listed in Table 1.1 are the microaggressions included in our shortened, 20-item measure of microaggression propensity, the Cultural Cognitions and Actions Scale (CCAS). The findings are based on nationwide survey data collected from a large number of Black ($N = 226$) and White ($N = 312$) adults throughout the United

Table 1.1 Opinions of Microaggressions by Race

Scenario	Microaggressive Item	Blacks Rating as Racist (%)	Whites Unlikely to Say/ Do (%)
1. Meeting a Black female with African-style dress and braided hair	"I've always wanted to go to Africa."	43.4	88.5
	"Why do Black women wear their hair in these sorts of styles?	64.6	92.0
	"Can I touch your hair?"	50.4	92.0
2. Discussion about White privilege at diversity training	"Everyone suffers. Not just Black people."	38.1	48.1
	"I am not a racist."	22.1	62.2
	"A lot of minorities are too sensitive."	74.8	77.9
3. Study session talking about various current events and political issues	"All lives matter, not just Black lives."	51.3	59.0
	"I don't think of Black people as Black."	37.6	72.4
	"Stay quiet so you don't offend anyone."	47.3	41.7
	"Everyone can succeed in this society, if they work hard enough."	36.3	57.4
	"Black people should work harder to fit in to our society."	82.3	83.3
4. A lost Black man asking for directions in neighborhood	Check that your wallet/purse is secure.	75.2	69.6
	Make sure not to make eye contact and just keep walking.	64.2	77.6
	Cross the street to avoid him.	73.0	78.8
5. Doing karaoke with friends and song with N-word comes up	Say the N-word loudly every time you hear it.	76.5	88.5
	Leave the room to avoid an uncomfortable situation.	10.6	61.5
6. Watching news about police brutality with diverse friends at sports bar	"I would be pretty scared—that guy looks like a thug."	85.4	87.2
	"The real problem is a lack of good role models in the Black community."	62.8	78.8
7. Talking to racially ambiguous lab mate about science project	"Where are your parents from?"	38.1	80.1
	"I'm not racist, but I really want to know what race you are."	49.1	90.7

States using Amazon Mechanical Turk (Williams, Muir, Ching, & George, 2019). Included are the percentage of Black participants finding the microaggressive statement objectionable in the context of the scenarios listed (i.e., rated as "a little racist" or "very racist") and the percentage of White participants who reported that they were "unlikely" or "very unlikely" to say or do each item. It is clear that despite some variability, there is much agreement on the unacceptability of most items ($r = .43$).

WHY ARE MICROAGGRESSIONS OFFENSIVE?

In our culture, "Where are you from?" is generally considered a normal and reasonable get-to-know-you question when interacting with new people. However, such a question may also be a microaggression depending on the context. To determine if the question is actually a microaggression, we can examine it to find out if it reinforces pathological stereotypes or communicates exclusion. Often, people of color are asked questions about their origins because the offender wants to know what "category" to place the target in to ascertain where that person stands on the socioracial hierarchy, and so the question may not really be about where the person is from at all. Because our culture places so much importance on race, people are very uncomfortable not knowing how to classify others, and so rather than asking what race they are (the question they really want answered), they ask it in coded language: "Where are you from?" For example, I am often asked this question in various ways, and when I answer "California," the other person is often not satisfied. If I want to avoid a long game of 20 questions, I might just tell the other person that I am African American to bring the conversation to a quicker end. Often, this reply is met with astonishment, if I do not look like what the other person thinks an African American should look like or the person is not used to meeting a Black academic. Remember, Black people are stereotyped as unintelligent, and being a professor runs counter to this expectation. If I do not volunteer my race right away, offenders will often keep asking questions to figure out how to classify me. And sometimes, even when I assert that I am Black, they may not believe it. Often, people stop asking me questions only after I explain that I was born in the United States, my parents both are African American, they were born and raised in two southern US states, and both of them had Black parents. Occasionally, I have been compelled to show pictures of my parents as proof. In these cases, rarely do offenders want to have a discussion about my heritage or want to learn about my cultural experiences growing up. They just want to know what "box" I belong in so they can attach their stereotypes to me. It is not until they are convinced I am truly Black that they stop asking questions. That is what makes this a microaggression and probably why so many people of color find this sort of questioning unsettling. But a genuine interest in my culture would not be a microaggression—it would actually be quite welcome.

As another example, when someone asks an Asian American where they are from, it is often a microaggression because the assumption is that the person is foreign-born. Many Asian Americans were born in the United States and have lived here for generations. It is tiresome to be constantly asked, "Where are you from?" and have the answer "Cincinnati" be unsatisfying to offenders. We can, however, imagine a situation in which it might not be a microaggression. For example, if someone is asking an Asian American woman where she is from because that person has been to Korea, wants to discuss Korean culture with her, and has a non-racist reason to believe she is familiar with Korean culture (because she has a Korean name, Korean art in her home, cooks Korean food, etc.), then that might not be a microaggression. But if the person is asking based on the simple fact that the woman has Asian physical features and he wants to know how to categorize her to attach his stereotypes to her, then it would be a microaggression. As previously noted, microaggressions are context dependent, and as such the same statement may or may not be microaggressive depending on the circumstances. However, the question may still be problematic, even if there is a non-racist reason for asking. A better query might be, "I am very interested in Korean culture, and I'm wondering if you are of Korean heritage." In this case, the person asking recognizes that simply asking, "Where are you from?" may not address what he really wants to know and he is sensitive enough to recognize that wording could be experienced as a microaggression, and so he provides a reason in advance for asking the question in the first place.

Figure 1.2 illustrates a similar example, with two couples at a get-together over dinner. Simply asking one of the guests, "Where are you from?" might not be a microaggression if it is for the sake of better understanding the other person. But when the person then comments on the guest's accent, it becomes evident that

Figure 1.2 Questions about where people are from can be a microaggression when some ethnic origins are devalued in comparison to others.

there was more behind the question, causing some concern and distress in the target, who fears that her answer will result in prejudice. When thinking about the harms caused by these types of microaggressions, consider there are many reasons this line of questioning is problematic:

1. White people who speak American English are almost never asked what country they are from, so the target may feel singled out for being non-White.
2. Implicit in the question is the assumption that the target may not be a true American, contributing to feelings of alienation and not belonging.
3. Assuming one is from abroad is wrong much of the time, and it feels awkward to have to keep correcting people. For example, more than 30% of Asian Americans were born in the United States.
4. If the target person says they are from someplace in the United States, the person asking the question probes for more information and this can be uncomfortable.
5. The assertion of "curiosity" is often untrue because often the person asking only wants the information in order to apply their stereotypes to the individual.
6. If the person is not a native English speaker, they may feel self-conscious or embarrassed about their accent.
7. If the person has a stigmatized heritage (e.g., they are Puerto Rican instead of Portuguese), the person asking may be disappointed with the answer, which is often apparent to the target.

Because just asking where someone is from may be a microaggression, one may wonder how a conscientious therapist can glean this information from new clients. It may be tempting to not ask at all. Although forcing someone to identify their race can be a microaggression, this is not the same as a situation in which someone is filling out a form and race is asked in order to better serve all clients, so you can keep this question on your intake forms. (Although it can be a microaggression if people are forced to choose a category that does not fit them.) But because this is so similar to a microaggression, anyone collecting racial and ethnic information should explain why they need it. In Chapter 5, there is more discussion on why therapists should collect this information and how to do it in a sensitive and non-microaggressive manner.

MICROAGGRESSIONS IN THE MEDIA

Microaggressions bombard us all through many avenues, including the media. Interestingly, there is a legacy of racism in soap ads, which has not completely ended. Historically, some brands of soap humorously advanced their benefits by featuring Black children turned White with the use of the advertised product. A recent Dove body wash advertisement followed suit by featuring a Black woman who removes her brown shirt and, as if by magic, underneath is a White woman in a white shirt. The ad was considered racist because it showed a Black woman transforming into a White woman, suggesting that dark skin is dirty and light skin is clean. This comes after an earlier, similarly criticized Dove ad that showed two women of color and a White woman standing in front of "before" and "after" signs. The Black woman was standing in front of an enlarged image of scratchy damaged skin, the White woman was standing in front of smooth healthy skin, and a Latina woman was standing in between.

The H&M fashion chain had to apologize after its website featured a Black child wearing a green hoodie emblazoned with the words "Coolest monkey in the jungle." In the same series of advertisements, a White child wore a hoodie that read "Survival expert." Of course, the chain apologized and insisted it meant no harm, but many were disgusted and outraged by the ad. If we examine this using our criteria for microaggressions, we can see the ad propagated hurtful stereotypes about Black people, who have historically been compared to apes and considered less evolved that Whites. And it was racially offensive to many. So, this ad would qualify as a microaggression.

Microaggressions appear in the news media as well. Such statements were made by a journalist employed by a major Canadian newspaper, the *National Post*. The title of the article was "Stop Calling People 'Racialized Minorities.' It's Silly and Cynical" by Jonathan Kay (2014). Kay states that

> Western societies have, to their great credit, taken further strides in removing race as a barrier to professional achievement. Indeed, one of the only barriers they have left to overcome is the effort of *Toronto Star* [competitor news outlet]-type liberals to convince them that anyone without white skin is constantly being racialized by the rest of us. They're not.

This writer is apparently praising his culture for fixing the racism problem without acknowledging major problems that still exist. He also fails to acknowledge that people of color *are* in fact racialized by others, and then he goes on to criticize those of us who would point this out. Finally, he calls the terminology "silly," which could be insulting to those who are racialized and also implies that he has the necessary authority or expertise that would give him the prerogative to weigh in on the issue, although he is not an expert on race relations.

Microaggressions are particularly harmful when made by prominent and powerful individuals. Politicians on both sides of the aisle have made a number of microaggressive statements throughout the years, and President Donald Trump is no exception. During his presidential campaign, he said,

> When Mexico sends its people, they're not sending their best. They're not sending you. They're not sending you. They're sending people that have lots of problems, and they're bringing those problems with us. They're bringing drugs. They're bringing crime. They're rapists. And some, I assume, are good people.

Here, we see a very public person advancing unfair and inaccurate pathological stereotypes about Mexican immigrants—that they are drug dealers and
rapists—that only fuels hateful biases. Such statements contribute to subsequent
stereotyping and fears about Mexican Americans that lead to real problems, including more microaggressions and larger problems such as hate crimes and even
racially motivated mass shootings.

Prominent democrats have also made microaggressive remarks. For example,
at a town hall meeting in Des Moines, Iowa, when discussing advanced placement programs in schools, former Vice President Joe Biden said, "We have this
notion that somehow if you're poor, you cannot do it. Poor kids are just as bright
and just as talented as White kids." In this sentence, he is equating kids of color
and being poor, even though most Americans of color are not poor. He is also
equating wealth and talent with Whiteness. We can see that Biden has some racist
associations around people of color that fuel biases and pathological stereotypes.

ENVIRONMENTAL MICROAGGRESSIONS

In a frequently used university conference room with which I am familiar, many
large framed pictures of impoverished Black children hang on the walls. It is
not immediately apparent why these pictures are there, as I noticed there were
no placards explaining the photos. The children were dirty, wore second-hand
clothes, and ate food off of plastic plates. These pictures could be considered
microaggressions at several levels: They promoted unfair stereotypes as Black
people as poor, needy, and unable to take care of their families. Were they
being rescued from their plight by White saviors? I did not see photographs of
impoverished White, Hispanic, or Asian children—and certainly needy children
of all races occupy the world. One of the students in my graduate class also saw a
similarly troubling picture in another room in the same facility portraying a poor,
crowded neighborhood with an AIDS symbol ribbon on every door. All human
characters in the picture had dark skin, perpetuating a stereotype that most Black
individuals in African countries have AIDS. One must wonder about the impact
of such images on those who use these facilities. It might promote feelings of stereotype threat in Black people and feelings of superiority in Whites, which could
influence the dynamics of meetings occurring in those rooms. I can only wonder
what diverse job applicants think and feel, seeing those images as a backdrop to
interviews.

"MICROAGGRESSIONS" VERSUS "EVERYDAY RACISM"

Microaggressions overlap with some similar concepts, so one cannot study
microaggressions without considering these other close constructs and the related literature base. Microaggressions are similar to the concept of "everyday
racism," which first emerged from the work of Essed (1991) and her studies

of Black women in various societies. She described how racism is transmitted through routine practices that seem normal to the dominant group, ensuring that the racism goes largely unrecognized and unacknowledged (Phillips & Lowery, 2018). *Everyday racism* is defined as unacknowledged racism, integrated into common situations through cognitive and behavioral practices that activate and perpetuate underlying power relations through familiar schemas in common situations. One example is the concept of "majority rule," which may be used to legitimize ignoring minority concerns, often dismissed as something of interest to only a small number of people. By this rubric, it becomes possible that no ethnic minority concerns will ever be addressed because those concerns impact a relatively smaller number of individuals, and yet we unthinkingly defer to majority opinion in many common situations. In fact, majority rule is considered a pillar of American democracy. Everyday racism is part of a larger system of structural racism that reinforces racial hierarchies resulting in a cumulative negative impact on people of color.

Everyday racism was followed by the concept of "everyday discrimination," which is well studied in terms of impact and outcomes. This describes subjective common discrimination or unfair treatment as a form of stress in society that is strongly related to race (Banks, Kohn-Wood, & Spencer, 2006). *Everyday discrimination* can be defined as minor daily hassles and recent experiences that often constitute an assault to one's character (Ayalon & Gum, 2011). Compared to microaggressions, everyday discrimination tends to have a greater focus on discrete discriminatory experiences, sometimes including blatant acts of prejudice, and tends to not include social exclusion or environmental assaults. This construct also sometimes addresses forms of discrimination other than race, such as gender or disability-related discrimination.

Like microaggressions, everyday racism and everyday discrimination, including covert prejudice, are common and are rooted in power differentials between groups. Therefore, many, if not most, microaggressions can be conceptualized as manifestations of everyday racism and discrimination. A robust body of literature utilizing national samples has linked everyday discrimination to various negative mental and physical health outcomes across racial and ethnic groups, as described in more detail in Chapter 3.

MICROAGGRESSIONS CAN BE DIFFICULT TO RECOGNIZE

When giving trainings about microaggressions, I typically show a slide with a list of categories and examples of related microaggressions. I notice that people are quickly snapping pictures of the slides with their cell phones, and many ask if they may have the list emailed to them. The problem, however, is that microaggressions are context dependent (Sue et al., 2007) and so cannot be defined simply on the basis of the exact behavior performed or the precise words used in a given sentence. A statement that might be microaggressive in one situation may not be a

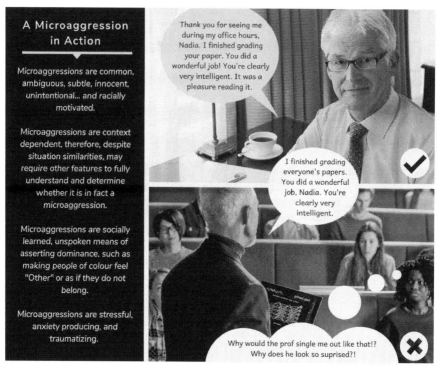

Figure 1.3 The same statement might not be a microaggression in one context but could be a problem in a different situation.

microaggression in another case. For example, as shown in Figure 1.3, telling a Black student that she is intelligent might not be a microaggression during office hours, but it might be if said during class with a look of surprise on the instructor's face (Williams, 2020).

Microaggressions are invisible to many White people because, as dominant group members, they usually do not directly experience them. Furthermore, they tend not to notice microaggressions levied against their peers of color (Alabi, 2015). However, those who are motivated to understand them can learn to identify microaggressions when they are happening to others, even if they are the observer and not the target. For example, a White parent who adopts a Hispanic child may start to notice microaggressions for the first time as they are leveled against the child or may even start to receive them from others who may be uncomfortable with an ethnoracially blended family.

People of color are at a social disadvantage that can at times lead to severe consequences (e.g., police violence, loss of employment, and eviction), and so out of necessity they may learn (from parents, peers, or their own experiences) to identify subtle signs of bias in order to most effectively navigate society. Some have argued this is critical for well-being (Stevenson, 1994), although it is worth noting that this discernment is an acquired skill and neither inborn nor an exact science. For example, groups of people living in the United States longer, for more generations, and/or with darker skin will tend to have more experience with racial bias than new immigrants or those who appear White (Keith, Nguyen, Taylor, Chatters, & Mouzon, 2017), and some ethnic groups engage in more racial socialization with their children than do others (Hughes et al., 2006). More racial socialization is correlated with both better identification of subtle racism and improved mental health (Brown & Tylka, 2010; Thai, Lyons, Lee, & Iwasaki, 2017). Furthermore, to the extent that some people of color may accept pathological stereotypes and vary in ethnic identity development, not all will be able to identify all microaggressions when they occur. In addition, due to the stress of confronting offenders directly about microaggressions, targets may make a conscious but effortful choice not to be offended, or they may engage in denial as a coping strategy (Nadal, 2018). And there are certainly some individuals who are simply not offended by anything.

Responsible individuals need to learn appropriate social habits in order to successfully navigate our increasingly multicultural society. Claiming ignorance is not good enough when one's behavior causes harm to others. For example, when one visits a foreign country, one is expected to familiarize oneself with the rules of the road before driving. Consider the case of a tourist who unintentionally strikes and injures a pedestrian because he was unfamiliar with the country's rules surrounding driving when pedestrians are near. Although the accident was unintended, the driver would still be considered culpable and possibly convicted for not being careful or knowledgeable enough. Claiming ignorance or even good intentions would not be adequate to absolve the driver. Stating that his American license is valid in the country he visited would not be adequate either. The problem is that harm was caused by the driver due to his failure to acquire the knowledge needed to manage that situation—knowledge that was freely available and that he was expected to acquire. The onus is on the driving tourist to find the information needed (rules of the road) in order to navigate the new country safely. By the same token, the onus is on therapists to learn the proper etiquette needed to interact appropriately with people from diverse cultures without causing harm. Ignorance ("I didn't know I needed to act differently"), arrogance ("Clients should adapt to my culture"), laziness ("I didn't have time to learn about her culture"), and naive good intentions ("I was only trying to help and didn't mean to be patronizing") are not acceptable reasons for causing harm, especially when the needed information for preventing harm is freely available.

2

Causes of Microaggressions

WHY DO PEOPLE MICROAGGRESS?

Why do people commit microaggressions? It has been suggested by some that microaggressions are mostly random behaviors that just happen because offenders are careless or unaware (Lilienfeld, 2017). Although it may be tempting to think of them as accidental acts, or even experiences imagined by targets, this idea is not theoretically or empirically supported. Microaggressions are learned behaviors, taught through observational learning and other social mechanisms from an early age. For example, racial socialization of African Americans typically includes parents teaching their children how to accurately detect racism and how to respond to encounters with racism, but typical racial socialization practices for White Americans are much different and may emphasize color-blindness (Pahlke, Bigler, & Suizzo, 2012; Priest et al., 2014). This process includes not acknowledging one's Whiteness, friendly joking about racial issues in the company of other Whites without calling it out as racism, and not talking about race at all around people of color. When race must be discussed, it is typically done using coded language, such as "low income," "quiet neighborhood," "inner-city kids," or "bad schools." As a result, White people are rarely proficient at having meaningful conversations about race, skillfully managing racially charged conversation, or calling out other White people on racist behaviors. This can be conceptualized as a skills deficit, and as such it can be remedied through education and practice (Williams, 2019b).

However, there is an additional component that also must be addressed, which is the fact that Whites are implicitly taught they are a superior race, even though explicitly they may be instructed otherwise. As a result, their actions or inactions continue to promote racism in subtle, microaggressive ways. As a historical example, during the era of legalized segregation, it was common to observe "caste behavior," such as Black people quietly deferring to Whites in public spaces, giving them the right of way on sidewalks and streets. Whites grew to expect this behavior, even if not consciously acknowledged, which reinforced feelings of superiority (Davis, 1989). It would be a mistake to argue that there was no intention to oppress the Black populace embedded in these subtle behaviors. Blacks deferred because they knew that failure to do so could result in harm. Most Whites would have denied doing anything harmful, aggressive, or intentional as they went about their daily business; it was simply what they had learned and what they had always done (Williams, 2020a).

Similarly, even people who may consider themselves unbiased learn that microaggressive statements and actions are an appropriate and harmless way of interacting with people of color, even if not taught this explicitly (as captured in Figure 2.1). This behavior is maintained because targets have learned that should they object, they risk suffering some degree of harm, such as invalidation (Sue et al., 2007), anger and defensiveness (DiAngelo, 2011), being called neurotic (e.g., Lilienfeld, 2017), or having one's character attacked (e.g., Campbell & Manning, 2014).

In addition, dominant group members may be rewarded by other White people for acting in superior ways and socially punished for calling out racism or pushing for equity. This is called *White solidarity*, and it prevents White people from speaking out against microaggressions, even when they see them happening and know something is wrong. Doing so puts one at risk of being considered a "race traitor." Consider that most White Americans have been subjected to powerful though often unspoken racial socialization processes that operate at a cultural level often outside of conscious awareness. This prevents individual

Figure 2.1 Even people who may consider themselves unbiased learn that microaggressive statements are an appropriate and harmless way of interacting with people of color.

agency in bringing about change. For example, one of my African American lab members gave a talk at a women's mental health conference recently—a place that was supposed to be a "safe space," filled with women who were strong advocates of social justice. During a panel discussion, one of the White women used the N-word (twice), much to the shock and horror of those in attendance and the other panelists (Reed, 2019). She was trying to describe an experience she had as a child surrounding her own learning about race, but she failed to consider how her words might be hurtful for people of color. My Black colleague was only a few feet away from the speaker, and the most distressing aspect of this was not that the N-word was used but, rather, that none of the other women corrected it. Those White women, all social justice activists, sitting on either side of a Black woman knew very well that saying this word was not ok. But not one spoke up or publicly corrected the White speaker. Rather, they all looked at the Black woman to see if she would respond. She got up and left. We processed this as a small group later, as I struggled to interpret the reason for their silence. The White women felt terrible. They admitted that they knew it was wrong, and they even knew what to do, but they just did not do it. Why? They did not want to hurt the speaker. The feelings of the White offender were more salient than the feelings of the Black victim in that moment. Their social conditioning around White solidarity was just too strong— even among social justice activists. I have seen very few instances in which a White person was willing to publicly advocate on behalf of a person of color and call out microaggressive behavior. And this seems even more unlikely to occur when the offender is considered a friend or colleague. It is no wonder that it is so difficult for people of color to fight against microaggressions at work or in other institutional settings. White people tend to close ranks and protect oppressors, and it may be automatic. These learning histories are difficult to overcome.

IMPLICIT BIAS

Implicit bias refers to biases in feelings, thoughts, or actions toward others, fueled by unconscious evaluative judgments and stereotypes. It has proven to be useful and important to understanding racial bias. The term's scientific foundations are from implicit social cognition, which attempts to explain observations that many mental processes function outside consciousness, and the term was soon applied to explain discrimination that could not be understood as resulting from explicitly expressed discriminatory attitudes. Tests that intend to measure implicit biases are diverse, ranging from tests of associative response latency, such as the Implicit Association Test (IAT; Greenwald, McGhee, & Schwartz, 1998), to sentence completion tasks and subtle behavioral indicators such as how close one chooses to sit in a waiting room beside a Black confederate. As noted by Kanter and colleagues (2019), White people respond, seemingly without awareness, in racially biased ways on all of these tests.

The IAT is probably the most popular means of evaluating implicit bias. It is a measure developed by social psychologists to detect the strength of a person's automatic association between mental representations of objects (concepts) in memory. Like one's blood pressure, the IAT does not produde the same score consistently, and its ability to detect bias can be affected by many extraneous factors, such as mood, attention, and motivation. But when taken over several administrations and across large populations, it does appear to measure something real. Using the IAT, research shows that most White people have a moderate pro-White, anti-Black bias, and this holds true for every state in America, with only minor differences based on geography. Furthermore, my own analysis of IAT data found nearly identical levels of anti-Black bias among White people in Canada, Europe, Australia, and elsewhere (Faber, Williams, & Terwilliger, 2019). White men and women and White Hispanic and non-Hispanic people also show a similar level of anti-Black racial bias. In addition, the same amount of implicit bias is seen in children as young as age 6 years as in 10- and 19-year-olds, although explicit bias decreases with age (Baron & Banaji, 2006). This means that children learn racism from an early age and continue to have these same biased attitudes into adulthood, although they will tend to profess a lack of bias as they grow older.

AVERSIVE RACISM

Implicit bias is thought to be a factor in the phenomenon known as aversive racism (Gaertner & Dovidio, 2005). Aversive racism differs from blatant, old-fashioned racism, and it is thought to characterize the racial attitudes of most well-educated and progressive White Americans. It is more indirect and subtle than the traditional racism, but its consequences are destructive nonetheless. Aversive racists outwardly endorse fair and just treatment of all groups yet harbor feelings of discomfort toward people of color that may be unconscious. Aversive racists are motivated by avoiding wrongdoing, and they may avoid interracial interactions to prevent any behaviors that could be considered racist.

Aversive racists may feel uneasy or threatened in the presence of people of color, particularly among those of equal or higher education level and socioeconomic status. Because aversive racists outwardly endorse egalitarian values, their biases do not manifest in situations in which there are clear social norms of right and wrong because to discriminate in such situations would compromise their egalitarian beliefs. Instead, aversive racists discriminate in situations in which the guidelines for appropriate social behavior are unclear, when the basis for decision-making is vague, or when their actions can be justified or rationalized on the basis of some factor other than race (Gaertner & Dovidio, 2005). For example, a therapist may opt not to take on a new client of color and justify it due to having a full client load already, although had the new client been White, the therapist would have found a way to squeeze the person in (Kugelmass, 2016). Thus, rejection of the client of color can be justified based on having enough clients already rather than the truth of the matter, which is that the therapist prefers White clients. People of color are highly attuned to this sort of behavior and will be quick to consider the possibility of covert racism, regardless of the stated intentions of the offender. Were the therapist to be confronted with the reality of the situation, the therapist has a ready explanation for the exclusionary behavior, making it easy to rationalize that no microaggressions occurred and perhaps the client is reading too much into the situation. This sort of reasoning can contribute to the misperception by some that microaggressions are not real.

MICROAGGRESSIONS AS AVOIDANCE AND INACTION

Bailey (1998) notes that schemas about how White people should behave include

> being nervous around people of color, avoiding eye contact with them, or adopting closed, uncomfortable postures in their presence. The repeated animation of these scripts, however, re-inscribes a racial order in which White lives, culture, and experiences are valued at the expense of the lives of persons of color, whose bodies are fearsome to Whites and who are cast as deviant, dirty, criminal, ugly, or degenerate. (p. 36)

I can recall an illustrative experience that happened to me not too long ago. I was invited to a prestigious Southern medical school to give grand rounds for the department of psychiatry. It was a wonderful experience, as the auditorium was full and people had many thoughtful and engaging questions. After the lecture was over, I waited in the lobby of an adjacent building for a ride from the doctor who had invited me. The lobby was mostly empty, but there was a long armless, concrete bench with a lone blonde White young woman sitting at the end working on her laptop. I also sat on the bench, at least 5 feet away. She did not make eye contact with me or acknowledge my presence, but over the course of the next 5 minutes, the woman slowly shifted her body 90 degrees until she was completely turned away with her back to me. As I noticed this, I saw that her new position was more uncomfortable than before because she no longer had the benefit of the back of the bench for support. I do not think she was conscious of the fact that she turned her back to me, but I do think it was motivated by racial biases about physical space between Blacks and Whites. And I definitely perceived it as a microaggression because it made me feel that my presence was unwelcome. It was a sad end to an otherwise quite positive visit.

Because of biased socialization practices and because interracial interactions put people at risk of committing microaggressions, some individuals find themselves avoiding people of color altogether. This does not solve the problem, however, because avoidance only heightens anxieties. Interracial anxieties may play a role in situations in which would-be offenders do not want to appear prejudiced and are motivated by a desire to avoid wrongdoing (i.e., aversive racism; Gaertner & Dovidio, 2005), but we know well that anxiety impairs performance. Thus, when people with interracial anxiety are in the company of people of color, they may stumble over their words, say something they did not intend, say nothing, or leave the situation entirely. Although wanting to avoid wrongdoing could be considered well-intentioned behavior, one must also consider what motivates the offender's discomfort as well as the consequences to the person of color in that interaction. Avoidance, exclusion, and ostracization are all forms of aggression, and some microaggressions fall into this category. We as mental health professionals certainly do not want people of color we encounter to feel avoided, excluded, or ostracized.

One mechanism for how these things can happen is that the offender may have had little contact with people of color because the person avoids them due to pathological stereotypes (e.g., assumed dangerousness), has had few opportunities at cross-racial interactions (e.g., due to segregated social experiences), and/or thinks a racial mistake will result in harsh response (e.g., stereotypes about people from certain groups being hostile). As such, the person unwittingly communicates their anxiety through body language (physical distancing, looking away, blinking, nervous laughter, etc.). The offender's comfort takes precedence over exhibiting courteous behavior, and instead of making the person of color feel welcome, the offender's behavior causes the target to feel out of place and unwanted or even feared. The offender does not attempt a genuine social connection but instead endures the presence of the person of color or may even look for opportunities to escape (Plant & Butz, 2006). Many people of color are keen observers of subtle signs of racism and will realize immediately that their presence is unwanted (Dovidio, Kawakami, & Gaertner, 2002). This is microaggressive behavior because it reinforces traditional rules that maintain separation between people of different races, and it reminds the person of color that social interactions outside of one's group are off limits and unwanted. Furthermore, it may also be driven by negative assumptions about the target based on pathological stereotypes. In our own research, we found that this sort of avoidance was significantly correlated with five separate measures of racism (Parigoris et al., 2018).

HOW ARE MICROAGGRESSIONS MAINTAINED?

Based on what we know about behavioral conditioning, we would expect that behaviors that are punished or unreinforced would eventually become extinct. Given that people of color are not positively reinforcing others for being microaggressive, and at least sometimes expressing their displeasure about it (punishment), one may wonder why such behaviors have persisted. Indeed, microaggressions are basically unchanged since Pierce first described them five decades ago. Microaggressions persist because the underlying cause of these behaviors (racism) reinforces social inequalities and hierarchies that are desirable to the in-group. According to social dominance theory (Pratto, 1999), group-based inequalities are reinforced through intergroup behaviors, including behavioral asymmetry and individual discrimination (Sidanius & Pratto, 2012). These behaviors are justified, both morally and intellectually, by widely shared legitimizing cultural myths (Sidanius, Pratto, & Devereux, 1992), including pathological stereotypes that ultimately serve to reinforce and propagate inequality.

These behaviors are maintained because they contribute to a sense of superiority in the dominant group.

Furthermore, although microaggressions are sometimes rebuffed by the target, they must often be accepted without challenge because of the power differential between the parties. Targets learn that should they reject microaggressive actions, they may experience social harm in the form of anger, defensiveness, and/or denial from the offender (DiAngelo, 2011; Smith, Allen, & Danley, 2007; Sue et al., 2007). Thus, targets are typically forced to endure these insults without recourse, which contributes to the perpetuation of the problem.

Fear of reprisal may not only perpetuate microaggressions but also lead to coerced behavior on the part of targets. For example, imagine a situation in which several students are attending office hours for a difficult computer science class (Williams, 2020). After one of the White students shares with the professor what a difficult time she is having, the professor points to a Chinese American student who is also waiting for help and suggests they work together, saying, "I bet David can help you out." Suppose David is also really struggling in the class, feels embarrassed to be doing poorly, and now feels tremendous stress and anxiety having been volunteered as a tutor. Imagine David says to the professor that he is not comfortable helping the other student and also feels a bit stereotyped by the whole situation. The professor could recognize the misstep and apologize, or he could get angry, defensive, and even covertly retaliate against the student. Imagine David has experienced angry retaliation in the past for pointing out a microaggression, so he decides it is just too risky and opts to help the other student rather than risk the possible harms of sharing how this affected him. He might even neglect other academic needs in order to meet the professor's stereotyped expectations. So, it is not simply that microaggressions are unwanted and offensive; it is also that targets are not truly free to reject them.

CAN PEOPLE OF COLOR COMMIT MICROAGGRESSIONS AGAINST EACH OTHER?

People of color are subjected to the same pathological stereotypes about various ethnic and racial groups as everyone else, and so they may hold negative views about other ethnic groups or even their own group if they are in an early stage of ethnic identity development (Sue & Sue, 2016). The stage of ethnic identity development and exposure to people from other groups may moderate the extent to which even people of color subscribe to pathological stereotypes.

People of color are generally cautious about discussing prejudice and conflicts between various oppressed racial and ethnic groups for fear that such issues may be used by those in power against them. For example, someone might assuage their own guilt about committing microaggressions by saying, "People of color are always microaggressing against each other, so why should I care if they're doing the same thing?" These types of problems may be used to divert attention away from larger problems such as structural racism by defining problems as residing between various racial minority groups rather than the greater issues (Sue & Sue, 2016).

It is important to understand that prejudice between various ethnic and racial groups occurs under an umbrella of White racial supremacy (Sue & Sue, 2016). Although people of color may discriminate, they do not have the systemic power to oppress on a large-scale basis. This means that although they might be able to cause hurt on an individual basis, they generally do not have the power to cause widespread harm, especially to White people. In fact, interethnic prejudice among minority groups may be encouraged by some White people because it benefits those in power by dividing groups that could have more power if they joined together to fight larger inequities.

So, the answer to the question, "Can people of color commit microaggressions against each other?" is absolutely yes. And, these behaviors hurt people of color while also advancing White supremacy.

3

How Microaggressions Are Harmful

MENTAL HEALTH IMPACT OF MICROAGGRESSIONS

Given everything discussed to this point, it should be no surprise that microaggressions are associated with several negative mental health outcomes. Here, I describe each major area that has been studied to date that connects microaggressions or everyday racial discrimination to psychopathology, along with some of the supporting literature. Most of the studies described are correlational, but many are prospective.

Stress

Torres, Driscoll, and Burrow (2010) studied the impact of racial microaggressions on the mental health of African American doctoral students and graduates of doctoral programs ($N = 97$). They found that underestimation of personal ability was associated with greater feelings of stress at 1-year follow-up, which in turn were related to greater depressive symptoms. They suggested that microaggressions which involve assumptions of low intelligence may be particularly salient for this sample of high-achieving individuals given that they occur in an important domain of professional functioning and academic success. Active coping was found to moderate the microaggression–stress link. In our own study of an undergraduate sample (Williams, Kanter, & Ching, 2018), we found that African Americans experience significant anxiety, stress, and trauma symptoms in connection with microaggressions that cannot be accounted for by negative emotionality. We found greater stress in connection with microaggressions against females, despite experiencing the same or fewer number of microaggressions as males.

Physical Ailments

Because microaggressions are so common and unrelenting, they can be conceptualized as a form of chronic stress that in turn results in physical problems, such as hypertension and impaired immune response (Berger & Sarnyai, 2015; Clark et al., 1999). Physical ailments can negatively impact mental health as well—for example, by reducing quality of life and contributing to other mental health concerns. Colen, Ramey, Cooksey, and Williams (2018) conducted a longitudinal study of middle and high socioeconomic (SES) Black and Hispanic Americans examining exposure to chronic discrimination using the Everyday Discrimination Scale. For Whites, moderate income gains over time result in significantly less exposure to any type of discrimination, whereas in this study, upwardly mobile African Americans and Hispanic Americans were significantly more likely to experience everyday discrimination (as well as more major discrimination). This explained worse health for African Americans in the sample.

Everyday discrimination was found to predict increased inflammation, a risk factor for future cardiovascular disease, over a 7-year period in non-obese diverse women (N = 2,490; Beatty Moody, Brown, Matthews, & Bromberger, 2014) and related memory decline in older adults over a 6-year period (N = 12,624; Zahodne, Kraal, Sharifian, Zaheed, & Sol, 2019). It was also predictive of chronic conditions such as heart disease, pain, and respiratory illnesses in Asian Americans (N = 2,095; Gee, Spencer, Chen, & Takeuchi, 2007), and low infant birthweight in African American women (Dailey, 2009).

Depression

Using a nationally representative sample of African American adults, higher SES men were found to experience greater everyday discrimination, with increased economic standing leading to greater likelihood of depression (Hudson et al., 2012). This finding may be due in part to higher SES men having jobs that require more time spent with White people, leading to more opportunities for microaggressions to occur and more structural barriers to advancement. Huynh (2012) studied first- and second-generation Latino and Asian American adolescents (N = 360) and found that microaggressions in the form of negative treatment predicted depressive symptoms. Nadal, Griffin, Wong, Hamit, and Rasmus (2014) examined a large diverse sample of community and undergraduate participants (N = 506) and found that higher frequencies of racial microaggressions negatively predicted mental health and that racial microaggressions were significantly correlated with depressive symptoms and negative affect, although correlations were small. In a large nationally representative sample of older adults (N = 7,493), everyday racial discrimination was correlated to symptoms of depression across all ethnic groups studied (Ayalon & Gum, 2011), with convergent findings in other studies as well (Clark, Salas-Wright, Vaughn, & Whitfield, 2015; Pittman, 2011; Torres et al., 2010; Torres & Taknint, 2015).

Self-Esteem and Self-Efficacy

In an undergraduate student sample ($N = 225$), Nadal, Wong, Griffin, Davidoff, and Sriken (2014) examined the relationship between racial microaggressions and self-esteem. They found that racial microaggressions negatively predicted lower self-esteem, with microaggressions that occurred in educational and workplace environments particularly harmful. Thai, Lyons, Lee, and Iwasaki (2017) studied emerging Asian American adults ($N = 87$) using Amazon Mechanical Turk and found a negative correlation between racial microaggressions and several facets of self-esteem, with racial socialization helping to buffer against this relationship. Forrest-Bank and Jenson (2015) studied microaggression among Asian, Hispanic, Black, and White American undergraduates at a public urban university ($N = 409$). Racial microaggressions were inversely correlated with academic self-efficacy; however, ethnic identity had the opposite relationship.

Alcohol and Substance Use

Clark et al. (2015) examined a national sample of African American and Caribbean Black adult respondents [the National Survey of American Life (NSAL); $N = 4,462$]. They identified four categories of everyday discrimination that they classified as low discrimination, disrespect and condescension, general discrimination, and chronic discrimination. Those exposed to chronic everyday discrimination were found to have elevated rates of substance use disorders. Gerrard et al. (2012) conducted an experimental study in which African American young adults ($N = 100$) were excluded from a cyberball game by a White confederate. Those who had previously endorsed substance use as a coping strategy reported more willingness to use substances after experiencing racial exclusion. In a study by Blume, Lovato, Thyken, and Denny (2012), undergraduates aged 18–20 years ($N = 594$) were asked to report on the frequency of experiencing 51 different microaggressions; students of color who experienced more microaggressions were at increased risk for underage binge alcohol use as well as the negative outcomes of alcohol abuse. Hatzenbuehler, Corbin, and Fromme (2011) reported similar findings in a mixed race sample for everyday discrimination. Lorenzo-Blanco, Unger, Ritt-Olson, Soto, and Baezconde-Garbanati (2013) found that everyday discrimination predicted smoking in a large ($N = 1,436$) sample of Hispanic high school students in Southern California in Project RED (Reteniendo y Entendiendo Diversidad para Salud).

Post-Traumatic Stress Disorder Symptoms

Several studies have found connections between microaggressions and trauma symptoms. Dale and Safren (2019) studied a sample of Black women living with HIV ($N = 100$) and found that gendered racial microaggressions and racial discrimination predicted higher post-traumatic cognitions. When controlling for racial discrimination and other variables, only gendered racial microaggressions contributed uniquely to both total post-traumatic stress disorder (PTSD) symptoms and total negative post-traumatic cognitions. In our own study of White and Black undergraduates ($N = 177$), we found that microaggressions related to being assumed to be a criminal by others, being eroticized, being perceived as low-achieving or part of an undesirable culture, being viewed as a foreigner or not belonging to society, and environmental omissions were all related to stress and trauma symptoms in African American students (Williams, Kanter, et al., 2018). In another study we conducted of trauma symptoms from discrimination that focused on African American and biracial students ($N = 123$), we found that both regularly occurring everyday discrimination and major discrimination over one's lifetime were significant predictors of trauma symptoms, despite sizable significant correlations between those two variables (Williams, Printz, & DeLapp, 2018). Furthermore, both general ethnic discrimination over one's lifetime and regular experiences of racial microaggressions were also significant predictors of trauma symptoms of discrimination, despite also being significantly correlated. This lends evidence to the hypothesis that all forms of discrimination are potentially traumatizing to targets, even types of discrimination that some might minimize or dismiss, such as microaggressions.

Suicide

Hollingsworth et al. (2017) studied African American young adults ($N = 135$) at a predominantly White institution in the Midwest. They found that specific types of racial microaggressions (i.e., invisibility, low-achievement/undesirable culture, and environmental invalidations) were associated with higher levels of perceptions of being a burden on others, which in turn were associated with higher levels of suicidal ideation. O'Keefe, Wingate, Cole, Hollingsworth, and Tucker (2015) examined a sample of Indigenous, Black, Hispanic, and Asian American adults ($N = 405$) to determine the relationship between microaggressions and suicidal ideation and depressive symptoms. Black American participants reported the highest frequency of microaggressive experiences among all groups, and Indigenous Americans reported the lowest frequency. Their analysis uncovered significant positive associations between frequency of microaggressive experiences and depressive symptoms and suicidal ideation. Depressive symptoms also significantly mediated the relationship between suicidal ideation and microaggressions.

Anxiety

Banks, Kohn-Wood, and Spencer (2006) examined data on everyday discrimination from African American adults in the Detroit Area Study ($N = 570$). Those who reported more everyday discrimination also had significantly greater anxiety and depressive symptoms, with women more likely than men to report experiencing anxiety symptoms in association with everyday discrimination. In the aforementioned binge drinking study conducted by Blume et al. (2012), students who experienced more microaggressions had higher anxiety. In our study of microaggressions in college students (Williams, Kanter, et al., 2018), we found that microaggressions related to being perceived as low-achieving, part of an undesirable culture, and environmental omissions were related to anxiety symptoms.

Somatization

Ong, Burrow, Fuller-Rowell, Ja, and Sue (2013) followed Asian American participants during a 2-week period and found that the experience of microaggressions predicted somatic symptoms and state negative affect, even after controlling for trait neuroticism. The participants encountered microaggressions frequently, with 78% experiencing at least one during the 2-week study period. Torres-Harding, Torres, and Yeo (2020) found that among college students of color, experiencing certain types of racial microaggressions was associated with more depression and perceived stress, which in turn were associated with more overall somatic symptoms. Also, microaggressions surrounding negative treatment emerged as the strongest predictor of somatic symptoms in the study of Asian and Hispanic American youth by Huynh (2012).

Obsessive–Compulsive Disorder

Using the NSAL data set, our lab examined symptoms of obsessive–compulsive disorder (OCD) in a nationally representative sample of African American adults ($N = 3,570$) and correlations between OCD symptom dimensions and experiences of discrimination (Williams, Taylor, et al., 2017). Two categories of discrimination were examined—everyday racial discrimination and everyday non-racial discrimination (i.e., due to gender, age, and weight)—to determine if racial discrimination had a unique impact on OCD symptoms. We found that everyday racial discrimination was correlated to all categories of obsessions and compulsions studied. Interestingly, everyday non-racial discrimination was not related to any of the categories of obsessions or compulsions. This suggests that racial microaggressions, as opposed to other types of microaggressions or slights, are uniquely related to OCD symptoms in people of color.

Overall Mental Health

A large epidemiological study (NSAL) examined associations between everyday discrimination psychiatric disorders in older African American adults ($N = 773$).

African Americans who experienced higher levels of everyday discrimination had higher odds of any psychiatric disorder, any lifetime mood disorder, any lifetime anxiety disorder, and more lifetime disorders as listed in the fourth edition of the *Diagnostic and Statistical Manual of Mental Disorders* (American Psychiatric Association, 1994), in addition to elevated levels of depressive symptoms and serious psychological distress (Mouzon, Taylor, Keith, Nicklett, & Chatters, 2017; see also Nadal, Griffin, et al., 2014). A nationally representative longitudinal study of older adults, spanning 2 years, found that microaggressions in the form of everyday discrimination had stronger negative effects compared to major discriminatory events, especially on emotional health (N = 6,377; Luo, Xu, Granberg, & Wentworth, 2012).

EXAMPLE OF PSYCHOLOGICAL HARM IN A HIGH SCHOOL STUDENT

Although the facts and figures connecting microaggresisons to psychological harm can be sobering, the pathway to mental health problems may be best illustrated with an example. Saleem, Anderson, and Williams (2020) describe a case in which a high school student named Lee develops depression and anxiety from experiencing microaggressions at his high school. Lee's parents immigrated to the United States before he was born; his father immigrated from China and his mother came from Palestine. As such, Lee was raised with a tricultural identity— Chinese, Palestinian, and American. Lee had a passion for music production, but his parents encouraged him to remain focused on academic advancement because they both immigrated for better educational opportunities as medical doctors. In high school, Lee was often called upon by teachers and asked for academic help from his peers, even though he did not perceive himself to be academically gifted. The pressure of the model minority stereotype caused stress and worry for Lee. In addition, negative depictions of Palestine in the media contributed to an uncomfortable racial climate at school. He experienced frequent microaggressions from classmates, including questions such as "Why does your mother wear that wrap on her head?" and "Do you think your family knows any terrorists?" On one occasion, Lee was sent to the principal's office by a teacher for wearing a shirt representing Palestine, and he was asked to change because it made others uncomfortable.

Due to the stressful racial climate, Lee began avoiding school when possible, dissociating, having nightmares about being racially targeted, and experiencing worry and hypervigilance about his performance and race. These symptoms were interpreted as an anxiety condition by teachers, who recommended a mental health consultation. Due to cultural mistrust, Lee's family was against the idea of mental health care and so they minimized Lee's difficulties, thereby preventing him from meeting with a counselor. By Lee's senior year, he was consumed with anxiety; feeling isolated from his peers; and experiencing frequent worries about police harassment because of his race, given the number of videos online showing racialized policing of Palestinians. Not only was Lee miserable but also his symptoms had a serious impact on his academic engagement and achievement.

ARE MICROAGGRESSIONS HARMFUL TO WHITE PEOPLE?

Several studies have found that discrimination for any reason can be harmful to the person on the receiving end, including discrimination due to gender, disability, religion, and sexual orientation (e.g., Cokley, Hall-Clark, & Hicks, 2011). Therefore, microaggressions can be harmful to targets, whether or not the victims identify as people of color. To explore this relationship further, we reanalyzed the data from our initial examination of microaggressions and symptoms of psychopathology in Black undergraduates (Williams, Kanter, et al., 2018) to determine if racial microaggressions were harmful to White students in the same way. Although White students reported far fewer microaggressions, we found the same relationships, with racial microaggressions being highly and significantly correlated to trauma symptoms, even after accounting for negative affectivity. In examining microaggression subscales by race, for White students, perceiving a lack of environmental representation or recognition was most traumatizing, followed by not belonging; for Black students, it was not belonging, followed by being part of an undesirable culture (Williams, Kanter, & Debreaux, 2017).

EXAMPLE INTERACTION: WHITE CLIENT WITH BLACK BOYFRIEND

Here, an example of a therapeutic interaction between a therapist and a client is presented. The client is a White female freshman at a large state college, and her boyfriend, also a freshman, is Black. She describes a recent encounter with campus police in which the two of them, along with two other friends (both White), were caught engaged in underage drinking. The police zeroed in on her boyfriend, interrogating him, while almost completely ignoring the three White students.

CLIENT: I couldn't understand it. I thought, why is this happening? Just because of the color of his skin? He is a great person. Everyone that I know in college drinks underage—it's not like something that defines his character. He is a hard-worker. He never does anything crazy against the law. He never is harming people. So I just couldn't pin why they were so adamant about being aggressive towards him.

THERAPIST: And you thought it was because of his race.

CLIENT: Yeah. I mean, given the circumstances and since they weren't talking to the rest of us at all, until they took our IDs. They acknowledged us and then said they were going to let us go. But the entire time that we tried to help the situation and explain to them what happened they were like, "No, we want to hear from him." Why? It's not like his story is going to be different than ours. It's not like we are trying to cover something up. It is not like any of us are here against our will. Why do you only need to hear the story from *him*?

THERAPIST: It's so hard to see someone you love being singled out because of their race. And to be singled out and mistreated and see the mistreatment happen right in front of you. It's really hard when you're close to that person, to witness it all, and then have to support him through all that.

CLIENT: Yes. Especially when I can't relate to it at all. It's not like I can say I understand. I can sympathize with him, but I can't really understand. I only feel what I see. I don't know what he's actually feeling. He tries to cover it up a lot, and act like he doesn't care, but I know he does.

THERAPIST: How have you approached him about this? Have you talked to him more about what happened in any detail?

CLIENT: Yeah. We discussed the situation afterwards, and I told him how I felt like they were being unfair to him, and he was like, "Oh, that's nothing" -- just brushing it off. To him, that was the best case scenario not the worst case scenario. You know? At least he wasn't harmed. But then I heard him tell another story about how his dad always told him if he ever had an interaction with cops to be very careful, because you don't know what is going to happen. You don't know if you turn your back on them if they are going to shoot, you know. Just because of the things you hear in the news and everything his dad always told him to be extremely careful with his words and the way he acts. So I know he is worried, and I know he is very concerned going into the future, but he doesn't like to admit that to me because I don't think he wants to think that he is afraid or that he can't handle it. But it is scary. I feel like he can't admit that it is something that should be a concern.

THERAPIST: And you know, it is brave how he can navigate situations like this with the kind of calmness you describe. But it does require great courage to be vulnerable, particularly with people that he loves.

CLIENT: Yeah, I know. I try to. Like there are times where he did admit to me that he was very nervous about how he looks. In the situation, he said he had a million different scenarios going through his mind. But, at the same time, that is all he will say. He won't talk about that he was scared, he won't acknowledge what could have happened. He will just say that there were other things that could have happened but they didn't. He doesn't want to come face-to-face with what could have happened despite the fact that there were three other people there. I think he is very brave for it. He is starting to realize this is an issue, and it's not okay to have people treat you like that based on your color.

THERAPIST: And what do you admire about him, you know, especially when you are seeing him in this particular situation and how he chooses to navigate it?

CLIENT: I admire his ability to not be angry and not internalize it all and become a bitter person because of it. He just takes it with a grain of salt and just says, "Well, if I can't get over it, then I'm going to be the person they want me to be." He is very strong about that, and I admire the fact that he is able to stay himself, despite the way he is treated at work or by the cops. He is still very diligent in his work. He is determined, he still gets good grades. He won't disrespect cops, no matter how many times they would come to talk to him, because he says that by being angry about it or being offended about it and changing who you are won't help the problem, it will only make it worse. I think that is very admirable about him.

THERAPIST: It sounds like, while there is a part of you that really wants him to fully express how he is feeling about the situation, there may be a part of you that is respectful of how he chooses to deal with the situation.

CLIENT: Yes. But, it bothers me a lot. I think about it more than I should, to be honest. And, it just makes me angry.

THERAPIST: I just want to say that I notice how you are reacting with anger but also managing to keep it under control, and also respecting his readiness to talk about it. That is very admirable, and I find it inspirational. You know, your willingness to be the person to support another person who is being discredited because of his race. I wonder how, like you said, you want to channel that anger into something, if you have ever thought about how you could support him while he is dealing with all this, and his readiness to talk about it, or how he chooses to present himself in similar situations.

CLIENT: When I think about it I get angry all over again. I want to distance myself from it because I wasn't the one being discriminated against or interrogated or anything, but just I don't want to sit back and do nothing. Even though I couldn't have helped that situation, I want to help prevent other situations, and it is a lot harder than it seems, but I definitely want to turn the anger into something positive. That way I can move forward with helping.

THERAPIST: I always say, you know, it's very important to have allies, and in our journey of combating discrimination, because, the whole experience of microaggressions or major forms of discrimination is very toxic. It wears you down, and you put in a lot of effort to combat that or to cope with it. From my personal experience, when I see a White ally putting in a similar amount of time and effort to increase awareness about these issues and be there for victims of color—that makes me feel warm inside, because I know at least they understand what it's like to spend time and energy to try and recover and support people who have been through similar experiences. It helps in my mind to create a sense of connectedness that I find to be absent if we were just to let this slide. To put in the time and effort, especially for allies to introspect about their privilege, and how privilege kind of shields them from events like this.

CLIENT: Exactly. And a lot of people don't realize that. In all honesty I had realized that, but that particular situation made me see that my privilege doesn't compare to anything that he experiences. It was very real to me. You hear everything in the news and you think, "Oh, that's never going to happen to me or happen to anyone I know." Then it does and you are like "Okay, this is a very real issue." Why is it that it is in every aspect in every person of color's life? It kind of woke me up a bit. It made me think that there needs to be more done about this. Yes, there were differences, but just acknowledging the differences isn't going to help take away the differences in how people are treated.

THERAPIST: Like being more actively involved and showing support in a caring way.

CLIENT: I am doing the best I can, and anyone who is White needs to offer their support.

THERAPIST: To use your privilege.

CLIENT: Exactly. In a way to help rather than harm.

THERAPIST: And being an ally can be tiring too. How in your day-to-day life you are coping in your efforts to support your boyfriend, in terms of self-care?

CLIENT: I have been trying to go to the gym a lot more just to keep myself busy, I guess, and just try not to think about all of the bad that happened. I am just trying to focus on the good. I do yoga a lot. I have an internship. I have another job with stage crew. I have been trying to surround myself with people I feel are like-minded and who can just, like I said, see the good in things rather than the bad. That's what I've been trying to do myself and keeping myself distracted and having these types of conversations with people I work with in different spaces. It's helping me realize that he is not alone, I am not alone—nobody is alone in the way they are feeling, and it is okay to just talk about it. So I have been talking about it a lot more, and honestly the more I do talk about it, the more I come to terms with what happened.

This situation shows how White people can also suffer from indirect microaggressions, such as when a microaggression is directed toward a person of color that may be a loved one. It was clear that the client was afraid for her boyfriend and believed he was in a dangerous situation. A therapist lacking a cultural understanding of police violence against Black men in America might have attempted to reassure the client and provide reasons why her boyfriend was not actually ever in any danger (witnesses present, no weapon, and cooperating with police). The therapist's cultural understanding of the situation and biases, including a belief in a just world, could influence the subsequent intervention, resulting in a microaggression of minimizing the client's fears. Fortunately, the therapist did not fall into that trap. He empathized with the situation, taking it seriously, and worked on processing the client's feelings about the experience. The therapist also helped the client better appreciate her boyfriend's strengths and formulate a plan for coping with racism, including being a stronger ally and supporting her attempts at self-care. See Chapter 7 for further discussion about allyship.

MENTAL HEALTH DISPARITIES AND BARRIERS TO TREATMENT

As described in the previous section, persistent discrimination in the form of microaggressions takes a physiological and psychological toll on targets, causing psychological and physiological stress leading to ethnic disparities in mental health. However, there are additional mechanisms by which microaggressions also lead to disparities, rooted in clinician biases. Some of these problems start before the client comes into the office. Bias can be seen in who therapists elect to treat, which can vary by race, income, and sex. It has been known for some time that these biases exist in the medical field, and the mental health profession is no exception.

Failing to Accept a Client of Color

Kugelmass (2016) conducted a study to determine if people of color were being discriminated against in terms of obtaining mental health services. To that end, 320 New York City-based psychotherapists, with doctoral degrees and solo practices, were randomly selected from a large health insurance provider's health maintenance organization plan. Each received voicemail messages from one purportedly Black middle-class and one White middle-class caller of the same gender or from one purportedly Black working-class and one White working-class caller of the same gender, requesting an appointment. The callers were evenly divided by race, class, and gender. Social class was cued through the caller's vocabulary, grammar, and accent, and the caller's name and accent were used to indicate race. All callers requested an appointment, specifying a preference for weekday evenings, and all had the same private health insurance coverage.

Half of calls from middle-class Whites and middle-class Blacks elicited a callback, compared to 45% for working-class Whites and 34% for working-class Blacks. Among middle-class people who contacted a therapist to schedule an appointment, 28% of Whites and 17% of Blacks received appointment offers, whereas appointment offer rates for both Black and White working-class prospective clients were 8%. The White middle-class woman was favored for the desirable weekday evening appointment; she received an affirmative response to a request for an appointment in that time slot from 1 out of 5 therapists contacted. By contrast, the Black working-class man needed to call 80 therapists to find even one who was willing or able to fulfill the request.

This is not an anomaly. Soon after the study by Kugelmass (2016) was published, Shin, Smith, Welch, and Ezeofor (2016)published another with very similar findings. The overall callback rates in both studies were low; in Kugelmass' study, for example, 56% of all callers did not receive a return call. This in itself is very concerning, but African American and working-class callers were hit hardest. It is not hard to imagine how those with the most stigmatized identities might give up searching in the face of repeated silence and rejection. Yet certainly none of the therapists who behaved in this discriminatory way would have admitted their actions were racially motivated/ This is an example of how microaggressive behaviors result in very real mental health disparities for people of color.

Clinician Implicit Bias

Racial disparities in mental health can have many causes, but there are three main pathways by which racial bias can lead to such disparities (Penner, Blair, Albrecht, & Dovidio, 2014). As shown in Figure 3.1, the most direct path is by means of daily persistent discrimination in the form of regular microaggressions, which leads to increased physiological and psychological stress for people of color. This increased stress has been linked to increased susceptibility to mental health conditions such as depression, as well as medical conditions such as hypertension, diabetes, and cardiovascular disease, which can also contribute to mental health issues.

The other pathways are more indirect, beginning with clinician implicit bias and leading to racial health care disparities (van Ryn et al., 2015), which in turn create disparities in mental health. As shown in Figure 3.1, clinician implicit biases can lead to errors in clinician decision-making, which then lead to racial mental health care disparities. For example, due to pathological stereotypes about people of color, clinicians may make wrong diagnoses or be less willing to

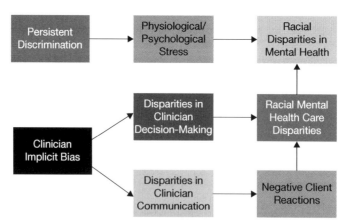

Figure 3.1 Bias and mental health care disparities.
Source: Adapted from Penner et al. (2014).

recommend certain treatments that White people would receive (Penner et al., 2014; Sabin & Greenwald, 2012). In the other pathway, clinician implicit bias leads to microaggressions impacting communications, which may manifest as clinician avoidance (ignoring racial topics), anxiety (faster speaking), and patronizing behavior (decreased client-centered care). This can cause negative client reactions, including lower levels of trust, satisfaction, and compliance, creating racial mental health care disparities (Cooper et al., 2012; Penner et al., 2014).

4

Microaggressions in Therapy

COMMON THERAPIST MICROAGGRESSIONS

Given that microaggressions are harmful to those who experience them, and therapists are generally invested in the well-being and care of their clients, the last thing a conscientious therapist would want to commit is a microaggression against a client. Unfortunately, therapists seem to be just as prone to microaggressing as the general public, and as a result, many people of color do experience microaggressions from their own therapists. In fact, one study found that 53% of multiethnic clients reported experiencing a microaggression from their therapist (Owen, Tao, Imel, Wampold, & Rodolfa, 2014).

Constantine (2007) studied microaggressions experienced by Black clients from White therapists. From focus group discussions, she identified 12 categories of therapist microaggressions: (a) color-blindness, (b) overidentification, (c) denial of personal or individual racism, (d) minimization of racial/cultural issues, (e) assignment of unique or special status on the basis of race or ethnicity, (f) stereotypic assumptions about members of a racial or ethnic group, (g) accused hypersensitivity regarding racial or cultural issues, (h) the meritocracy myth, (i) culturally insensitive treatment considerations or recommendations, (j) acceptance of less than optimal behaviors on the basis of racial/cultural group membership, (k) idealization, and (l) dysfunctional helping or patronization. Racial microaggressions were found to be a major predictor of dissatisfaction with counseling by African American clients, as clients subjected to such comments were understandably less satisfied with the counseling experience. They believed that such therapists were less competent and, unsurprisingly, the therapeutic alliance suffered. Here, we review some common examples of microaggressions committed by therapists.

Welcome to My Practice!

Microaggressions can start before your client even walks into the office. Your website is your public face, and it is usually the first thing clients see. Therefore, it is critical to take stock of the messages embedded in the online presence provided

r clients. For example, stock photography with only White faces may commu-
...cate threat to people of color (Purdie-Vaughns, Steele, Davies, Ditlmann, &
Crosby, 2008). If you are part of a practice group, put pictures of the therapists on
the website so that people of color can ascertain if there are others like them in the
practice. Add material about services for people of color and how you are willing
and able to address their specialized needs. Be specific. For example, our clinic has
a specialization in post-traumatic stress disorder (PTSD) and has a web page that
states the following:

> The traumatizing effect of racial discrimination, which is similar to
> posttraumatic stress disorder (PTSD), is sometimes called *racial trauma*.
> Racial trauma is caused by a combination of stressors, including historical/
> cultural trauma, community trauma, overt and covert racial discrimination,
> and/or microaggressions. Microaggressions are brief, everyday exchanges,
> in the form of seemingly innocuous comments and subtle gestures that send
> denigrating messages to people of color because they belong to a minority
> group. Microaggressions are a primary source of racially biased experiences
> on a day-to-day basis and are also a barrier to treatment for patients of
> color when committed by mental health professionals. This has important
> applications for many groups, including ethnic minorities as well as refugees
> who may have experienced ethnic violence in their countries of origin.
> The ability of clinicians to accurately understand and assess their clients'
> difficulties is the essential first step to effective treatment.

This paragraph is educational because it explains the connection between racism
and PTSD, and it also signals to people of color that clinicians care about their
experiences of microaggressions and have an awareness that this can be a problem
in life and in therapy. It is hoped that it also communicates our desire to treat all
clients respectfully in the treatment process. Do not assume that putting a generic
anti-discrimination statement on your website will attract people of color and put
them at ease. It will not. It will likely be viewed as obligatory and may even be
worse than having nothing at all.

Pay careful attention to the appearance of your office space. Individuals are
part of a social context, which refers to the immediate physical and social setting
in which people live or in which something happens or develops. It includes the
person's culture and the people and institutions with whom they interact. Given
the importance of social context, there are many factors to be considered when
creating a comfortable space, which differs by culture. Deliberate measures may
be needed to create a welcoming venue. A lack of diversity in artwork, reading
material, and decorations may communicate to people of color that the practice
was not built with them in mind. Clinicians should always consider the décor of
the facility. Color schemes, music, choice of magazines, and cultural office artwork can all be critically important in making clients feel comfortable and welcome (Williams, Beckmann-Mendez, & Turkheimer, 2013).

Ensure that your front desk staff are well trained to treat all clients in a respectful and courteous manner. Despite how culturally informed, aware, and/or humble you are, if your receptionist is committing microaggressions against your clients of color, their visit is already going badly before they have even seen you. Ensure that all staff, especially those who interact with clients, are well trained, whether or not they are therapists.

Basic Interactions

Initial greetings are an opportunity to make people of color feel welcome or alienated. Often, the dynamics of these interactions are communicating something different to the two (or more) parties involved. For example, Dovidio, Gaertner, Kawakami, and Hodson, (2002) assessed White participants' explicit racial attitudes (based on self-report) and implicit racial attitudes [using the Implicit Association Test (IAT)] before they engaged in an interracial interaction. The researchers then asked both White and Black participants how the conversation went. White people who had reported they were not prejudiced thought they behaved in a friendly manner during the interaction. But for conversations with Whites who were aversive racists (low in explicit prejudice based on self-report but high in implicit prejudice based on the IAT), Black and White participants had very different opinions about the quality of the interaction. Although White participants believed they behaved in a friendly and nonprejudiced way, and that the interaction was positive and productive, Black participants did not agree. The Black partners perceived White participants as *less friendly* than White participants thought they were, and Black participants were *less satisfied* with the conversation. Interestingly, Black and White participants were completely unaware that the other person viewed the experience differently than they did. Thus, the interracial interactions were characterized by fundamental misunderstandings. Similarly, this means that therapists and clients may walk away from a session with very disparate impressions of an interaction after a therapeutic encounter.

Dovidio et al. (2002) found that people tend to base their perceptions of interracial interactions on two different sources of information, with White people relying more on verbal behavior, such as actual words spoken, and Black people relying more on nonverbal behaviors, such as blinking and decreased eye contact. This can be thought of as "racism radar," with people of color picking up on these subtle signs that are typically unnoticed by most White people.

The good news is that new responses can be learned. Among aversively racist people, recognizing the disparity between their personal standards and their actual behaviors can lead to monitoring their prejudicial behaviors and performing them less often. Furthermore, when practiced consistently, these monitored behaviors become increasingly less disparate from the values of the individual and can eventually suppress negative responses that were once automatic.

Minimizing Cultural Experiences

In a mixed methods study, Constantine (2007) used the Racial Microaggressions in Counseling Scale, a 10-item, Likert-type scale (0 = "this never happened," 2 = "this happened and I was bothered by it"), to quantify the frequency and impact of microaggressions experienced by clients. She found that the most common microaggression committed by therapists was not an act of commission but, rather, avoidance of discussing cultural issues in sessions. An example of this is when a client begins to discuss a racial or cultural experience or belief and then the therapist changes the subject. This type of behavior can make clients believe that the therapist is minimizing the importance of cultural issues or is unaware of the important role of race and racism in clients' lived experiences. It might also signal to the client that the therapist is not skilled in addressing such issues, leading the client to believe the therapist is not competent or possibly even racist.

Constantine (2007) provides an example in which the therapist says, "I'm not sure we need to focus on race or culture to understand your depression." Consider the impact of these words on a client, who has just advanced their own explanation for their distress. This statement not only minimizes the client's concern but also illustrates the therapist's own discomfort with the idea that race and mental health can be linked—in opposition to research that clearly makes this connection (Mouzon, Taylor, Keith, Nicklett, & Chatters, 2017), as discussed in the previous chapter. Furthermore, how can the therapist possibly know if race is a factor in the client's mental health problems when the therapist will not even take the time to listen and learn? This client is quickly discovering that this therapist will not take such concerns seriously.

Sometimes when clients describe an experience, the therapist responds in a way that minimizes the cause of the event. For example, the clinician might say, "Let's hope you weren't treated that way due to racism. What are some other possible explanations?" (DeLapp & Williams, 2015). The therapist probably thinks this statement will help the client feel better because racism is a terrible thing to experience, but this is actually invalidating. This dismissal fails to acknowledge the reality of racial discrimination as a problem in our society. It also tells the client that discussion of racism will not be entertained and that racism is not a valid explanation for mistreatment. It may further communicate that racist behaviors from others are the fault of the client (blaming the victim) rather than the person who perpetrated the act.

Pathologizing Cultural Values and Collectivism

Being familiar with a philosophical framework reflected in the values and attitudes of those from non-White ethnic groups can help clinicians become more culturally competent and reduce their chances of committing microaggressions. By understanding and appreciating the role of the client's culture, therapists can better tailor treatment to the individual. Just as any client may have individual differences that need to be considered, cultural differences are equally important. Cultural differences are not to be confused with pathological stereotypes. Remember, *pathological stereotypes* are overgeneralized or false ideas about a group used to justify or explain inequities. *Cultural values* are actual measurable differences in the beliefs, attitudes, and practices of a particular group. Obviously, not everyone in a given cultural group identifies with all of their group's cultural values, but most people in that cultural group will understand and appreciate the values, or defend them, even if they do not adhere to them.

Therapists should avoid challenging core cultural values whenever possible. Unfortunately, so many therapists have been socialized and trained in Western ways of thinking that different cultural values may be mistaken for psychopathology. One common example of pathologizing cultural differences occurs when individualistic norms are imposed on people from collectivistic cultures. Most ethnic groups are collectivistic in their values and behaviors. In collectivistic cultures, people emphasize the needs and goals of the group as a whole over the needs and desires of each individual. In such cultures, relationships with other members of their community and the interconnections between people are central to each person's identity. Collectivistic cultures include social norms focused on promoting selflessness and putting community needs ahead of individual needs. Working as a group and supporting others are critical, people are encouraged to do what is best for their communities, and family life is central to well-being.

Common areas in which Western therapists risk microaggressions against their clients of color include the following:

- Advancing Western models of child-rearing and discipline as morally superior, when in fact Western approaches may be considered permissive and disrespectful to clients of color.
- Encouraging young adults to pursue their own happiness over the needs of their families—for example, many cultures expect children to care for elderly parents as a way of paying back their investment in rearing children in the first place, and nursing homes are not an acceptable option.
- Pathologizing young adults living with parents or intergenerational households—in fact, many people of color expect unmarried children to live at home, and moving out would be considered a family crisis.
- Failing to appreciate the importance of participation in family and community social events and that missing such events may be considered deeply disrespectful to family members.
- Expecting parents to confront their children's teachers or a school principal when issues at school arise. In fact, many cultural groups highly respect teachers and consider challenging such persons disrespectful. Therapists may need to help advocate in such cases.

There may be situations in which cultural values need to be challenged for the sake of the client's well-being and mental health. However, when this is necessary, therapists must tread very lightly to prevent a permanent rupture and prema- ture termination. Therapists must ensure they deeply understand and respect the basis of the cultural belief before challenging it, and they should be very aware of the social consequences faced by the client for opposing their group norms. Advantages and disadvantages must be weighted carefully. Therapists should help prepare clients when clients must behave in a way that violates their community standards.

Trying Too Hard to Be Culturally Sensitive

Many therapists are aware of the importance of being culturally aware and sensi- tive to their clients of color. They are genuinely making an effort, but because they still believe pathological stereotypes, they fail in the execution of their egalitarian goals. Related microaggressions are often meant to be supportive, and yet a person of color may find these responses troublesome. These include situations in which the therapist offered extra help that was inappropriate because it was offered based on group membership rather than need, or the therapist was accepting of dys- functional behaviors due to stereotypes.

Constantine (2007) shares the following example: "I don't normally do this, but I can waive your fees if you can't afford therapy." This is an example of dysfunc- tional helping, which is patronizing to the client. It sends the message that the therapist believes the client and all members of the person's ethnoracial group are poor and in need of handouts. Many clients of color work hard to present them- selves as financially capable to combat negative stereotypes about being poor, and for the therapist to express this belief based on race alone can be hurtful and demeaning. Certainly there are cases in which a fee reduction is helpful or even essential, but this should be based on income and not race; otherwise, it is not appropriate.

Another example is when the therapist says, "It might be okay for some people to cope by drinking if that's normal for their culture" (Constantine, 2007). Such a statement shows a troubling acceptance of problematic behaviors based on path- ological stereotypes about certain ethnoracial groups. The client may be seeking help for an alcohol problem and the therapist is not doing the client any favors by communicating approval of the behavior for any reason.

Overidentification

Another common microaggression is when a therapist denies having any cul- tural biases at all. Constantine (2007) provides the following example: "As a gay person, I know what it's like to be discriminated against due to race." In this sit- uation, the therapist is engaging in overidentification, whereby he is denying or minimizing his own potential bias because of assumed similarity. The therapist is saying, "Your racial oppression is no different than my form of lived oppression, so I can't be a racist because I'm just like you." However, being gay is not the same as being Black (or Hispanic or Asian); both may be difficult but not necessarily in the same way. Furthermore, anyone can behave in a racist manner, even a sexual minority or someone who is a person of color. No one is completely immune to the negative social messages and pathological stereotypes that disproportionately denigrate people of color. The therapist's statement shows the reverse of what he is trying to convey—that he really does not know what it is like to be a person of color.

Insensitive Remarks

Therapists may make insensitive remarks about a cultural group when trying to understand or treat concerns or issues. Belief in pathological stereotypes about a client's cultural group may be conveyed by therapists even though not expressed directly. Insensitive remarks can be particularly harmful to vulnerable clients, who may already feel stigmatized and exposed by just attempting therapy in the first place. Clients of color may find it difficult to respond to racist comments in counseling situations due to self-doubt and power dynamics. This then contributes to feelings of distance from the therapist, unwillingness to disclose sensitive information, and early termination from treatment. Thus, due to therapist microaggressions creating a barrier to treatment, clients may be unable to overcome the condition for which they sought help. The amount of harm therapists may cause in this way is unknown and probably greatly underestimated (Constantine, 2007).

Specific examples of insensitive remarks include the therapist making statements that indicate an underestimation of client capabilities or strengths based on cultural group membership or implying that the client is overly sensitive about cultural issues. Although the following examples are from Constantine (2007), I have heard such statements made by therapists many times:

Stating "Your English is very good. Where are you from?" to a non-
White client with no accent: This backhanded compliment sends the
message that the client is not a real citizen. Asian Americans and Latino
Americans are often assumed to be foreign-born, making such clients
feel as if they are aliens in their own homeland. It may also communicate
a belief that people from the client's group typically lack proper
education, refuse to assimilate, or are in the country illegally.
"I don't see you as a person of color. I just see you as a regular person": This
tells the client that the therapist finds the client odd or irregular in some
way because they are not White. It is as if something is wrong with being
a person of color and the therapist is going above and beyond the call of
duty to politely ignore differences.
"If Black people just worked harder, they could be as successful as other
people": This shows that the therapist has uncritically accepted the

pathological stereotype that African Americans are just plain lazy. By extension, the client is also lazy and would be successful and happy with a bit of good hard work. It also ignores social forces, such as institutionalized racism, and other barriers that make it more difficult for people of color to be successful. Finally, it overlooks problems such as John Henryism in Black men that cause physiological problems due to working too hard and eschewing self-care. (Named after a folk hero who competed against a steam engine, John Henryism is a dysfunctional coping strategy for managing stressors such as racism by overexertion, leading to accumulating physiological costs.)

"Don't get so sensitive about the racial stuff. I didn't mean anything bad or offensive": In this case, the therapist made a racist remark and this client was brave enough to call it out. Does the client get an apology from the therapist or even a discussion of the occurrence? No, in a typical blame-the-victim fashion, the client is accused of being hypersensitive. After all, the therapist meant well, right? In my own lab, we found that comments such as this were strongly correlated to multiple measures of racism (Kanter et al., 2017).

EXAMPLE OF RACISM DISMISSED BY THE THERAPIST

I have a blog on *Psychology Today*, and I received an email from a distraught reader who had been subjected to some serious microaggressions by his therapist. I have heard from many others who have experienced this problem, and equally as many who need therapy but avoid it for fear of being misunderstood. Here, I share part of one of these letters and offer some helpful suggestions (Williams, 2014):

WRITER: Currently, I am experiencing trouble with my therapist, and I am in need of advice. I brought up my experiences with racism, and it was the only time in any form of psychological treatment that I mentioned it. It was a hard thing to bring up, and it puts me in vulnerable position because of how my community treats racism and their post-racist mentality. He responded to my distress about my experience of racism by saying we can work on "[my] perception" to keep things in control and kept derailing away from the topic of racism saying he wants to "keep things controlled." I cried because I feared this was going to happen. . . . Part of me expected it, but I thought I was being negative, so to see this happen anyway and the one time I brought up racism while feeling vulnerable made me cry.

I tried to explain to him why I was upset, but he cut me off and concluded that I have a chemical imbalance in my brain. At the end of therapy I tried to explain it to him again. He rolled his eyes and said, "I mean if you want to 'fight'[racism . . ." (*using finger quotation on the word* *"fight"*). At my next appointment I found out that he wrote all this in my records. He wrote about my views on racism as he saw it: oversensitive, chemical imbalance, etc.

It worries me because my insurance only covers the therapists and social workers in that clinic, and the notes written down about me from one therapist/social worker is what every mental health professional in that clinic reads before they meet me. It heavily influences on how they treat me. So this prejudgment about me plus this post-racist mentality has caused more microaggressions, dismissal, and pathologization.

MY REPLY: The first thing I want to say is that this situation should never have happened. Even if a client tells me that he saw Elvis in Central Park, I am not going to roll my eyes or use air quotes. To me this is an indication of your therapist's own internal biases. That he said, we need to "keep things controlled" illustrates his own insecurity over being able to professionally manage your distress. And the way he refers to the problem as your "perception" insensitively communicates disbelief over your report. I want you to know that I believe you.

This racial disconnect is a tough problem and potentially tricky issue. White people in our culture are socialized not to see themselves as racial beings, and thus experience themselves as non-racial. Therefore it can be difficult to understand the perspective of ethnic minority clients, who typically live and struggle with racism on a regular basis. Racism is something we must fight to maintain our dignity, sanity, and self-esteem, so this struggle falls squarely within the realm of mental health. Fighting the deleterious effects of racism can lead to what scholars have termed "racial battle fatigue"—which leads to the same kinds of anxiety traumatized soldiers experience when returning home from war.

Pointing out racist behavior to an offender is usually not a useful strategy, as people are quick to become defensive when called out, and no one wants to be considered a racist. And pointing racist behaviors out to therapists can be even more difficult, as they are seen by many (and themselves) as objective, progressive and open-minded. As a result they may become dismissively closed off from the possibility they may be part of the problem, and even blame you for pointing out the issue. Although most new therapists are emerging from training programs with at least some basic multicultural education, there is a whole generation of practitioners who were never exposed to any multicultural training at all. As a result, these unfortunate experiences are tragically common.

I posed the question you asked to my classroom of doctoral students in my Clinical Psychopathology course. We had just completed a segment on the mental health effects of racism, and I thought it would be useful to brainstorm this problem. They broke into groups of two and came up with several excellent suggestions.

First, I should point out that there was a broad consensus that you, as the aggressed-upon client, should stop seeing this therapist and find someone else who can actually intervene therapeutically. I agree with this suggestion, since the therapist described above is only making you worse by doing the very thing that others have done, resulting in so much emotional pain. I would not worry too much about what your therapist wrote in the chart. Any good therapist will want to hear your perspective before drawing any important conclusions about you. However, finding another therapist is not always easy or possible, especially depending on where you live, your resources, and insurance options. If you must continue with this person, here are a few suggestions.

1. Do your best to share how your therapist's response made you feel. Let him know that you feel marginalized and invalidated because he didn't take the time to understand your experience. You might even write out your thoughts in advance to help you organize your points while in session.

2. Ask the therapist if he knows what it feels like to be discriminated against. And if so, ask him how it would feel if he had that experience dismissed by important people in his life.

3. Trick him into hearing the experience by describing the event without framing it as racism, and let him pathologize the experience rather than his attribution of it.

4. Suggest he take a cultural competency course so he can better relate to his clients of color. (I actually offer a webinar on this topic every other month, so that's one easy possibility.)

5. Offer him research literature about cultural differences and how racism can affect mental health outcomes.

EXAMPLE OF THE STRONG BLACK WOMAN

In a seemingly reverse pattern, stereotypes can cause therapists to overestimate client capabilities or strengths based on cultural group membership. This often occurs with Black women, who may be stereotyped as strong, independent, and sassy. This stereotype might seem mostly positive at first, but it has origins in the US practice of slavery, where Black women had to be strong to protect their families and survive in a world of forced servitude and rape, and where families were routinely torn apart when children were sold to new owners. So although being a "strong Black woman" may seem like a desirable trait, even among Black women, it can actually have some very destructive consequences. This stereotype overestimates desirable qualities and underestimates limitations. A Black woman who is told she is "strong" by her therapist may be left feeling that she now has to live up to the therapist's expectations to be superwoman and therefore cannot be free to share her weaknesses and vulnerabilities. In fact, the strong Black woman archetype keeps many Black women working multiple jobs, overcommitted to family responsibilities, and constantly in motion, resulting in problems such as high blood pressure, binge eating disorder, and absolutely no time for self-care. And when there is no time for self-care, therapy is the first thing to go.

In an essay titled "To the Therapist Who Called Me a 'Strong Black Woman,'" Contessa Cooper (2017) shares the following story:

> I knew at the age of 16 that life wasn't going to be easy as a teenage, single parent. Somehow between the late nights and early days, I was able to walk across that stage and receive my high school degree. That was just one of many obstacles I battled through.
>
> My son was nonverbal until he was 5 years old. There were times he was upset and could not tell me why. It took years of fighting with doctors, teachers and other professionals to finally get some answers. My son has autism, which is characterized by challenges with social skills, repetitive behaviors, speech and nonverbal communication, as well as unique strengths and differences. There was nothing I could do but be the best mother I could be.
>
> After that, life kept handing me one stressful situation after another. Miscarriages, a failed marriage ending in divorce, having to work as a stripper because I could only get someone to watch my son at night. One day I couldn't take it any more. I gave away everything I owned, so the children and I could move back home.
>
> The stress and the pressure that was my life was too much to bare. I could barely make it out of bed. There were days that I just . . . cried. I tried to keep it together, but I couldn't. I drank more than I should have. I wasn't living; I was just surviving.
>
> I confided in my mother about being completely overwhelmed with life. I needed some help. I suggested therapy to help me cope. She was totally against it. "Don't you go telling them people what happens in this house. What goes on in this house stays in this house. They are going to blame me anyways. They always blame the mother. Plus, you need to pray about it," said Mom.
>
> It would be weeks of replaying that conversation (over and over again in my head) before I would pick up the phone and call your office. I had to force myself not to turn the car around, and go back home several times. I made myself sit in your waiting area against the words of my mother and my faith.
>
> Why am I telling you this? I wanted you to know I was hanging on by a thread. You were my last hope. I didn't know what else to do, so I turned to a therapist. The drinking, crying and feeling helpless could have been signs of depression. You were supposed to help me. You didn't.

I told you about me, my struggles and how I was feeling inside. You sat there in your expensive clothing, your perfectly decorated office and smiled at me the entire time. When I finished being open, vulnerable and raw, you said words that would haunt me to this day.

"You seem like a strong black woman, and found ways to cope. I'm proud of you. Please come back if you feel like life is too much to handle."

Why didn't you hear me? Why didn't you acknowledge the internal battle between me, my culture and my faith that I had to overcome? Why didn't you see all of me? Why did you ignore the tears that streamed down my cheeks? Why didn't you know I had had enough of being "strong"?

Perhaps you believed the stereotype that black women are strong and conditioned to handle stress better than a white women like yourself. Maybe you accepted the belief that this is my lot in life. I'm destined to struggle and somehow, make things work out. That's what you see on television, usually solved by the end of a sitcom's episode, or a movie: the strong, single black mom making it all work out in the end.

I'm not strong because I want to be, or because I'm trained to be. I'm strong because I have to be. You invalidated and ignored my pain, allowing me to nearly drown in my own sorrow because you didn't care enough to know me.

I'm now speaking on Decolonization and Microaggressions in Therapy. Not only do I share my story, but I share stories from other women who had similar experiences.

No, you didn't save me. Maybe I can help save someone else from just being "A Strong Black Woman" and coping with it themselves.

Withholding Answers

Due to a variety of factors, people of color may not seek treatment until problems are severe. As illustrated in Contessa Cooper's poignant narrative, communities of color have taboos against sharing problems outside of their community, and mental health literacy is often a problem because people may not initially recognize their difficulties as signs of a mental disorder, meaning they do not seek care until they absolutely must (Cheng, Wang, McDermott, Kridel, & Rislin, 2018). At the onset of treatment, clients of color may expect therapists to provide expert advice to help them resolve urgent problems. The common therapist catchphrase, "You are the expert on you," is likely to feel frustrating and shaming. Clients come to a therapist to benefit from the therapist's expertise. If the client could have figured out the problem and solved it already, they would have. Cognitive–behavioral therapy (CBT) is particularly well-suited for people from different ethnic groups because it tends to be direct and clear, with mechanisms of change well-articulated to clients.

Nonetheless, as a profession, we sometimes put too much importance on making people find their own solutions, even when we know the answers. If we can reduce suffering by providing an answer in a single meeting that would have taken someone months to uncover through Socratic questioning, it is better to provide that answer directly. If clients are able to take action based on this new information, their suffering is reduced and they save time and money. This is particularly important to understand because people of color tend to get frustrated and suspicious when they believe that important solutions are being pointlessly withheld from them by elite people with power. Many people of color have encountered medical professionals who have not taken their complaints seriously and sent them home without the care, medications, or tests that were needed. For example, many medical doctors falsely believe that Black people have a higher pain tolerance and are more likely to abuse pain medicines, and so doctors withhold basic treatment and these patients end up unmedicated for their pain (Hoffman, Trawalter, Axt, & Oliver, 2016). If people of color think this may be happening in therapy, they will stop coming and may never get the help they really need.

Furthermore, different people learn new things in different ways. Some learn best by figuring out things after struggling for a long time, some learn by watching others fail or succeed, and some learn by seeking out expert advice. I have had clients say, "I just want to talk things through and use you as a sounding board so I can figure things out on my own"; other times they have said, "What can I do to make this stop happening to me?" Culturally informed therapy means that we give answers when clients ask for them. Keep in mind that this is not the same as pushing unwanted solutions on clients. Clients of color should always be free to accept or reject solutions provided. If you do not know the answer, you can say, "I am not sure just yet, but the more I learn about you and your situation, the better I will be able to help."

Acceptance and Commitment Therapy

Acceptance and commitment therapy (ACT) is an empirically based psychological intervention that uses acceptance and mindfulness strategies with commitment and behavior-change strategies to increase psychological flexibility. It is used by many CBT practitioners to help clients be present with what life brings and to move toward behavior that is in alignment with a person's values.

To use ACT effectively with people of color, therapists must be aware of the expectations of clients of color and account for them to build rapport. Because, as noted previously, new client problems may be urgent and clients may be desperate for answers, a non-directive approach could be experienced as frustrating, unhelpful, and invalidating. For this reason, a clear explanation of the mechanism of ACT is essential because therapeutic concepts may seem foreign, mysterious, or counterintuitive. For instance, the idea of "acceptance" may be misinterpreted as a need to continually accept inequitable and hurtful treatment from others rather than noting and allowing whatever emotions are experienced as a result of maltreatment. Clients must be validated in their lived realities before acceptance can take place. Furthermore, among people of color, the idea of "commitment" may be experienced as an extension of racist cultural assumptions about an unwillingness to be accountable. "Committed action" could then be more neutrally described in terms of identifying small practical steps to live a fuller or more meaningful life in line with the client's cultural values, eliminating any implied link with a lack of commitment and retaining the meaning of this mechanism within ACT. In summary, therapists should take care to use the language of ACT carefully. Concepts can be described in a number of ways—for example, ACT protocols for topics such as chronic pain routinely omit the use of the word "acceptance" while retaining the core principles in practice (McCracken, 2005).

COMMON CONSEQUENCES OF THERAPIST MICROAGGRESSIONS

Most therapists go into helping professions because they care about people. Because many microaggressions may seem positive at face value (e.g., backhanded complements or patronizing statements), therapists may not realize how these have affected clients. Most people of color have experienced microaggressions many times and may be willing to give their therapists an occasional "pass," realizing that the therapists mean well, despite the blunder. However, such statements communicate to clients that they are not understood and their experiences as a person of color will not be addressed in a safe or useful way. Clients of color may prematurely end therapy or simply decide to share only limited information with their therapists as a result of microaggressions.

HOW TO REPAIR THE THERAPEUTIC ALLIANCE

As previously mentioned, microaggressions are quite common in therapy. If you are a White person working with a client of color, it is likely that you have already committed a number of microaggressions. If you are a therapist of color working with people of color from other ethnic groups that you are not a part of, you may have microaggressed against them as well. And if you are a therapist who works exclusively with people from your own cultural group, it is less likely you have committed microaggressions in therapy, but it is still possible. All that to say, unless you are in that tiny last group, you should assume you have at some point microaggressed against your clients of color. It is hoped that reading this book has shown you ways in which you may have done this.

The good news is that if your clients of color have not stopped seeing you, they think you have enough good qualities such that they are willing to tolerate occasional microaggressions. However, you should not assume that simply because you have clients of color who seem to appreciate you, your microaggressions have gone unnoticed. If your clients have not pointed out your microaggressions to you, it is because they do not trust that you will be able to respond productively to what they have to share. This also indicates that there may be other important facets of their lives that they are unwilling to entrust to you. So it is likely they will appreciate that you are now in a place to own these problems and work on repair. Repair is not always easy, but it will help improve the therapeutic relationship and the quality of your work with your clients of color. Research shows that it is not the presence of an alliance rupture but, rather, an absence of repair that results in undesirable therapy outcomes (Gaztambide, 2012).

If Your Client Points It Out

The first time a client points out a microaggression is a critical turning point in the therapeutic relationship. The way you respond will set the stage for the future of your therapeutic interactions. The client may not use the term "microaggression" but instead may say that they feel stereotyped, disrespected, misunderstood, or that you behaved in a way that was "slightly racist." It is important to recognize the difference between an action being called racist and a person being called racist. If the client pointed out one problematic statement or behavior, that does not mean they think you are a reprehensible a human being. They are just explaining that you did something hurtful, and that is the right thing for your client to do. Chances are you are being called out over a microaggression, but if a client says you are an entirely racist and bigoted human being, this suggests a larger problem. Maybe you have committed several microaggressions or did something major that came across as racist. Either way, this is an opportunity to learn something about yourself and your client. Recognize and appreciate that they trust you enough to share this difficult information with you. You might even say, "Thank you for trusting me enough to bring this to my attention."

Defensiveness is the biggest trap that people fall into when a microaggression is pointed out. Do not get defensive under any circumstances. Do not make excuses for what you did. Do not attempt to prove you are not a racist by providing evidence of your goodness. Mentioning a diversity award, a lecture you did on multiculturalism, a mission trip to Guatemala, or your time volunteering with disadvantaged children is not going to help. Talking about your ancestry or other stigmatized identities is not a good idea either; just because your grandparents were Holocaust survivors, your parents were immigrants, or you do not identify as White does not mean you are unable to commit microaggressions. Not all racists are hateful people brandishing flaming tiki torches in the middle of the night, and you can accidentally do racist things even while actively working against racism most of the time.

Take it seriously and agree there is a problem to be addressed. Pointing out a microaggression is difficult for the client and is generally not done lightly. Really listen to their concerns. Let the client talk first before you respond; do not interrupt. Preemptively apologize, and show that you care about the client's feelings. The client may be afraid of what you will say or do, so do your best to put them at ease. Show concern on your face. You could say,

I'm sorry that I said something hurtful and insensitive. I want you to feel safe and relaxed around me, so if I'm making clients like you feel uncomfortable that is a problem. I want to hear more so I can learn from it.

This shows that you are a caring person who is willing to listen. Keep in mind that in many cultures, medical professionals are viewed as experts and there may be a power imbalance, so clients may be afraid to speak to you about the problem in detail.

If it is not completely clear to you what you did and why it was wrong, ask for more information and pay careful attention to what your client says. Keep in mind that people of color are generally better at identifying microaggression than are White people, so go into the conversation assuming your client is correct, especially if you are White. As you listen to their response, communicate caring and openness with your body language (e.g., make sure your arms are not folded and you are not grinding your teeth). It is okay to say, "I don't understand why that's racist. Would you please explain it for me so I can better understand?" Show cultural humility (Hook et al., 2016).

Validate your client's pain and frustration. Ask if they have experienced behavior like this from you before or from others in the past. Show sympathy for past microaggressions or other acts of racism they have faced. Make it clear that you care about their pain. Some of the client's distress might be connected to these other experiences that were not your fault, but your microaggression is compounding it. Ultimately, you want to relieve the distress you triggered and re-establish trust. For example, you might say, "I am sorry that you have had to deal with that, and now here I am doing the same thing. You deserve better."

Acknowledge your biases and blind spots. Many people unthinkingly accept pathological stereotypes and do not realize that these are racist beliefs. You probably have biases that you have not yet completely weeded out. Think about our culture's history with respect to the structural challenges working against true fairness and equality. You have most likely absorbed some biases without realizing it. Remind yourself that in places like the United States and Canada, where the federal government and municipalities have long been controlled by White men, everyone is influenced by racism and other biases to some degree or another. Explain to your client that some unconscious and unwanted racial bias still exists in you (they will not find this admission surprising), and commit that you will do better.

The last step is to clarify any misinterpreted statements or behaviors. *It is critically important that you do not start here or you look defensive and make the client feel invalidated.* Furthermore, you may want to bypass this step altogether if you really did, in that moment, mean what you said or did. Certainly, it may have been that you said something that seemed microaggressive, even if that is not how you meant it. If so, apologize for the misunderstanding and any distress you caused by failing to recognize that your words or actions appeared microaggressive and then clarify what you truly meant. For example, you might say,

> I am sorry, Ms. Davis, I really did not know you were in the waiting room for so long. I hate to keep anyone waiting, and I know that this could look like I don't value you as a client or a human being. It makes sense that you would think that, given how poorly you've been treated by so many others when you didn't deserve it. I feel horrible for making you feel unwelcome.

In this situation, you can even make your response more personal and impactful by letting the client know how much you have been looking forward to seeing her and how much you appreciate her as a client and a person.

Do not pathologize your client for pointing out your microaggression. Unfortunately, this is a very common maneuver therapists use to deflect attention away from their own issues. This approach is racist and will ultimately harm the therapeutic relationship. You likely know other therapists or even a supervisor who will quickly take your side against the "angry" or "neurotic" client who dared to criticize or question you. You can easily dismiss this as projecting, distancing behavior, or the product of unresolved internal conflicts on the part of the client. Any or all of these may be true, and at the same time, you may still have been microaggressive. So do not go there. This is a situation in which you are better off searching for psychopathology in yourself rather than your client.

You may have committed a microaggression in the past that you only later realize. If this happens, you can check with the client. You might say something like, "I was thinking about our conversation from last week, and I realized I might have said something insensitive." Describe what you said or did that was possibly a microaggression. "How did that make you feel? I want to apologize for that." The client may say they were not offended, but do not assume this is actually the case. Most people of color are used to shrugging off microaggressions, and so they may not feel comfortable telling you the truth right away. Nonetheless, your gesture at sensitivity will most likely be appreciated, even if they did not detect a microaggression.

Once you have addressed the issue, do not over-apologize or keep checking in on how the client feels about you. This is not about them helping you feel ok with yourself; it is about what is best for your client. All they probably need is an acknowledgment and short apology. Too much apologizing and checking in creates a situation in which the client becomes the emotional caretaker and must now soothe and heal the therapist. Many people of color have gotten into the habit of soothing White people who may be unsettled by their very presence (e.g., *Whistling Vivaldi*; Steele, 2010). It is not the client's job to help repair your wounded identity as a progressive and fair-minded individual. Excessive apologizing is aversive to the client and will make them feel like they cannot disclose future microaggressions to you because you are too fragile to handle it. Ultimately, you want them to let you know every time you microaggress so that you can initiate a repair and learn from the experience.

Although addressing your own errors in therapy can feel overwhelming and frightening, the same skills you have developed for navigating other therapeutic challenges can work with microaggressions as well. Be willing to experience the discomfort of having made a mistake. Chances are, if addressed properly, it can actually strengthen the therapeutic alliance. Because people of color rarely experience apologies from those who microaggress, your efforts can be an appreciated and corrective experience.

If you are uncertain about how you are impacting clients of color, cannot retain clients of color, or have been unsuccessful in addressing racial issues in therapy, you might need to seek more professional guidance. You may be best served by consulting with a clinician who has expertise in racial issues to help you navigate these challenging experiences and improve your work with diverse clients. There are peer support groups for addressing multicultural issues and anti-racism groups for people who are willing to do the hard work of addressing their own biases and shortcomings in the service of improving their work with clients of color.

RESPONDING TO MICROAGGRESSIONS COMMITTED BY CLIENTS

Therapists may be uncertain about how to respond to clients who make microaggressive statements against people of color. This may be a frequent occurrence for White therapists, who may have White clients who feel comfortable expressing vaguely racist sentiments in the company of someone from their same ethnoracial group. Certainly, however, people from any ethnoracial group can make biased statements about any other group. Many therapists have been trained to ignore such statements. They may believe that if it is not the goal of the client to change their beliefs about people of color, then it should not be a topic of therapy. This perspective is common but incorrect. Microaggressions and underlying racist attitudes are always an appropriate target for therapeutic intervention. Clients who continually microaggress in session are likely harming others in their lives, hurting other relationships, and contributing to the public health problem of racism in general. Therapists should address these behaviors in session to help increase understanding, awareness, and empathy in clients. Simply being silent can be misinterpreted by clients as agreement with microaggressive sentiments. Ultimately, conscientious therapists will want to actively promote prosocial behaviors.

When working with clients who express racially biased thoughts, feelings, or behaviors, it is important to search for the origins of the underlying beliefs and the functions that these biases serve in the clients' lives. A good first step is to determine where the attitudes came from. Assessing the client's experiences with race, social and familial history with prejudice, and parental reactions to culturally different people in childhood can provide valuable information about learning history surrounding these ideas. In response to the expression of a pathological racial stereotype, a therapist might say, "How did you come to feel this way this about that particular group?" It could be that these biases were formally taught by parents, or it could be that they were simply acquired due to living in Western culture and being exposed to American media. Understanding this allows the therapist to better empathize with and validate the client's current belief system instead of responding in a way that might make the client feel shamed or judged. The therapist can both validate the client in how they came to acquire the belief and also introduce some doubt about the veracity of the belief. Although we have emphasized that questioning a belief is not appropriate when someone reports microaggressive experiences, just the opposite is warranted when microaggressions are committed by clients. Even simply having the belief gently questioned may signal to the client that they have embraced poorly considered ideas, which have lead to problematic statements and behaviors.

Simply providing correct and accurate information may be sufficient to remove the biases, but if the client resists, it is an indication that the biases may serve an important function in the client's life. With further discussion, you may discover that, for your client, looking down on others is a maladaptive means of coping with the client's own fears and anxieties. For example, stereotyping a certain group as lazy may reflect the clients own challenges with workaholism. Disparaging comments about affirmative action may be fueled by worries about a client's own ability to find a good job. Clients who have suffered due to feelings of powerlessness may feel more capable when they can quickly categorize large numbers of others as inferior (Bartoli & Pyati, 2009). As such, the content of microaggressive statements can be a compass pointing to areas where therapeutic work is needed for growth and healing.

Example of Microaggressive Statements by a Client

A White undergraduate student, Amelia, has been seeing a therapist, a Filipino American woman, at the college counseling center for approximately 6 weeks for stress and anxiety. At the session, she enters the office looking visibly upset.

THERAPIST: It's great to see you. How are you today, Amelia?

CLIENT: I'm OK (*frowning*). I mean, I had this class today, it was like a debate class and, you know, we talked about race which . . . to me, I don't really see color. So, it was a little strange to try and point out people's skin tone and talk about different experiences you've had based on that, because I think there is only one race which is the human race. And you know, to me, that made a lot of sense, and I've talked to my Chinese friend about this before and he completely agrees, but I was in this class and this Hispanic girl just started getting mad at me. She was telling me that I was completely wrong, and I just felt like a lot of the class was against me . . . which I think was ridiculous and it made me feel very singled out. And I'm very upset that people wouldn't have enough sense to understand that we're all just people and race isn't something that should be, like, brought up as a theme, I guess.

THERAPIST: Wow, that sounds really tough.

CLIENT: Yes. I know you understand because we've done this for a while, and we haven't had any problems even though technically, to some people, we would be very different people based on our skin tones, but you and I know that there is only one race, so there shouldn't even be a conversation about that, like we had in that stupid debate class.

THERAPIST: I think I could understand why some people of color might think about it a little differently.

CLIENT: I don't get it.

THERAPIST: Well, I think as a White person, you don't have to think about race whereas people of color, they always have to think about race, because they get treated differently.

CLIENT: I've never seen anybody being treated differently because of their race, and I don't think it would necessarily be fair to say that just because I'm White I have it better in some way because of my skin tone. Technically, people always want to have a tan, they were always into that, and so me as someone who is very pale, I can't get a tan, and I don't think it's very fair. I think people should adopt this view more instead of the idea that we should be looking at race, and we should just accept people because of their personality and not their race, you know, just like Martin Luther King Jr. said, that we should all be judged on our character rather than our race.

THERAPIST: Yes. Why do you think he had to say that?

CLIENT: Because back then people were very racist and segregated, and it was a tough time but we have come way further than that now, and for people to still be debating about it makes no sense.

THERAPIST: I'm wondering why you think that so many of the people in your class saw it differently.

CLIENT: I don't know what they think they're gaining, from it. Maybe they're still stuck in that time period, when there was something wrong. If they just opened their eyes they would see that everything is actually fine.

THERAPIST: I wonder why they would be so upset if everything is fine.

CLIENT: I have no idea. I don't understand those people at all. And I'm frankly just glad that I'm not sitting there with them anymore.

THERAPIST: Yeah, it sounds really uncomfortable.

CLIENT: Very.

THERAPIST: I think that sometimes, it's easy to turn away from things that are uncomfortable and unpleasant. And problems like race in our society are very unpleasant and so it makes sense for you to want to get out of that class and not think about it.

CLIENT: It is very unpleasant.

THERAPIST: At the same time, it is also important to understand where your classmates are coming from—even the ones that you don't agree with.

CLIENT: I mean they had very good points, I think. They were talking about, like, police issues and, you know, our police force is one of the things that keeps us safe, and for them to be bashing on them like they're some kind of racists was ridiculous to me. I've met police officers and, you know, they have never done anything like they were saying in class. And for the people that they do hurt, it is always in self-defense. And at the end of the day, they've done more good than harm, and for people to use the police as an excuse to say something like that. . . . It doesn't make sense to me.

THERAPIST: Sounds like you've had mostly good experiences with the police.

CLIENT: Definitely, yeah. You know, people who've had bad experiences with police probably did something they shouldn't have done.

THERAPIST: We've had a few sessions together, you and I. What would you think if I told you that I was afraid of police?

CLIENT: I would be surprised and certainly confused because you don't seem like someone who would do something bad.

THERAPIST: I wouldn't do a crime, but sometimes police make assumptions about me, simply because my skin is brown. I've been stopped by police before, jogging in my own neighborhood, and questioned and that was very frightening. One time I was assaulted, and I needed the police to come and help me and they came and they didn't help me because my skin is brown.

CLIENT: Did they say it was because you were Filipino?

THERAPIST: No, they just opted to believe the assailant who was White. And then I had to go to court later and get a restraining order against that person. It was a difficult time in my life, and I don't want to go into details cause it's not about me it's about you. But I do want you to understand that sometimes police do things that have more to do with how the person looks than the actual realities of the crime.

CLIENT: I mean, they do need to make snap judgements, and I'm not saying police can't make mistakes now and then, but I don't think that it has to do with racism. I'm sure that there are some bad police officers. I'm also sure that the bad ones get fired or get taken care of and there is a lot of, I think, mainly good police officers that make mistakes. And I'm really sorry that you are afraid that things happen, but I think most of the time we can rely on that police force.

THERAPIST: I think it is wonderful that that is true for you. And, at the same time there are many people where that's not true for them—people who support and pay for the police force with their tax money that would be afraid to call them if they needed them because of the color of their skins. To me, this tells me that there is still a lot of work to do in our culture around racial issues.

CLIENT: I mean the idea sounds terrifying, but I don't know if everybody really feels like that.

THERAPIST: No, people like you don't feel that way, and if you've had good experiences, why would you? I think some people might say that's true for you because you are White, and yet I know people of color have had bad experiences and they feel like it is because they're not White.

CLIENT: I think if more people adopted the idea that everybody is just a person and that skin color isn't even something to think about, maybe things would be better, but I see now that perhaps that isn't completely true.

THERAPIST: I do agree with you, if people wouldn't judge people on their skin color we wouldn't have problems like this. I think that is a wonderful goal. The problem is, I think, we've not quite achieved it.

CLIENT: I have never met somebody like what you've described that doesn't think the way that I do. I haven't met somebody that is racist. It seems strange to me that people that technically go to my school and shouldn't really be too far off from where I live, say that they've had experiences with racist people on, like, an everyday basis. It doesn't sound realistic to me.

THERAPIST: Yes, I understand why that could seem confusing, because a lot of people think of racists as people who just use the N-word or run around in White hoods, chanting at night and burning crosses, whereas I think a lot of people of color see racism in other places too. Maybe it's racism that is a little more subtle, and because it has happened to them a lot, they are able to recognize it more quickly than for people it doesn't happen too. Perhaps many White people don't notice it because they don't have to.

CLIENT: Maybe they're just assuming that it is because of race and it is not actually because of race.

THERAPIST: Yes, well racism is pretty unpleasant, and people who experience it don't want to believe that they're being mistreated due to race either.

CLIENT: Maybe . . . I think it is a possibility that I haven't thought of before.

THERAPIST: Maybe this is something you can talk to with your friends of color and ask them some of those questions and see what their experiences are.

CLIENT: I don't think they'll have any of those kinds of experiences, but I could certainly ask them.

THERAPIST: I think it would be worthwhile. You could ask them if they've encountered racism or people who have treated them differently due to their race and if that's been hurtful for them.

CLIENT: I could do that.

In this example, the client shared some microaggressions she committed in class that led to an upsetting conversation. The therapist was able to empathize with her distress while also gently challenging her color-blind ideology and unfair judgments about people of color. She leveraged her own relationship with the client to help expand the client's thinking on these issues and judiciously used some self-disclosure to challenge incorrect beliefs about a just and equitable legal system. It ended with the client agreeing to do homework involving having a conversation with another person of color, with the intention of developing empathy and understanding around everyday racism. This one interaction did not correct all of the student's biases, but it is one conversation among many that will help move the client toward more prosocial thoughts and behaviors.

MICROAGGRESSIONS AGAINST THERAPISTS OF COLOR

What do you do when you are the therapist and also the target of a microaggression? Therapists of color may find it challenging to put their best foot forward when a client is continually committing microaggressions, and this may be compounded when supervisors and mentors are unable to help or even understand the situation. Literature focusing on cross-racial psychotherapy tends to emphasize the relationship between a psychotherapist who is White conducting psychotherapy and a client who is a person of color. As a result, mental health professionals who have marginalized identities are rarely provided with the guidance they need to help them navigate microaggressions encountered in clinical settings. Often, they resort to the strategies they have used in their own lives, the most common of which is to ignore the experience. As a result, clients may not be aware of the harm they are inflicting or that the behaviors are causing tension to arise in the therapeutic relationship.

As an African American psychologist, I have experienced many microaggressions from clients and even supervisors. When I first started my career after my internship, I worked at a large clinical research center at the University of Pennsylvania Medical School. At that time, there was no website with pictures of the therapists, so patients generally just got whoever was available based on insurance and diagnosis. So when new clients walked into my office, this was usually the first time they saw me. Most of the time, I could tell they were surprised to discover their therapist was a Black woman. Usually, they recovered from the surprise quickly, but sometimes they needed reassurance that I was actually qualified to help them. What made this unpleasant was not that my skin shade was unexpectedly different than the White American norm but, rather, the pathological stereotypes attached to my ethnoracial group that caused clients to have concerns about my competence and ability to help them.

Although I graduated from a top psychology program and had a number of expert supervisors, I was not given any training on how to address these experiences. As a result, I had to find my own ways of managing such situations. Knowing that my competence would be questioned more so than my White counterparts, I professionally framed all of my awards, diplomas, and certificates and put them on the wall opposite where the clients sat so they were easily seen. There were no other people of color at my workplace, and I could not get the professional mentorship and support I needed as a Black woman in academic medicine. I found outside mentorship from leaders in the Delaware Valley Association of Black Psychologists—a chapter of the Association of Black Psychologists (http://www.abpsi.org)—which was invaluable as a source of advice, camaraderie, support, and learning. Therapists of color should look for mentorship specifically for such issues as needed, and local or national organizations for therapists of color are an excellent resource.

From Clients

Microaggressions against therapists of color are common and can be quite stressful to therapists experiencing them (Hernandez, Carranza, & Almeida, 2010).

Although these therapists may become upset, usually they recognize that becoming defensive or aggressive in the session is counterproductive to helping the client. Many therapists of color are then left unsure how to respond to clients who microaggress against them. They worry that by pointing it out, they are making the situation about themselves and not focusing on the client's needs. However, nothing could be further from the truth. As noted previously, microaggressions are harmful broadly, and it is our duty as mental health clinicians to help make clients aware of dysfunctional or antisocial behaviors for the purpose of bringing about growth and positive change. Clinicians of color are in a unique position to effect such change by leveraging their existing relationship with the client to be helpful, including helping to dispel pathological stereotypes, speaking authentically about the harms caused by microaggressions, and modeling healthy cross-racial interactions.

There is no exact recipe for how to address a microaggressions committed by a client against a therapist of color. How best to respond depends on many contextual factors, including the client's racial and ethnic identity development, the clinical significance of the behavior, the strength of the relationship, and the form in which the intervention by the therapist would occur (Sue & Sue, 2016). The therapist must recognize the microaggression for what it is and think carefully about the most effective intervention. This may be warranted in the moment or at a later time in order to best maximize the enlightenment of the client. Finally, because the therapist of color will be addressing racial issues, to succeed the therapist must feel competent in their ability to engage in a potentially difficult dialogue on race (Sue & Sue, 2016).

In the case of a new client making microaggressive statements, I usually do not recommend confronting the microaggression immediately. Clients who are naive to issues about race may have considerable fragility around these topics and so a gentle approach may be needed. If a client commits microaggressions in the first session, chances are this is a pattern and it will occur again, leaving plenty of future opportunities to address the problem. In the interim, the therapist can take some time to understand the client better in order to best proceed with addressing the underlying misinformation and racism within the client that are fueling the commission of microaggressions. The therapist might open the conversation by saying, "Mr. Fairfax, I notice that in the course of our meetings you've made a few comments that I think could be misunderstood or hurtful to others. Would you be open to having a discussion about this?" Any CBT techniques that are helpful in addressing and dispelling other cognitive distortions can be helpful here as well, including psychoeducation, Socratic questioning, and even behavioral experiments.

From Supervisors

Therapists of color may also experience microaggressions from supervisors. When supervisees attempt to address these experiences within the context of supervision, supervisors sometimes communicate invalidation and lack of empathy toward the supervisee's experience rather than support and knowledgeable guidance. These invalidations by the supervisor can result in the perpetration of further microaggressions against the trainee, potentially causing damage to the supervisory relationships and trainee efficacy (Oshin, Ching, & West, 2019).

Constantine and Sue (2007) identified seven ways that Black psychology supervisees reported experiencing racism in the form of microggressions from White supervisors:

1. Invalidation of racial/cultural issues (e.g., "I think that client sees a lot of racism when it isn't really there.")
2. Stereotypical assumptions about certain clients of color (e.g., assuming a Latinx client is low income, will not pay, or will drop out of treatment)
3. Stereotypical assumptions about supervisees of color (e.g., assuming peer difficulties are the Black trainees' fault without considering the role of racism in the training setting)
4. Reluctance to provide performance feedback for fear of being viewed as racist (e.g., telling a Native American supervisee that all her work with clients of color is just fine because they "understand each other")
5. Overemphasis of clinical weaknesses or lack of conformity to White normativity (e.g., scolding a trainee for nonstandard administration of a test when a Black client objected to a naming task that included a picture of a noose)
6. Blaming clients of color for problems stemming from oppression (e.g., saying that the client of color needs to take more personal responsibility for legal problems without considering the client's version of the facts or racial profiling)
7. Advancing culturally insensitive treatment (e.g., asserting that an Indian American client with strong family ties should not be responsible for his parents' failing health and should "live his own life")

Supervisors should be aware of the ways racism may manifest in their relationship with their trainees of color in order to avoid it or self-correct when it happens, without defense and with humility. To that end, it is recommended that supervisors establish procedures when beginning individual or group supervision, emphasizing mutual respect in the training context, particularly with regard to topics related to cultural diversity. By compassionately facilitating conversations around race and inviting exploration from trainees with the goal of deepening mutual understanding and connection, supervisors can help therapists of color feel more willing to correct misinformation, particularly in group settings, and to challenge notions of privilege. Supervisors should consistently convey a sense of authenticity and humility to cultivate an enriching, inclusive, and positive learning environment. This can help repair "ruptures" or misunderstandings in the supervisory relationship and setting, and it can help prevent microaggressions or defensiveness from other trainees around conversations about diversity (Oshin et al., 2019).

Therapists of color are more likely to share their experiences of discrimination when supervisors authentically relate their own personal challenges related to experiences of exclusion from various settings. Thus, supervisors should be willing to model personal growth and exploration of biases to their trainees. Furthermore, supervisors should remain aware of the impact of current events on trainees of color and ensure that diversity topics are continually included and not just an "extra" topic that only is covered in an obligatory way (Oshin et al., 2019).

5

Assessing the Impact of Microaggressions

MICROAGGRESSION MEASURES OVERVIEW

Several classification systems for microaggressions are represented in the literature and have been developed into validated psychological measures. Sue et al.'s (2007) original nine categories of microaggressions were based on the subjective reports of people of color, but since that time, classifications arising from quantitative analyses have emerged that are based on Sue et al.'s taxonomy or some variation. Measures of microaggressions have largely focused on diverse individuals' self-report of these experiences. These measures vary in their applicability across specific racial and ethnic groups, with some being designed for people of color broadly and others tailored for very specific groups with multiple stigmatized identities. Some scales are designed for specific settings, such as counseling or research. In the following sections, I describe a few of the validated self-report measures available for surveying and quantifying microaggressions experienced by clients. At my clinic, we use several of these as part of our intake materials for clients of color.

Self-Report Measures for Targets

The Racial Microaggressions Scale (RMAS; Torres-Harding, Andrade, & Romero Diaz, 2012) is a 32-item scale that can quantify microaggression frequency. Exploratory and confirmatory factor analyses were used to assess dimensionality, and six factors (categories of microaggressions) were identified and included in the total scale. These partially map onto Sue et al.'s (2007) taxonomy and include items about (a) feeling invisible due to race, (b) assumptions of criminality by others, (c) eroticization, (d) being low-achieving or part of an undesirable culture, (e) being a foreigner or not belonging, and (f) environmental omissions. Sample items include "Others suggest that my racial heritage is dysfunctional or undesirable" and "Sometimes I feel as if people look past me or don't see me as a real person because of my race." For each item, respondents are asked to indicate how often they have encountered a particular racial microaggression on a 4-point Likert-type scale (0 = "never," 1 = "a little/rarely," 2 = "sometimes/a moderate amount," 3 = "often/frequently"). The RMAS was found to have good psychometric properties.

The Racial and Ethnic Microaggressions Scale (REMS; Nadal, 2011) is another important measure of microaggression frequency. The REMS was validated with a large sample of African Americans, Latina/os, Asian Americans, and multiracial participants. It has a six-factor structure that includes (a) assumptions of inferiority, (b) second-class citizen and assumptions of criminality, (c) microinvalidations, (d) exoticization/assumptions of similarity, (e) environmental microaggressions, and (f) workplace and school microaggressions. This structure was confirmed using exploratory and confirmatory factor analyses, and the measure was found to have good psychometric properties. The REMS measures the frequency of microaggressions experienced in the past 6 months (1 = "I did not experience this event in the past six months," 5 = "I experienced this event 10 or more times in the past six months"). Respondents answer items such as "Someone told me that all people in my racial group look alike." There is also a 28 item version (Forest-Bank et al., 2015).

The Ethnic Microaggressions Scale (EMA; Huynh, 2012), designed for Latino/a and Asian American adolescents, comprises 12 items and includes three general factors. The structure of the scale was assessed using exploratory and confirmatory factor analysis with structural equation modeling. The three scales are (a) emphasis on differences, (b) denial of racial identity, and (c) negative treatment. The items for this measure are rated on a scale from 0 to 5 ("never" to "almost every day"), gauging how often respondents experienced microaggressions in the past year. The assessment is scored by obtaining an average total score, with higher total scores indicating higher frequency of microaggressive experiences. Participants are also asked to indicate how much the event bothered them on a 5-point scale for a reactivity score. The EMA was validated with a representative adolescent sample of Asian, Latino/a, European, and participants of other multicultural backgrounds.

The LBGT People of Color Microaggressions Scale (LGBT-PCMS; Balsam, Molina, Beadnell, Simoni, & Walters, 2011) was created based on the theory regarding the cumulative nature of minority stress. Individuals who are both sexual and racial minorities are found to be more susceptible to microaggressions according to this 18-item, three-factor structure, which includes (a) lesbian, gay, bisexual, and transgender (LGBT) racism; (b) people of color heterosexism; and (c) LGBT relationship racism. The validity of this measure was supported by parallel analyses. These items form the basis of a survey scaled from 0 to 4 (from "did not happen/not applicable to me" to "it happened, and it bothered me extremely"), determining the occurrence of the microaggression and how it affected the individual. Responses are added to yield a summed total ranging from 0 to 90, with higher scores equating to more frequent experiences of microaggressions.

The Inventory of Microaggressions Against Black Individuals (IMABI; Mercer, Zeigler-Hill, Wallace, & Hayes, 2011) is a reliable and valid measure that assesses the extent to which Black Americans experience microinsults and microinvalidations. Exploratory factory analysis along with assessment of local independence determined that the measure is unidimensional, or has one factor. The 14 item IMABI uses a 5-point Likert scale ranging from 0 to 4 (from "this has never happened to me" to "this event happened and I was extremely upset"), allowing respondents to report the extent to which they experienced a certain situation and the extent to which they were troubled by the event. The items are then averaged to obtain a total score, with higher values implying greater frequency and impact of microaggressions. The IMABI was found to have good psychometric properties and a strong association with general distress.

The Gendered Racial Microaggressions Scale for Asian American Women (GRMSAAW; Keum et al., 2018) was developed using an intersectionality and microaggressions framework. Items were developed based on literature review, focus groups, and expert review. Examples of items include "Others expect me to be submissive" and "Others have suggested that all Asian American women look alike." Factor analyses suggested a four-factor structure with the following subscales: (a) Ascription of Submissiveness, (b) Assumption of Universal Appearance, (c) Asian Fetishism, and (d) Media Invalidation. The 22 items assess frequency and stress appraisal. GRMSAAW scores were found to be associated with sexism, racial microaggressions, depressive symptoms, and internalized racism.

With the Multiracial Microaggression Scale (Johnston & Nadal, 2010), participants rate the frequency with which they experience certain multiracial-specific microaggressions. The investigators created this scale based on qualitative data describing multiracial individuals' experiences with microaggressions. The 16-item scale measures the frequency of microaggressions experienced (from 1 = "not at all" to 5 = "a great deal"). Scale instructions are "Given both your current and overall experiences in life, how often have you experienced the following incidents?" An example item is "People around me felt uncomfortable about not knowing my racial background."

The Racial Microaggressions in Counseling Scale (RMCS; Constantine, 2007) was originally developed to understand African American clients' perceptions of White counselors. RMCS is a 10-item, 3-point Likert-type scale (0 = "this never happened," 2 = "this happened and I was bothered by it"). The RMCS measures client perceptions of racial microaggressions that they have experienced in the context of counseling, along with the impact of the microaggressions. Scores can range from 0 to 20, with higher scores being associated with greater perceived number and impact of microaggressions in counseling.

For more information about the previously discussed measures and others, see the review by Wong, Derthick, David, Saw, and Okazaki (2014).

Clinical Interview for Experiences of Microaggressions and Trauma

We recently designed a survey called the UConn Racial/Ethnic Stress and Trauma Survey (UnRESTS; Williams, Metzger, Leins, & DeLapp, 2018) to assess for racial stress and trauma to guide clinicians in asking clients difficult questions about their experiences surrounding race. The survey includes questions to assess ethnoracial identity development, a semistructured interview to probe for a variety of racism-related experiences including microaggressions, and a checklist to help determine whether the individual's racial distress meets the fifth edition of the *Diagnostic and Statistical Manual of Mental Disorders* [DSM-5; American Psychiatric Association (APA), 2013] criteria for PTSD. The format of the UnRESTS is modeled after the DSM-5 Cultural Formulation Interview (CFI; APA, 2013). Unfortunately, neither the CFI nor its supplementary modules examine racism or discrimination, despite the CFI having been developed as a cultural assessment. Therefore, it is important for clinicians to also have access to an interview such as the UnRESTS specifically designed for the assessment of discrimination and its impact. The interview is available in both English and Spanish (Williams, Mier-Chairez, & Peña, 2017). There is a short version that assesses the impact of racism and other forms of discrimination as well (Williams, Reed, & Aggarwal, 2020).

OTHER MEASURES FOR UNDERSTANDING CULTURE AND EXPERIENCES

Demographics Forms

It is important that clinicians capture and understand the human experience as best as we can. Although this may seem unnecessary or even intrusive, when collecting demographic information from clients or research participants, always ask for race and ethnicity. Take some time to review your intake materials to ensure the language is current, accurate, and inclusive. Be sure to offer write-in "not listed, please describe" responses for all questions that allow participants to self-define, if the available options may not fit their identity. Do not simply provide a box or space that states "other" because this can be insulting. In addition to potentially compromising validity, offering limited identity options has negative emotional repercussions. Asking a participant to fill out a form with checkboxes that does not include an important part of their identity or experience can be harmful and off-putting. It makes clients feel like their clinicians do not understand or value who they are, and it may reduce engagement in psychotherapy. As clinicians, we want to do our best to avoid contributing to clients' feelings of marginalization, and their experience of microaggressions can happen as early as when asked to complete intake paperwork.

Wadsworth, Morgan, Hayes-Skelton, Roemer, and Suyemoto (2016) published an article in the *Behavior Therapist* titled "Ways to Boost Your Research Rigor Through Increasing Your Cultural Competence." This article includes an appendix for the UMass Boston Comprehensive Demographics Questionnaire, a culturally informed demographic assessment that can be adapted for use in clinical and research contexts. This form is an excellent starting point when trying to develop an inclusive means of data collection. It sensitively collects information about clients' racial and ethnic identities, as well as gender identity, sexuality, and sexual orientation. I have put together a demographics form based in part on this measure but adapted for outpatient use; it is provided in the Appendix and can also be accessed at http://www.oxfordclinicalpsych.com/microaggressions.

Cultural Interview

One of the more useful but underappreciated means of better understanding clients of color lies at the back of the DSM-5. APA's CFI has been carefully designed to help enlist the client's own narrative of their mental health issues. It consists of a manualized set of standard questions that can precede every psychiatric evaluation. This includes gathering a cultural definition of the problem, cultural perceptions of the cause of difficulties, context and available support, and cultural factors affecting coping and help seeking. The CFI has both patient and informant versions, and it is available in multiple languages. There are several supplemental modules that can help gather additional information as needed. There are modules about the client's explanatory model of illness, level of functioning, social network psychosocial stressors, religion, cultural identity, coping and help seeking, the clinician–patient relationship, school-age children and adolescents, older adults, immigrants and refugees, and caregivers.

The CFI can be used in clinical encounters with all clients and all clinicians, not just with non-Whites or in situations of obvious cultural difference between clinicians and clients (DeSilva, Aggarwal, & Lewis-Fernández, 2015). However, it may be most useful when working with people of color, first- and second-generation immigrants, and those from unique cultural backgrounds. All students and trainees should have experience using the CFI, and after becoming familiar and comfortable with the questions, clinicians can incorporate the material into their own intake style to use more flexibly.

Self-Report Measures of Related Cultural Constructs

There are many good measures that can be used to better understand client experiences related to race, ethnicity, and racism. Here, I discuss several that I have used or developed for practice and research. Therapists can administer these early in treatment and then have a discussion with clients about findings and/or track their symptoms over time.

The Trauma Symptoms of Discrimination Scale (TSDS; Williams, Printz, DeLapp, 2018) is a 21-item self-report measure that focuses on anxiety-related trauma symptoms surrounding the experience of discrimination, including avoidance, negative cognitions, social fears, and anxiety. The following is an example of the items: "Due to past experiences of discrimination, I often cannot stop or control my worrying." Items are rated from 1 ("never") to 4 ("often"), where ratings are based on the amount of distress caused specifically by discriminatory acts. The measure is scored by summing all items. This is a good measure to provide to clients who are dealing with stressful experiences of racism.

The Multigroup Ethnic Identity Measure (MEIM-12; Roberts et al., 1999) is a 12-item scale validated in adolescents of various ethnic groups. The MEIM has also been validated in a nationally representative sample of African American and European American adults, aged 18–35 years, with excellent reliability ($\alpha = .91$; Williams, Duque, Chapman, Wetterneck, & DeLapp, 2018). Items are scored from 1 to 4, with higher numbers corresponding to greater agreement of items. Our research team also developed a 6-item version (MEIM-6; Williams, Duque, & Wetterneck, 2015). This is a good measure for all clients, but it is especially useful for adolescents and young adults struggling with ethnic identity issues.

The General Ethnic Discrimination Scale (GEDS; Landrine, Klonoff, Corral, Fernandez, & Roesch, 2006) is used to measure the frequency of ethnic discrimination over one's lifetime and resulting stress. Respondents are asked how often they have been treated unfairly in various situations due to racism during the past year and in the course of their lifetime. They are also asked how much stress resulted from each experience. The GEDS contains 18 items, rated on a Likert-type scale from 1 to 6, with higher numbers indicating more experiences of discrimination or greater stress. In the validation sample, mean scores for lifetime discrimination (GEDS-Lifetime) were 42.4 for African Americans and 26.5 for European Americans; mean stress from discrimination was 43.0 for African Americans and 25.9 for European Americans. This is a good measure to provide to all clients of color, but especially those who are dealing with experiences of racism.

The Schedule of Racist Events (SRE; Landrine & Klonoff, 1996) is an 18-item self-report inventory that assesses the frequency of racial discrimination (specific, stressful racist events) in the past year (recent racist events) and over one's entire life (lifetime racist events). It also measures the extent to which this discrimination was evaluated (appraised) as stressful (appraised racist events). The SRE has high internal consistency and split-half reliability. It was found to be related to psychiatric symptoms and cigarette smoking. The SRE is considered a good measure of (culturally specific) stress, particularly for clients who are dealing with racism.

The Everyday Discrimination Scale (D. Williams, Yu, Jackson, & Anderson, 1997) is a scale of global perceptions of everyday unfair treatment that has been widely used in research. This scale consists of nine items and measures encounters with discrimination in the respondent's day-to-day life with good reliability ($\alpha = .88$). Representative items include the following: "How often have you been treated with less courtesy than others?" and "How often have other people acted as if they are better than you?" The final two items ask about more serious events— that is, being "called names or insulted" and being "threatened or harassed." Items are asked of respondents regardless of the attribution for the unfair treatment. Responses are scored on a Likert scale ranging from 1 ("never") to 6 ("almost every day"), where higher total or mean scores indicate more discrimination. Follow-up questions can be asked of those answering "A few times a year" or more frequently (e.g., "What do you think is the main reason for these experiences?"). Although the experiences listed mostly overlap with microaggressive experiences, item 9 is stronger than a microaggression. Our own research found that removing this last item from analyses did not change the predictive value of the measure in a regression predicting trauma symptoms of discrimination, probably because being threatened or harassed is a relatively low-frequency event (Williams, Printz, et al., 2018). Thus, this measure can be a good proxy for microaggressive experiences. This scale is used widely in research but is also useful clinically for anyone of any race. Both short and expanded versions are available.

The Major Experiences of Discrimination Scale (MEDS; Forman, Williams, & Jackson, 1997; D. Williams et al., 1997) has two versions: One consists of nine items and a more recent short version comprises six items. Items include being fired from a job, being harassed by police, or being denied housing. Items are scored as 0 = "Never," 1 = "At least once in the last 12 months," and 2 = "At least once in my lifetime." A follow-up question is asked after each item: "What do you think was the main reason for this experience?" The MEDS is used widely for research, including for the National Survey of American Life and the 1995 Detroit Area Study. This is a good measure for people who may be highly stigmatized, and it is useful clinically for anyone of any race.

The Cross-Cultural Counseling Inventory–Revised (CCCI-R; LaFromboise, Coleman, & Hernandez, 1991) is a 20-item, Likert-type (1 = "strongly disagree," 6 = "strongly agree") scale designed for assessment of counselors' cross-cultural counseling competence. This single-factor scale was formulated on the basis of the cross-cultural counseling competencies identified by the Education and Training Committee of Division 17 of the American Psychological Association. The CCCI-R comprises items representing three areas: cross-cultural counseling skill, sociopolitical awareness, and cultural sensitivity. CCCI-R scores range from 20 to 120, and the measure appears to have good content, construct, and criterion-related validity. Higher scores on the CCCI-R correspond to higher ratings of cross-cultural counseling competence. This is a good measure to use with trainees who are just learning to work across ethnic differences and therapists who want to improve the quality of their cross-cultural work.

The Racial Microaggressions in Counseling Scale (RMCS; Constantine, 2007) is a 10-item, 3-point Likert-type scale (0 = "this never happened," 2 = "this happened and I was bothered by it"). The RMCS measures respondents' perceptions of racial microaggressions that they have experienced in the context of counseling, along with the perceived impact of these microaggressions on them. Scores for the RMCS range from 0 to 20, with higher scores being associated with greater perceived number and impact of microaggressions in counseling.

The previously discussed measures are just a few of those that are available. When selecting a measure to use with clients, ensure that the measure has been validated on the ethnic group to which your client belongs. The racial landscape is changing fast, so you should also ensure the instrument is current and uses up-to-date language.

6

Helping Clients Manage Microaggressions

STARTING A CONVERSATION ABOUT MICROAGGRESSIONS WITH CLIENTS OF COLOR

Therapists should ask clients of color directly about experiences of microaggressions early in the therapeutic relationship. Clients may not be familiar with the term, so you can describe it in a variety of ways. It is not essential to use the term *microaggressions* per se, but it is important for clients to have a language for these experiences. Many therapists who are not used to talking about race may not know how to start a conversation about microaggressions. Clients may not be quick to raise the issue either because they do not yet have enough trust that the therapist is able to understand and validate their experiences. This could be because the therapist has committed microaggressions against the client in the past, or it could simply be because of negative experiences the client has had with other professionals.

In any case, it will be important to provide the client an opportunity to share their struggles surrounding microaggressions, and using validated measures to understand the impact of microaggressions on clients (such as those described in Chapter 5) can be an easy way to start the conversation. Ideally, measures can be administered before or during the first meeting, but they can be given at any time and then used as a springboard for further conversations. For example, the therapist might say, "Ms. Juarez, I see on this questionnaire you completed that you are having some stress at work due to discrimination. Can you tell me more about that?"

Broaching Racial Issues in Therapy

Broaching racial issues in therapy is important and can occur as soon as the first meeting. This can be especially challenging when therapists have been working with a client of color for some time and there have been no conversations about racial issues. It is not too late to start the conversation. The following are suggestions that you might try in your practice:

- Administer at least one of the cultural scales with a client. Pick one that seems potentially salient to issues the client has mentioned. Then, as noted previously, discuss the results with the client in the next session.
- Ask a client to share with you something about their cultural heritage you might not be aware of. For example, if a client mentions a cultural holiday or event, the therapist could ask the client to share more about it.
- Ask a client of color about experiences with racism. Given that nearly every person of color has experienced racism, asking a question such as this will likely be productive. You can say, "How has your job been? Do you have to deal with much racism or bias in the workplace?"
- Acknowledge and apologize for a microaggression you committed. You can say, "I don't understand your culture as much as I'd like to. As a result, I may have said some things that were insensitive or even hurtful to you without realizing it. Will you let me know if that has happened? Or if it happens in the future?"
- Describe a time you felt dismissed, ignored, misunderstood, or stigmatized (this can be in any area, not just about race). Ask your client if anything similar has happened to them to open the door to their sharing experiences of mistreatment.
- Let your client know that you are searching for ways to keep improving your work together and to that end you will be administering a short post-session satisfaction questionnaire after each session. Then, ensure the questionnaire includes at least one item about therapist sensitivity to cultural issues.

THERAPEUTIC INTERVENTIONS FOR MICROAGGRESSIONS IN SESSION

When a client shares a microaggression in session, therapists can follow the guidelines for how to respond effectively. Of course, every situation is different, and not all of the following steps may be appropriate in every situation. But for therapists who feel lost, confused, stuck, or defensive, these guidelines can help provide a path forward:

1. Show concern in your face and body language.
2. Ask questions to more fully understand the problem.
3. Reflect back the essence of what was said to you to ensure the client felt heard and understood.
4. Validate the client's experiences.
5. Validate the client's feelings.

6. Discuss some of the mental health consequences of racism to help put your client's experiences, feelings, and symptoms into perspective.

7. Connect difficult feelings to experiences of racism—explore the impact of the different types of microaggressions on the consequent symptoms of psychopathology.

8. Discuss specific coping mechanisms for dealing with the microaggressions.

9. Problem-solve surrounding the issue.

10. Strengthen self-esteem to better enable the client to manage future (unfortunate but inevitable) experiences of racism.

I am fairly behavioral in my approach, and other therapeutic traditions may have some equally effective means of helping without being as directive. I would also likely share some of my own experiences of racism to help normalize the experience, feelings about those experiences, and my feelings about the client's experience (Miller, Williams, Wetterneck, Kanter, & Tsai, 2015). However, there are many therapists who do not share much about their own feelings and experiences but who can still be helpful in processing such experiences with clients.

EXAMPLE OF LISTENING TO A CLIENT OF COLOR WHO HAS EXPERIENCED A MICROAGGRESSION

The following is an example of a therapist discussing a microaggression with a client of color. Look for some of the previously described elements in the conversation, and also think about what could be improved.

CLIENT: Something really disturbing happened at work yesterday. I mean, actually it probably seems like something small but it bothered me a lot. And it bothered a couple of my co-workers of color as well so I thought maybe I could talk to you about it.

THERAPIST: Of course, you can talk to me about anything.

CLIENT: Great. So, what happened was what we are doing this research study and recording a participant on video, which is automatically uploaded to the cloud where it's reviewed by independent raters. One of the members of our team was helping the participant get set up for her video. He was captured on the video before the assessment really got started. Then later I got this kind of angry email from the rater asking, "Who is that Black male on the video? What's he doing there?" And it was in boldface! I thought it was kind of like—weird and alarmist. They could have just asked us, "Who is that person who is helping out?" I mean they must have known it was someone on our study team, because who else would it be? But the way that they wrote it, like as if it's some sort of crime sketch, was a bit jarring.

THERAPIST: (*Nods looking concerned and thoughtful*)

CLIENT: I thought it was just me, but then our study coordinator who is Black was copied on the email and read it, and so did the student who was the one who was captured on film (*who actually isn't even Black; he's Chinese*) and they were both offended. They were like, "You need to talk to somebody about this." But I'm not even sure what I would say, and I don't know how they will react. I'm sure that the raters are just trying to do their jobs.

THERAPIST: Who do you think you would tell about this?

CLIENT: I don't know if I should speak directly to the rater or talk to her supervisor about the way she worded that email.

THERAPIST: Has this rater behaved in this way before?

CLIENT: I have experienced this sort of thing from this team before. And I've talked to people about this stuff in other situations, and sometimes they get really angry and defensive. So I'm kind of afraid to offend them. And I don't know the rater at all; she's new, actually.

THERAPIST: If these are bigger issues with this organization, maybe you can talk to her and someone higher up as well.

CLIENT: You think so? I know the higher-ups pretty well. But they're all White, and I don't think they really understand any of this. In fact I think they would all call themselves pretty liberal and progressive, so it'll probably be shocking if I say, "Hey you know what? One of your raters was a little bit racist."

THERAPIST: If it's bothering you that much, that probably means you should find a way to address it.

CLIENT: I'm sure I could think of something, but do you really think I should even bring up?

THERAPIST: It's bothering you and others on your team too, so that says something important right there.

This therapist did a decent job responding to the microaggression. He did not fall into any of the most common pitfalls, such as questioning the accuracy or the negative impact of the experience. He recognized it was important and supported the client in taking action. However, this interaction could have been more effective. The therapist might have done better in terms of showing empathy, helping the client process her feelings about it, and putting the experience in the context of her daily life as a person of color.

The following is an example of a therapist using the guidelines described previously. The client is a Mexican American male, meeting with a racially ambiguous therapist to talk about his challenges adjusting to college. He is having trouble making new friends, and he describes a microaggressive classroom interaction with a peer.

CLIENT: Last Tuesday, something happened that kind of hurt my feelings. One of my classmates, I had just met him, and, we were just kind of talking, and it seemed like a totally normal conversation. Then he was like, "Oh yeah, where are you from?" And I was like alright, "I am from Chicago which is kind of in the Midwest." We are not there, so it was understandable for him to be interested. Then he was like "Oh, ok, but where are you really from?" So I said, "Well, I mean, it is a small town outside of Chicago, but you know, it's like an hour away from Chicago, the Chicago area." He said, "No, like, where are you from, like where are you *really* from?" (*Deep breath*) And it was then that I realized that he wasn't really concerned about my background but more about my race and about my ethnicity, and that was really all that was on his mind.

THERAPIST: Yeah . . . (*with concern in her voice*)

CLIENT: I don't know. I kind of felt hurt by his lack of interest in my individual background, because it was more of just like him getting to the root of who I am ethnically, and if I meet his criteria, is how I experienced it.

THERAPIST: That sounds difficult and really uncomfortable. What for you signaled that it was more about your race and your ethnicity than just your location.

CLIENT: Well, when he asked, it was his tone of voice. It kind of changed from like, just curiosity to more like, "Where are *you from*?" It really signified to me that he was asking for my ethnicity and, you know, it felt kind of undermining in a sense. Like he was trying to undermine and make me feel like I had to meet his standards to continue to be a candidate for his friendship.

THERAPIST: I'm so sorry that happened to you, especially in a classroom. You are looking for peer relationships and to connect with someone -- and then to be minimized to just where your family has come from and your race and ethnicity versus seeing you for fully who you are . . .

CLIENT: Yeah, yeah, I agree. That is exactly how I experienced it.

THERAPIST: What did you say back? How did you handle the situation?

CLIENT: Well, I told him that I am Mexican and that my family is from Mexico, and he was like, "Oh, ok cool." And we just kind of went back to class to the coursework, and I didn't really reach out another hand to make more of a connection with him because I didn't feel comfortable anymore, and he didn't extend another hand to continue the conversation, so that was that.

THERAPIST: I would imagine having that experience is a bit hurtful. I know that I have had experiences like that, of being kind of rejected and pushed aside for being different.

CLIENT: Yeah.

THERAPIST: That's really hard. I'm so sorry that happened to you.

CLIENT: Yeah (looking down).

THERAPIST: These kinds of experiences can really get people down. It would be totally normal to feel depressed, angry, or sad. What was it like afterwards for you? How did you feel later in the day?

CLIENT: I don't let that kind of stuff get to me. I didn't really think too much about it. And I kind of just, you know, I didn't think about it. But in the moment it did affect me, but since then—it is what it is.

THERAPIST: It sounds like something you are kind of used to by now. Just from your tone you are just sort of like, "Well, it happens," and you keep moving.

CLIENT: Yeah, it happens—that's a good way to put it I would say. It happens, and you can't let anybody else's ignorance affect the way you feel about yourself . . . so I just move on.

THERAPIST: How are you able to move on and forward from this situation?

CLIENT: Just by thinking about past experiences and knowing that, you know, it's not my issue with my background. It's sort of their issue, and I think about it as it's their come-up. It's the way they were raised that has brought them to be intolerant. I didn't really do anything to cause that, so you can't let it really get to you or else you start thinking it was your fault, that you are the way you are, but that's not the case.

THERAPIST: So, really kind of resting on the pride that you have in your ethnicity and realizing that those interactions are not about you. They are not about your heritage. It's really about that other person and their own ignorance.

CLIENT: I believe so, yeah.

THERAPIST: (Pause) How are you feeling now talking about it to me?

CLIENT: Honestly, I just feel like you wouldn't understand. You are a White woman, and I don't think you can really understand.

THERAPIST: Yeah, and I think that's a fair thing to say. I mean, as someone who has been able to move up in the world and looks sort of the same as most of the people that are out there, I could imagine how you would look at me and think, "How do you know my experiences?" And even if

I did have those experiences, mine would always be different than yours. But my job here is to listen and support you in your journey, and so I really want to understand your experiences from your point of view.

CLIENT: Mm, hm.

THERAPIST: How is it, talking to someone who looks different than you and who may have different experiences with race?

CLIENT: Like I said, you do your best to understand, but, you know, you will never know what it's like to be a Mexican in America right now. And, well, sometimes I don't even know . . .

The therapist did a good job validating the client's feelings and experiences, but the client still did not feel completely understood. Also, he misperceived the therapist as White, and upon reflecting on some of what she shared, he started to wonder if her experiences were more like his own. They discussed this more, and upon questioning, she shared a bit of her heritage—that her mother immigrated from Portugal and her father was African. She said,

Although again my experiences are going to be very different from yours, I have had experiences where racism has impacted me. Your experience and how you have reacted to these things are much more important to me, but if understanding this about my heritage is something that makes you feel closer to me and better understood, I don't mind sharing.

Note that the therapist did not lead with her own experiences of discrimination, but she was willing to talk about them in response to the client's questions and in a way that was supportive of his process. She also made use of techniques from Functional Analytic Psychotherapy, a behaviorally-based form of interpersonal therapy, to help strengthen the cross-racial therapeutic connection (Miller et al., 2015).

EXAMPLE OF PROCESSING MICROAGGRESSIONS EXPERIENCED BY A CLIENT OF COLOR

In the following situation, a female African American college student is having a session with a therapist at the student counseling center about challenges she is having on campus. She describes that her White academic advisor committed a microaggression against her, as have so many others since she has started college.

CLIENT: I recently had this experience, and I'm trying to process it and understand it, because I also feel that it's starting to trickle into other areas of my life.

THERAPIST: Tell me about that.

CLIENT: I was a part of a club on campus, a student organization, and I sat down with my advisor for a meeting. So we've already established a good rapport and have a relationship, and throughout the semester I changed my hairstyles regularly. Some days I'll have braids, and some days I'll rock my natural curls, then I might decide to relax it and wear it straight. And I remember I had straightened it, and when I had my meeting with her she basically told me that she really loved my hair. She kept saying how it looks so much more professional compared to my other hairstyles. And from her point of view, I can see she was probably trying to give me a compliment, but that was a very backhanded compliment. In that moment I kind of froze a little bit. I was a bit taken back that she actually would say that. And she actually thought it was a compliment. I spoke with the president of the club, but I didn't tell her what happened. I just left. I really didn't want to be around in that space at all anymore. I just felt so uncomfortable.

THERAPIST: That's a horrible thing to have happened to you, and from someone that you trust, in a supervisor's role. And someone who's supposed to mentor you and give you a lot of good advice on how to further your interests in that setting. It must have been really shocking to hear that coming out of her mouth.

CLIENT: Yes, it was really upsetting. And yet, I wonder how I could have reacted differently. I wonder how other people, I guess, would react to a microaggression like that. Is it a thing where, you know, we all kind of freeze up a little bit, or go in a state of shock and then moments later replay the situation in our head and think how we could have handled it differently? I just wonder about different ways that people cope.

THERAPIST: So your experience typically was to freeze up and then replay the situation?

CLIENT: Yeah. Probably out of shock and not expecting someone to really say that.

THERAPIST: You can have some level of vigilance, but when it actually happens you're not really prepared for it.

CLIENT: If I choose to engage with them verbally, how do I not come from such as a defensive standpoint, because I was offended. I'm kind of figuring out basically how to navigate that situation.

THERAPIST: Everyone has their process and you know, it can be hard to know if one process is better than another. Do you feel like that's the way that you tend to handle these situations?

CLIENT: I'd definitely say it's been unhealthy just because, like I said, I'm an overthinker. So even after the situation that's passed, I'm rethinking how I could have handled it better, how that person could have learned from it. Whereas, if I had said something in the moment, I could just cross it off and I don't really have to think about it. Things do tend to just linger in my mind when I don't address it. But I also feel like, I haven't addressed it because most of my experiences have been with people who are older than me, and, you know, growing up learning to respect your elders and kind of figuring out how to behave respectfully. I guess engaging in a productive dialogue with them would be my struggle.

THERAPIST: I want to say that, that's the very pernicious nature of what we call microaggressions. Actually, you know, there is a level of ambiguity to them that is extremely toxic, which makes you deliberate upon whether the intent was there when it was delivered or not. And that causes, I would argue, a lot more stress than the actual moment of the microaggression. And it's the whole process of like, what did he really mean by saying that? And that's time taken away from, you know, living a really fulfilling life. Not to say that you reacted that way. It's just naturally how people would react to these really ambiguous messages.

CLIENT: I think I should have done more, but I don't know what.

THERAPIST. It's pretty common for people to react with some level of responsibility, feeling like it is their fault. But you know, we're living in a pretty sick society where there are stereotypes about prejudice and discrimination that allow for these moments of microaggressions to go unchecked. There's always something else we could have done, but certainly in that moment it was the best that you could do—to just roll with it. But maybe there's the option, then of thinking that you have no responsibility for what happened to you and, you know, how could you? You didn't see that coming. I also will say that we can't possibly will people to change. They're going to have to want to step up. And it's just the very nature of the society that we live in and we navigate these challenges. I've learned how to cope with them. I hear you, and I definitely understand where you're coming from with wanting to arm yourself with more strategies to cope with these experiences, rather than just taking it. If you were to confront someone who said that to you, if you could redo that situation, let's think, what would you do?

CLIENT: In the situation with my advisor, I'd probably just say, I don't even want to say thank you, but I think I would say "thank you"—

THERAPIST: Hm. You thank her for her intent . . .? Yet she is hurting you,

CLIENT: Uh, then I'd explain to her why what she said essentially was not a compliment. It doesn't feel validating to any person to really hear that. And then maybe briefly go over a quick history of issues about African American hair, because I can't even really blame her not knowing based on her background. I don't know if she grew up around, you know, other people who don't look like her. So, I guess I would just explain to her why that essentially is not a compliment. Explaining to her, just very briefly, about my experience and maybe what other Black women might feel and then leave it at recommendations. Because I don't want to give her a whole PowerPoint presentation about the history behind it, and tell her what she has to do about this, but maybe just giving her some recommendations for things that she can Google and educate herself about. That is the best way I can really see myself doing something differently.

THERAPIST: And I want us to not forget that this is a situation where there's—maybe a power differential.

CLIENT: Yeah, she was my advisor. So just saying "thank you" really didn't make me feel good. It really wasn't a compliment. I don't know if I don't want to get too personal because it wasn't like we were best friends or anything, but maybe just encouraging her to do a little bit more research on certain things before she speaks so freely.

THERAPIST: And then you have the burden of having to educate.

CLIENT: Yeah, there's definitely that. But at least I would rather say something and not just freeze up and say nothing at all.

THERAPIST: I like your idea. And, I think it's important to have compassion for how you did react in that situation. That's certainly the best that you could have managed in the moment. Who knows what I would have done? In that situation, I could've just shouted and yelled and done crazy stuff like that. And that would have caused the whole situation to go really wrong, with more dire consequences. So I think it makes a lot of sense to talk through this here and have a plan that you feel good about for next time.

In this situation, a Black student was complimented and encouraged by her advisor to conform to Eurocentric norms of appearance (hair pressed straight). Because her hair, like that of most Black women, is naturally curly, wearing it in straight styles requires extra labor. The student believed her hair's natural appearance was less acceptable to her advisor, which has been a centuries-long area of contention for Black women who have to battle against Eurocentric standards of beauty to maintain positive self-esteem and body image.

The therapist might have been tempted to use cognitive–behavioral therapy (CBT) techniques to help the client reframe the microaggression as a compliment, but that is not what was needed in this situation. Instead, he affirmed the impact of the racial insult buried in the advisor's communication and subsequently validated the client's offense. The therapist then helped process the client's unhelpful response (freezing up and thanking the advisor for the insult) and aided the client in problem-solving for how she might respond differently next time. Finally, the therapist validated and supported the client, recognizing the challenge and burden inherent in the situation.

HELPING CLIENTS COPE WITH MICROAGGRESSIONS

Harmful Coping

Sometimes, the emotional weight of ongoing microaggressions can lead people of color to engage in maladaptive coping, such as remaining in denial, engaging in substance use, aggression, self-blame, and, in extreme cases, suicide. Despite the immense news coverage focusing on the Black Lives Matter movement, something we hear very little about is the mental health of the activists on the front lines. Unfortunately, it took the suicide of MarShawn McCarrel, a 23-year-old Black Lives Matter activist in Ohio, to bring this issue to the forefront of the conversation. In a final post to his Facebook page, McCarrel wrote, "My demons won today. I'm sorry." He then shot himself on the steps of the Ohio Statehouse. I was interviewed by *The Washington Post* about McCarrel's story to shed light on the psychological pressure experienced by many Black activists (Lowery & Stankiewicz, 2016). In a society that likes to imagine itself as post-racial, it can be a shock and traumatizing to experience ongoing hate, often in the form of microaggressions, with an intensity not experienced before.

Doing this work means being constantly engaged with hurtful reactions at every level. Jonathan Butler, a University of Missouri graduate student, led a hunger strike in 2015 that led to the resignation of the school's president. In assessing the communal impact, he said, "You're being faced with the reality that I'm more likely to be killed by the police, that I'm being discriminated against. You start to see all of the microaggressions."

As a scholar with a relatively large platform to facilitate discussions about race, I receive a great deal of unwanted comments. It is common to receive blatant hate and racism posted online in response to my blogs or media appearances, but in person I am more likely to experience microaggressions. Often this is in the form of unwanted advice or assertion of pathological stereotypes as if they were helpful novel information for me. For example, I recently moved from the United States to Canada, and when I would tell colleagues my area of study (multicultural psychology), a common response was, "You know, Canadian culture is different." For some reason, many people seemed to think this was new information for me and that by sharing it they were being helpful. It seemed bizarre that as a scholar of cultural differences, one could imagine that this fact could have escaped my notice or consideration.

All people of color experience microaggressions—whether or not they recognize it—and as a good therapist, you want to understand how your clients have been managing them. This holds whether or not racial issues are the main focus of therapy. Microaggressions are stressful, and stress impacts the success of treatment for all conditions broadly. Assess for harmful versus functional coping methods of managing these experiences. Examples of harmful coping include denial, substance abuse, aggression, self-blame, self-harm, and even suicide attempts.

EXAMPLE OF PSYCHOPATHOLOGY RELATED TO MICROAGGRESSIONS

Amy was a 21-year-old, Japanese American college student at a large, public, predominantly White university in New England. She decided to seek out therapy after an emotionally charged conflict with her White boyfriend's twin brother, Tom. She described the incident as "the straw that broke the camel's back." There was a painful interpersonal exchange that happened during a Super Bowl party. While drinking, Tom made increasingly racist comments about Black football players. "These Black players are only in here because they needed them to make up numbers," he snarled. Tom used the N-word repeatedly and hurled other derogatory racial epithets at players as they appeared on the television screen.

Amy told Tom several times that she was hurt and angered by his behavior, only to have the vicious verbal responses turned on her. "Shut up, you stupid b***!" he said. "What the f*** do you know about football, you slant-eyed b****? Your people don't even f***ing play football!" Racial tensions in the room became increasingly elevated. Amy felt flushed and angry but did not know what to do. She looked around the room for support, but neither her boyfriend nor his parents said a word. She expected that her boyfriend would stand up for her against the barrage of racist insults, but he looked away and ignored the conversation. Amy finally left the house in tears, feeling shaky and vulnerable. A week later, her boyfriend broke up with her, which only worsened her sense of betrayal and abandonment (Williams, Printz, Ching, & Wetterneck, 2018).

After these events, Amy became increasingly depressed. She was anxious and had difficulty falling asleep. Despite being an achievement-oriented student, she lost her motivation to excel academically and her self-esteem suffered. She began having nightmares about the Super Bowl incident and actively avoided her ex-boyfriend and his brother on campus. Reminders of the incident, such as seeing her younger sister wearing her ex-boyfriend's sweatshirt (which he had left at their home), triggered strong emotional reactions, including what Amy said felt like panic attacks.

Amy was administered the UConn Racial/Ethnic Stress and Trauma Survey by her new therapist and was found to have post-traumatic stress disorder (PTSD) symptoms as a result of her experiences. After a careful assessment, it was determined that Amy's symptoms of PTSD were a result of racial trauma. It would be tempting to place the blame for Amy's condition entirely on the actions of her ex-boyfriend's brother, whose comments were arguably stronger than what we would consider microaggressions. However, the main source of her pain was not his racist statements but, rather, the betrayal she felt from her ex-boyfriend, who did nothing to support or protect her. In therapy, Amy responded well to strong initial affirmation of her ethnoracial identity, as well as values she identified with that were part of her cultural heritage. This was facilitated by racial similarity with her therapist, who was of Chinese heritage, and a sense of closeness and relatability to him, which was enabled through the use of culturally-senstive FAP (Vandenberghe, 2008). Amy's subsequent treatment plan included self-care and academic organizational skills training, as well as empathic support in processing the racist incident. Over time, this allowed her to experience substantial symptom improvement and regain her academic motivation and self-confidence, in line with her personal values.

Adaptive Coping

Utsey, Giesbrecht, Hook, and Stanard (2008) found that race-related stress was a more powerful risk factor than even stressful life events for causing psychological distress. Greater psychological resources had a significant direct effect in minimizing psychological distress, and social resources had a significant stress-suppressing effect on race-related stress. This implies that there is an important role for psychologists in helping clients strengthen their emotional coping skills and utilize their social support resources for help.

A way of coping grounded in the subdiscipline of positive psychology is *proactive coping*, which characterizes how individuals detect, interpret, and prepare for anticipated stressors in their daily lives. This coping approach describes how people may minimize the onset of stress in advance. People of color socialized into American culture have used proactive coping to maintain self-control in anticipation of microaggressions and to manage the situational dynamics of an interracial interaction in which a peer or colleague may behave in a biased manner. Literature (albeit limited) demonstrates that stigmatized groups, including people of color, use proactive coping to manage stigma-based stress (DeLapp & Williams, 2019).

Some research in our lab has examined how African Americans proactively cope with racism, especially when they anticipate that a peer or colleague may behave in a racist manner toward them (DeLapp & Williams, 2016). We noted that participants used a range of tactics to prepare, including suspending judgments about the meaning of a peer's comment until further information is obtained (reserved judgment), reconfiguring one's perception of their peer to be more positive in nature (cognitive reappraisal), effortful control tactics to avoid impulsive reactions, disclosing personal information to encourage one's peer to view them as an individual rather than as a negative stereotype (individuating information), and pursuing information about the nature of a peer's racial biases to guide coping efforts throughout the interaction (information seeking). Collectively, the purpose of these strategies is to enable one to persevere through a racially hostile encounter.

However helpful, these proactive coping responses will not typically prevent microaggressions. Moreover, such strategies may not even ameliorate the emotional distress experienced from anticipating microaggressions. As such, people of color may (and often do) utilize a toolbox of coping strategies to deal with the lingering effects of racial stress. In a therapeutic context, you can help your clients cope with microaggressions through steps that include placing the blame where it belongs (on the perpetrator and, secondarily, our cultural dysfunction), seeking social support within one's community (e.g., close friends, family, other people of color, and people who "get it"), temporarily limiting one's exposure to cues of racism (e.g., signing off social media), utilizing religious or spiritual practices for comfort (e.g., prayer and meditation), seeking distraction from cues of racism (e.g., engaging in pleasurable activities), and participating in restful and relaxing activities (self-care). Also, many people of color nationwide have sought solace, received social support and validation, and pursued systemic change through peaceful activism (making meaning from pain). They may also find it rewarding to educate others by working to facilitate mutual understanding, but people of color should never feel required to take on this responsibility because the ultimate responsibility lies with the offender. Regardless of the deployed strategy, adaptively coping with racism is an ongoing, evolving process.

As discussed previously, microaggressions can even be traumatizing. This is particularly true if one is exposed to microaggressions repeatedly, the microaggressions are coming from superiors, and/or when there is clear malicious intent. Most of the clients seen in my clinical practice who are suffering from racial trauma have become traumatized by unchecked microaggressions in the workplace or repeated harassment by law enforcement. You should determine whether the microaggressions experienced by your clients have been traumatizing and, if so, whether they are still happening. Although microaggressions are everywhere, progress in treatment will be slow if they are occurring at a high frequency and unchecked, as victims need space to heal. You need to help your client identify the major sources of microaggression-related stress. If it is not possible to stop the bad behaviors, you should work with your client to make a plan to change the environment. This could mean major life changes, such as finding a new job, moving to a new neighborhood, or removing toxic people as close friends. These types of changes are not easy, but they are often necessary for a client's mental health.

HELPING CLIENTS RESPOND EFFECTIVELY
TO MICROAGGRESSIONS IN THEIR DAILY LIVES

Although microaggressions are relatively common, they are also disturbing and sometimes even shocking. People of color are often at a loss for what to do when microaggressions occur. Sue and colleagues (2007) describe this as the catch-22 that people experience when they experience (or witness) microaggressions. First, the individual may question if a microaggression has really occurred (e.g., "Did I hear him correctly?" or "Did she mean it in that way?"). Next, the target (or observer) must decide whether or not to take action. If the person does respond, there is a likely negative outcome, such as denial, arguments, defensiveness, or additional microaggressions in the form of victim-blaming. If the target/observer does nothing, there is also a negative outcome, such as feelings of regret, anger, resentment, shame, or sadness. Even the process of deciding how to respond to a microaggression can be stressful in and of itself.

It is not always possible or safe to respond to a microaggression, but clients should be encouraged to respond if they are able to do so safely. Microaggressions can occur at any time, and clients of color and White allies alike will benefit by feeling prepared and empowered to respond effectively in the face of this inevitable but troubling occurrence. We do not yet have research definitively showing that tactful responses to microaggressions will protect against the negative sequelae of such events. However, based on what we know about oppression and learned helplessness broadly, we have good reasons to believe that it would be beneficial for a client's mental health to take valued actions in the face of such attacks rather than being a passive victim.

Derald Wing Sue was born in Portland, Oregon, yet he receives frequent complements from others on his grasp of English. He says, "I usually will reply with, 'Thank you—I hope so. I was born here.'" Sue, who is Asian American, notes that when people make comments such as this, they unaware that they are sending out a metacommunication, a hidden message stating their belief that he is a perpetual alien in his own country (Jagannathan, 2019). Sue and colleagues (2019) provide some guidelines for how to respond to microaggressions such as this that may occur in everyday situations, which are described further in this section. You can role-play some of these situations with clients so that they feel prepared to respond effectively when such events occur.

Make the Invisible Visible

Sue et al. (2019) suggest undermining the metacommunication, challenging the stereotype, describing what is happening, or asking for clarification as ways to make the invisible racism in microaggressions more apparent. They provide the example of a situation involving an Arab American college student in a chemistry class who overhears the following comment from a fellow student: "Maybe she should not be learning about making bombs and stuff" (p. 137). The metacommunication here is that all Arab Americans are potential terrorists. The target might respond by saying, for example, "You are making some very hurtful assumptions, and that's really not alright." This draws attention to the underlying pathological stereotype and also informs the offender that the statement is inappropriate. She might also broaden the ascribed trait to a universal human behavior and say, "Anyone can be a terrorist." Or she can ask for a clarifying statement, such as "Tell me more about that. What is your point?"

Disarm the Microaggression

Microaggressions thrive when unchallenged. When a microaggression occurs, it can be disarmed by expressing disagreement in some way. This can include voicing disagreement in the moment, using nonverbal communication such as shaking your head, or interrupting and redirecting (e.g., "Hey, let's not go there."). In this example scenario, a colleague makes the following statement about a new employee who is a Native American: "He only got the job because he's an Indian" (Sue et al., 2019). The metacommunication is that people with minority racial identities receive unfair opportunities through special accommodations rather than through their own capabilities or merit. In this case, the target can state values and set limits, saying,

> You know that respect and tolerance are important values in my life and, while I understand you have the right to say what you want, I'm asking you to

show a little more respect for me by not making racially offensive comments.
(p. 136)

Another response could be to describe the consequences of the statement: "Every time I come over, I feel uncomfortable because you say hurtful things like that." This can be particularly effective when there are others around, and it communicates to everyone that this is not all right.

Educate the Offender

Microaggressions are typically rooted in faulty information (pathological stereotypes), which creates many opportunities to educate the offender on how and why their actions were hurtful. In the example about the student in the chemistry class, an educational response could be, "The majority of Arab Americans are completely against terroristic acts. How would you feel if someone assumed something bad about you because of your race?" (Sue et al., 2019). Targets and allies can try appealing to the person's own values around inclusivity and equity, or even suggest how they might benefit from learning more about pathological stereotypes. Be sure to separate intent from impact, and focus on the behavior and not the person. If a person tells a racist joke, for example, one's response could be, "I'm sure you meant that to be funny, but here's why that particular joke might hurt people's feelings . . ." You can also add that such jokes can cause harm by promoting negative thoughts about certain groups that may then result in negative behaviors against people in those groups.

Education can take place at a broader level as well. If repeated problems tend to happen in a specific setting, such as the workplace, it might be possible to advocate for office-wide training. For example, initiating a speaker series on microaggressions or addressing the issues at staff meetings on what types of comments are and are not condoned could help shift the landscape.

Seek External Intervention/Help

Sometimes microaggressions are so frequent or egregious that help is needed. When an offender will not stop, the behavior could be considered racial harassment. In such cases, victims should keep a record, documenting what was said, the date and time, and any witnesses who were present. Then the person can email this information to a friend for documentation and support. Even if the person does not want to act on it in the moment, there will be a record of it. So if it does get to the point where the client needs to file a report, the facts are all there (Jagannathan, 2019). If making a report to human resources, do not have high expectations, but do give staff a chance to investigate. Give them an opportunity to determine what happened and whether they can do anything to improve the situation. Even if they are unable to assist, the very act of filing a report alerts people in charge about the problematic individual, and future complaints from others will be taken more seriously. If the problems persist, clients can file a discrimination charge with the Equal Employment Opportunity Commission (EECO). It can be difficult to get justice from the EEOC because the legal standard is so high, but clients can talk to a civil rights lawyer beforehand to explore options.

In addition to getting support in therapy, clients can be encouraged to get outside help from friends, colleagues, co-workers, or even a community leader. Clients can also collaborate with other people who have shared experiences. The unfortunate fact is that victims cannot always rely on human resources or upper management to spontaneously do the right thing. Often, superiors do not want to look like the bad guy or break racial solidarity (e.g., a White supervisor faced with reprimanding a White employee for a microaggression against an employee of color), and so they do nothing (Bailey, 1998). But there is power in numbers, and if several people make a complaint together, it is much more likely to get attention and, thus, a positive outcome is also more likely.

Should Clients Always Challenge Microaggressions?

As noted previously, Sue et al. (2019) suggest undermining the metacommunication or challenging a stereotype as one way to address microaggression in the moment. To demonstrate how this could be done, the authors provide an example in which a Black man steps onto an elevator, and then a White woman who is already inside clutches her purse in fear. (This really happens.) To make the implicit visible, Sue et al. note that the Black man could respond by saying, "Relax, I'm not dangerous" or "Do you realize what you just did when I walked in?" (p. 136). Generally, I think Sue has a great deal of wisdom with regard to the topic of microaggressions. And although I agree that this is an excellent way to shed light on the racial stereotypes underneath this microaggression, a word of caution is advised. Consider that this woman is already fearful about being in a tight space with someone she perceives to be dangerous. For the Black man to confront her in this manner may escalate her fear to the point that she ends up calling for help or even reaching for the pepper spray.

Few people today recall that the largest act of domestic terrorism occurred in Tulsa, Oklahoma, in 1921 when an entire Black town called Greenwood was burned to the ground because a White woman became fearful in an elevator that she shared with a Black man (Oklahoma Commission, 2001). She told other White people about her anxieties, and in response all of Greenwood suffered. Black people were lynched by a frenzied mob of White men, and the community was firebombed by a fleet of planes operated by the US National Guard. Because, historically, White men did not want to compete with Black men for their women, law enforcement was a part of the system designed to enforce these divisions. Any inference that a Black man had designs on a White woman could result in a legal response or mob violence and lynching of the suspected offender (e.g., Emmett Till, an adolescent violently killed by White men for allegedly whistling at a White woman; Farzan, 2019).

Even today, White women yield an astonishing amount of power with regard to controlling and punishing Black people. One simply needs to watch the news to find multiple instances in which police were called by White women in response to Black people who were doing nothing dangerous or illegal at all. Examples include playing ball in a parking lot, picking up trash with a gripper stick, gardening, and standing under an awning in the rain waiting for an Uber. In 2018, one of these events made headlines in Philadelphia when two Black men were waiting to meet a local businessman at a Starbucks in Rittenhouse Square. The Black men arrived a few minutes early, and one asked to use the restroom. The Starbucks manager, a White woman, told him he could not use the restroom because he was not a paying customer. Soon thereafter, she approached their table and asked if they needed help. After they said no, she called the police. Three police officers showed up, and the men were told to leave immediately. Bystanders were shocked and took videos of the two Black men being handcuffed and taken away for doing nothing wrong. Starbucks subsequently implemented anti-bias training for all employees (Abrams, Hsu, & Eligon, 2018).

In consideration of the suggestions offered by Sue and colleagues (2019), I decided to conduct a short informal poll of a few professional Black men I know to ask them if they thought Sue et al.'s suggestion for disarming the elevator microaggression was a good idea. I described the situation and proposed intervention to seven African American men, then asked, "Good idea: Yes or No?" Six of the seven gave a resounding "No," and the seventh was equivocal. While admittedly this not a rigorous scientific investigation, I find their responses informative. One of the respondents, a psychologist, noted that although the intention is to provide a "corrective experience" in the moment, it could have a paradoxical effect, reinforcing preconceived racist attitudes about being ostensible and aggressive. Another said, "That would place me in a more uncomfortable position when, really, I just want to get out of the elevator ASAP!" Another was just upset altogether by the very suggestion, "No. It's not going to put her at ease, and it's confrontational which will lead me to jail or put me in danger." The final respondent, who did not give a definitive answer, offered that the intervention

> puts the targeted individual at risk, if the one microaggressing against them is in a position to considerably gaslight or otherwise do harm to them. It is taxing enough to experience microaggressions, so the feeling would be doubled or tripled by attempting to call attention to every one without proper precaution.

The theme of risk and danger seems evident in these responses (Williams, 2019c). Sue and colleagues do advise us to consider the consequences of microaggression interventions, especially when a strong power differential exists between offender and target. However, they may underestimate the extent of the harm that can come to people with highly stigmatized identities when they try to push back. So, although microaggressions should be challenged when possible, I advise safety first. When considering how to respond to microaggressions, you should generally ask your client if they think any proposed interventions would be safe and take seriously any concerns voiced about what could happen.

However, in this scenario, there may be an important role for a White ally, who could safely say things that would be too dangerous for the Black man to proffer. For example, as suggested by Sue et al. (2019), an ally could say, "He might be Black, but that does not make him dangerous" or "You're clutching your purse. Are you afraid of him?" Allies can often contribute to the war against microaggressions in ways that the most stigmatized among us cannot. However, it remains to be determined if this intervention would be helpful or still result in a distressing conflictual situation. There is more about Allyship in Chapter 7. One suggestion that seemed worthy of consideration is for the Black man to mirror the frightened expression of the White woman, and anxiously look around the elevator for signs of danger and seem frightened, as a way to cue her regarding her visible biases.

IMPROVING THE ETHNIC/RACIAL IDENTITY OF CLIENTS

We have touched on ethnic and racial development in clients, and this is one of the few known moderators of harm caused by racism. Racial, or ethnoracial, identity consists of a sense of commitment and belonging to an ethnic/racial group, positive feelings about the group, and behaviors that indicate involvement within the group (Avery, Tonidandel, Thomas, Johnson, & Mack, 2007; Roberts et al., 1999). Positive ethnoracial identity is a sense of self, which has been demonstrated to be a protective factor related to identity development among African Americans and other people of color. Positive ethnic and racial identities are essential to the personal and collective well-being and resiliency of ethnic minority youth. Most research on psychological correlates of ethnoracial identity has focused on youth because the process of developing an ethnoracial identity is thought to typically begin in childhood. Among adolescents, positive identity has been found to be associated with self-esteem, coping, sense of mastery, and optimism; conversely, loneliness and depression have been negatively related to ethnoracial identity (Roberts et al., 1999). In adults, positive ethnoracial identity has been associated with self-esteem and reduced anxiety and depression (Lorenzo-Hernandez & Ouellette, 1998; Williams, Chapman, Wong, & Turkheimer, 2012). Having a negative ethnoracial identity has been linked to poor self-esteem, problems with adjustment, poor school achievement and dropout, delinquency, depression, eating disorders, and substance abuse (Rivas-Drake et al., 2014).

EXAMPLE OF STRUGGLES SURROUNDING ETHNORACIAL IDENTITY

Ethnoracial identity is a process that starts in childhood and can evolve over the lifespan. Here, a professional woman of color shares her struggles surrounding ethnoracial identity development in the face of ongoing negative social messages about her cultural group (Spatz, 2004).

We are born into a culture, and whether we like it or not we usually first adopt the value system of that culture. This value system may be consistent with our personal idea of what we would like our values to be, or it may be quite inconsistent with what we believe. It may be inconsistent with our cultures laws or stated values as well. Take this statement from the American constitution, ". . . all men are created equal and endowed by their creator with certain rights . . ."

Many Americans today (including myself) would agree with this statement, however beliefs are borne out by actions, and I must say I find myself at times judging the worth of a person based on their looks, status, or numerous other characteristics. I do not want to do this, nor do I think it is correct. However, if you grow up and every moment you are bombarded consciously and unconsciously with things like "thin is beautiful," "greed is good," "the poor deserve to be poor," "brown skinned people are worth less than white skinned ones," it is difficult to then believe in the core of your being that all are created equal. It does not matter if you yourself happen to be not thin, or poor, or brown skinned. I take on these values from my culture. At some point I recognize the inconsistency and attempt to disabuse myself of these notions.

It would be naive to think that I could grow up in a culture in which racism exists and think that I would somehow not be affected by it. Until my nineteenth year of life, I was myself afflicted by racist ideas. If racism means to value one people group or culture higher than another and to use the characteristics of a group of people such as hair or skin color as a sign of their lesser worth, and to think that beauty or intelligence is determined by skin color, then I would have to say that I was a believer. Not to say that I did not want to believe that all peoples intrinsic value was equal. I had in fact believed myself to be free of such biased thinking, but I could not help it, I did not yet have the tools to allow myself to be free of this kind of thinking, I had not even made the first step which is to recognize it in myself.

How did I find out that these seeds of racism live in me? I knew because I was not satisfied with my own skin color or my own culture. I believed myself to be ugly and stupid. I observed my own country and my TV, and I saw that those of my skin color were the poorest people. These same people were the most uneducated people and that a large amount of the men were in jail. To accompany this I was told that if anyone works hard enough, then that person will make it, they will become rich and prosperous. I was told that every person regardless of his race had the same chance to be educated and rich. I was told that the proof that there is no racial obstacle to wealth and education is that people of many cultures and ethnic backgrounds had come to America over the years and been able to "make it." And I had believed this. I must have at some point come to the following conclusion: If every people group has the same chance, and my people remain poor, then it can only be their OWN fault. They must have something in them to prevent them from getting to the top. I never made this logical conclusion consciously. But no one at my school, or on TV or in the newspaper or in the magazines gave me any other options for why my people remained at the bottom. In fact no one really wanted to talk about it at all. My culture made it impossible for me to find any other solutions for my internal conflict. For this reason I hated myself and my people. I thought they had some intrinsic flaw which prevented them from becoming successful.

How did I change my opinion? When did I change my mind? Do I think that all people have the same intrinsic worth? Sadly, I still have to say no. I am still too much a product of my country and my culture. I have been the most successful in changing my mind when I have found out that my culture has lied to me.

I have found out that people are not poor because they do not work hard enough. Some people are unlucky. Some people are abused. I have found out that all people do not have the same chances. I found out that "privilege" exists (based on wealth, skin color, accent, etc.). I did not find out these things from my school teachers or the TV or my text-books, or the main stream society, or my friends. These people never wanted to talk about any of this. In as much as I found out where and how and to what extent my own culture lied to me, exaggerated or told me half-truths, have I been able to change my opinion about myself and my worth in a way which is reflected in my actions and my subconscious, and not just like some parroted truism. For this reason the truth is so important to me. It is the truth that sets me free from self-hatred and bias.

To what extent have the lies our culture has told us has crept into our thinking? The words we say and the emphasis and implication of what we say and, do not say, become very important—for they reveal the real cultural value behind the "believed" or stated idea. The disease of anorexia is an example of how our cultures lies distort the idea of self-worth. These young women believe the lie our culture tells that beauty and self-worth is dependent on weight. Neither their doctors nor their parents not even their friends can convince them that it is the culture that lies—that their self-worth is not dependent on their weight. If they do not believe it for themselves, how can they believe it for others?

As demonstrated in the previous narrative, social biases against various groups can result in difficulties developing an adaptive ethnoracial identity. As noted previously, research has identified racial socialization as a protective factor. For cultural groups that have lived in the United States for several generations, families are instrumental in the process of racial socialization by transmitting values, beliefs, and ideas based on cultural knowledge of the competencies needed for optimal functioning as a stigmatized minority in US society. Racial socialization influences a young person's emerging sense of identity and self-concept, beliefs about the world, strategies and skills for coping with and navigating racism, and inter- and cross-racial relationships and interactions. Children of color who learn that others may think negatively of them but have cultivated values, beliefs, and knowledge of a positive ethnoracial identity are less likely to have negative outcomes and more likely to be resilient in adverse conditions. However, people of color who are new immigrants or those raised by White families are less likely to have received the type of racial socialization necessary to successfully navigate experiences of racism in their new home country. An emphasis on empowerment is essential. This can be facilitated through acknowledging social, emotional, and cultural strengths; encouraging self-advocacy; bolstering racial pride; and supporting traditional spiritual practices.

Thus, clinicians should assess and routinely consider the client's stage of ethnoracial identity development when working with people of color. This might occur in the form of clinicians encouraging and supporting clients in the exploration of their ethnoracial identities to help improve overall psychological well-being. CBT interventions might include discussions of what the client likes about their ethnic group, learning more about their history and the achievements of others from their group, explicit rejection of stereotypes, and increased involvement in traditional cultural activities to build a greater sense of ethnoracial pride. In addition, critical-mindedness could help protect against the damage that experiences of discrimination can cause and facilitate a beneficial critique of existing dysfunctional social conditions. Understanding cultural differences can promote flexibility and provide the tools needed to adapt to the difficult cognitive, emotional, and social situational demands that people of color must often traverse (Williams, Chapman, Buckner, & Durrett, 2016).

ADDRESSING CLIENT AVOIDANCE IN THERAPY

Many mental health professionals do their best to treat all groups fairly; thus, it can be difficult to understand why they might encounter guarded suspicion when working with their clients of color. Most people of color have already experienced discrimination in other medical-like contexts and thus may take a defensive posture as they are evaluating the safety of a new situation. Therapists should pay careful attention to the behaviors they use to form the therapeutic alliance. If a client has acknowledged the experience of microaggressions, either in an assessment or verbally, but is unwilling to discuss that situation with the therapist, this could indicate a lack of trust that the therapist will be able to respond in a supportive and helpful manner. Rather than take it personally or pathologize the client, the therapist should openly acknowledge and validate the client's mistrust. The therapist might say,

> I can understand why you might not want to talk to me about ways you have been disrespected, disbelieved, or even harmed due to race. It wouldn't surprise me if you've had many negative experiences with people who look like me. I really do want to understand what you've been through, and I hope we

can build the trust needed for you to eventually feel like this is a safe place to talk about anything you've experienced. But we can wait until you are ready and we have had a chance to get to know each other better.

Some clients of color will admit to having experienced microaggressions or having witnessed them but will deny that these are a source of distress. The research indicates that microaggressions are indeed stressful, so if any client denies this is the case, their assertion should be further explored. Because of the stress of confronting offenders directly about microaggressions, targets may make a conscious but effortful choice not to be offended, having resigned themselves to being unable to prevent microaggressions from occurring. However, there are certainly some individuals who are very easygoing temperamentally and are simply not unraveled by anything.

To the extent that some people of color may accept pathological stereotypes or be new immigrants still in the process of acculturation, not all people of color will be able to identify all microaggressions when they occur. But there are some people of color who will deny ever having experienced microaggressions, which is simply at odds with the realities of Western culture. For example, in one study of Filipino Americans ($N = 199$), 99% reported at least one microaggression in the past year (Alvarez & Juang, 2010). Therefore, this is perhaps the most concerning presentation because it may represent either a complete lack of awareness and understanding of social behaviors or very low self-esteem. When people experience microaggressions without an ability to attribute them to racialization, they may begin to believe that they have caused the microaggressions and are deserving of maltreatment. Therapists should carefully assess for *internalized racism*—a disdain of one's own ethnic group and belief in pathological stereotypes about oneself. It is also possible that such individuals are engaging in avoidance and denial surrounding the reality of microaggressions, which would constitute a maladaptive coping strategy (Nadal, 2018). Unfortunately, pretending microaggressions do not exist is neither an adequate mental health strategy nor an effective method of coping (Alvarez & Juang, 2010). In such cases, gentle probing or questioning with the goal of bringing these experiences into the forefront of awareness and ultimately into the therapeutic space would be appropriate.

CAN THE TARGET OF A MICROAGGRESSION BE MISTAKEN?

It has been argued that microaggressions are really a subjective experience and, as such, if a person believes they have experienced a microaggression, it must be so. Because microaggressions are subtle and must be interpreted in context, it can happen that a person believes they have experienced a microaggression but is mistaken. However, when someone describes a microaggression, approaching such a situation with the notion that the other person "could be wrong" sets the stage for more microaggressions and relationship damage (or further relationship damage if the offender is the one claiming the target may be wrong). The main problem is that the typical response a person of color gets when they point out a microaggression is denial from the offender, with the implied or explicit assertion that they are mistaken. This is a second microaggression and only compounds the damage from the initial assault.

In a therapeutic context, when a client describes a microaggression, if the therapist assumes the client is mistaken, the therapist adds insult to injury (Williams, 2020b). This shifts the authority of interpretation from the person who experienced it (who is usually in the best position to make this determination) to the person who is learning about it secondhand (i.e., the therapist, who was not present for the event and does not understand the full context of the situation) or the person who committed the microaggression (who is motivated to deny racist wrongdoing to preserve self-esteem or for impression management). As such, the default response should always be to believe and support someone reporting a microaggression. You should assume that your client's perspectives are as valid as your own. Even if the client is mistaken, suggesting this at the onset will be counterproductive, so give the client the benefit of the doubt.

If it is ever the case that another person believes a microaggression occurred when it positively did not happen, and there is an important need for absolute accuracy in the situation, then the appropriate response would be to have a careful and sensitive discussion about the situation. The response should never be "You are certainly wrong" or "That was not a microaggression and here's why . . ." This is simply replicating the harmful and invalidating messages people of color frequently experience when trying to engage in important conversations about this problem. The therapist might instead start the conversation as follows (Williams, 2020b):

> I can see why that felt like a microaggression, given the many times you've experienced that situation in other contexts. If I had experienced all of the ignorance and bias from others the way you have, I would think that too. But this particular case seems a bit different to me. May I tell you why?

This approach shows empathy, recognizes that microaggressions do occur with some regularity, and invites the client to explore alternatives rather than flat out saying the client is wrong; as a result, such feedback will be more effective and experienced more respectfully.

MICROAGGRESSION DISCUSSION SCENARIOS

Microaggressions are not always easy to identify. The following example scenarios are based on true stories. As you read them, try to determine if a microaggression occurred and what, if anything, should have been done differently or could be done to address the situation.

Possible Profiling

A new client, who is gender nonbinary and identifies as Filipino American, makes an appointment for a consultation for social anxiety. At the first appointment, the intake administrator asks the person for a picture ID. The client complies, and the administrator makes a copy of the ID card, noting that the participant's stated name does not match what appears on the card. After the first session, the client emails a complaint to the therapist stating that they feel like they were singled out and possibly racially profiled by the request. The administrator says that obtaining a picture ID is standard procedure for new clients.

Academic Conflict

A Black female professor planned and organized an anti-racism workshop and invited two White male professors from other institutions to help as co-trainers. At several points, she had to veto exercises advanced by her two colleagues for being culturally problematic. Several months into the planning process, one of the White males demands to take charge of the workshop, arguing that his name was listed first on the event advertisements. Not wanting further conflict with him, and feeling somewhat disempowered as a Black woman working with two White men, she acquiesced and allowed him to take over the planning and implementation of the workshop. The White professor subsequently made several unkind remarks to the Black professor during the training event, and later accused the Black female professor of undermining him.

Practicum Student Dress Code Conflict

A queer, African American practicum student had a meeting with the site supervisor and clinical director, also a Black woman. As she had done with many of the clinic practicum students, the supervisor informed the student that her style of dress fell outside of the clinic guidelines and dress code. When the student asked for more details, the supervisor pointed out scruffy shoes, a hole in her stockings, unshaved legs and armpits, and unkempt hairstyle—a very large, thick, uneven Afro with faded orange tips. The student became upset and started to cry. She said she was trying to reclaim her feminism and Black identity and did not think she would have to deal with microaggressions such as this from another Black woman. She refused to attend further supervision meetings and soon thereafter switched to a different clinic placement.

CLASSROOM CONFUSION

A White professor is teaching a small graduate CBT course to a diverse group of counseling graduate students. In an effort to learn everyone's names, the professor asks each student to wear name tags. A few weeks into the course, he stops asking for the students to use the name tags. Two female Black students who always sit next to each other end up switching seats that day, causing the professor to accidentally mix up their names. He immediately realizes his mistake and apologizes. A Hispanic student approaches the professor after class and tells him that he is not comfortable in class due to microaggressions in the classroom, such as the professor not being able to tell people of color apart.

7

Preventing Microaggressions in Therapy (and Life in General)

BRINGING THE HIDDEN TO LIGHT

We have been discussing microaggressions for several chapters, and yet it is likely that some readers may struggle to grasp some concepts simply because they have not experienced or seen microaggressions occur. This makes it difficult to understand why microaggressions are so distressing to victims and how to help those who are suffering.

Microaggressions seem invisible to many White people because, as previously discussed, they are socialized not to see them (Phillips & Lowery, 2018); they usually do not directly experience microaggressions, and as dominant group members, they do not need to be aware of them for their own personal safety and well-being. Research shows that White Americans have more difficulty identifying microaggressions, and they generally do not to notice microaggressions committed against their peers of color (Alabi, 2015). However, those who are motivated to understand microaggressions can learn to identify them.

Some ways therapists can make microaggressions more visible in their own lives include the following (Williams, 2020a):

1. Educate yourself on the serious problem of subtle prejudice and develop an appreciation for how people may have very different life experiences due to racialization.
2. Cultivate close professional and personal connections across race to help broaden your cultural perspective. Learn about other people's racialized experiences and share information about yours.
3. Ask others you know to point out when microaggressions occur in real time to increase awareness and better understand their ubiquity.
4. Examine the racial and ethnic diversity of those in positions of power, such as supervisors, board members, and organizational governance. Advocate for more inclusion, and examine any internal and external resistance you encounter.

FEARLESS SELF-EXAMINATION

Are you a racist? You probably do not have a Klansman robe hanging in your closet, but as previously discussed, just about everyone has some degree of bias. Even if you think you would never hurt someone because of their race, deeply embedded racist beliefs can have an effect on the way you treat people, leading to microaggressions. Bringing hidden racism to light is essential before you can make a change; as such, it is important that all clinicians take stock of their biases through a fearless moral inventory. This section presents some important steps to help determine if your attitudes about people of color are problematic.

Do you think some races are inferior to others? Do you think that White people are better? The belief that some races are superior while others are inferior is the foundation of racism. If you believe deep down that one racial group has inherent qualities making that group better than others, that is racist thinking. Be honest with yourself about what you believe.

Do you stereotype people based on their race? For example, it would be racist to believe that all members of a certain race lack good moral character or emotional stability. It is equally racist to believe that all members of a certain race are smart or industrious. Applying any one stereotype to all members of a race is racist thinking. Many people who practice this type of racism believe that it is harmless. For example, they might think that assuming a person of a certain race has a higher intelligence than average is a compliment. However, because this assumption is based on a racial stereotype, it is racist. It also implies that members of other groups are less intelligent. Judging people based on stereotypes leads to microaggressions and other racist acts. For example, innocent people are frequently targeted as criminals due to their skin color, even when they have not committed any crimes.

Pay attention to the judgments you make when you meet someone. First impressions always come with a few immediate judgments, but are yours generally racial in tone? Do you feel uncomfortable if you cannot place a person in a specific racial category? Do you assume certain qualities about the person based on skin color and other features associated with race? Those are racist tendencies. Racism is not limited to judging based on skin color. If you make sweeping judgments based on someone's culturally preferred attire, hairstyle, jewelry, or other aspects of their appearance related to their race, those judgments also fall into the racism category. If you are judging them because they have an accent, that could be racist as well. Keep in mind. the judgments you make can be positive or negative, but in either case, they are racist. Whether you assume the person is sophisticated, sexual, antagonistic, or any other quality, you are still making an unfair judgment, probably based on a pathological stereotype.

Do you tend to dismiss concerns about racism? When you hear or read that someone else has pointed out something as racist, do you try to understand their point? Or do you get defensive and tend to think it is not really racist? Racism is a major problem in just about every country in the world. If you do not notice it, this is not because racism is not present; rather, it is because at some level you are working hard not to see it. Racism can be difficult to spot when you have been socialized to ignore it. But when someone dismisses concerns about racism out of hand without trying to understand the problem, it probably means the person has strong racist tendencies.

Think about whether you usually notice racial injustice. In a perfect society, people of all races would have equal opportunities and enjoy equal wealth, but that is not the case. For example, in the United States, White families have seven times the wealth of Black families, and this ratio has remained unchanged since the 1960s. This inequity is due to systemic racism, meaning that dominant groups have put policies in place to allow them to take more for themselves and leave others with less (Salter, Adams, & Perez, 2018; Thompson, 2018). Failing to acknowledge racial injustice perpetuates racism by allowing it to continue unchecked. For example, if you believe that all races have equal access to education and that races underrepresented in universities are just not trying hard enough to succeed, you have made a racist judgment without examining the root of the problem. The reason certain groups are better able to afford college and graduate with a degree is that they have historically had more privilege than others, including more wealth (Williams, 2019a). Likewise, if you believe that the criminal justice system is fair and that so many more people of color are incarcerated because they tend to have more criminal tendencies, you are viewing the world through a racist lens. This bias is important because, for example, it will impact how you react to people who have criminal records and almost guarantee that you will commit microaggressions against such individuals.

CHALLENGING PERSONAL STEREOTYPES

Before working with people of color, clinicians must be willing to examine and correct any stereotypical beliefs. For example, consider a Black college student visiting a counseling center during the second semester of her freshman year because she is concerned about getting lackluster grades, which could put her scholarship in jeopardy. As noted in Chapter 1, negative stereotypes about Black people include notions such as being lazy, poor, and unintelligent. This might also include seemingly positive stereotypes, such as being athletic and musical. If therapists believe these stereotypes, then this will become evident in the course of conversations and therapeutic interventions through the commission of microaggressions. For example, if a student is struggling in school, the therapist may suggest a tutor when in fact a quiet study area may actually be what is needed. In this case, the therapist would have been better off taking more time to understand the problem rather than jumping to a solution informed by negative stereotypes. The suggestion that the student needs a tutor is a reflection of the therapist working from an assumption of decreased aptitude. A more open conversation with the student about the obstacles to getting good grades could uncover that the student lives with extended family (which is more common in communities of color) and as a result the home too noisy or distracting. So a quiet place to work in a library or other location turns out to be the appropriate solution. Furthermore, due to stereotypes about athleticism, the therapist may assume that the student has a sports scholarship and express concern over the difficulty of the courses being taken, only to subsequently discover that the client is a pre-med student. Expressing directly or indirectly the belief that the client is a student athlete would be a microaggression because it is an assumption that places her in a stereotypical role. Thus, it is critical that therapists learn to actively challenge their biases so that their interventions can be informed by facts and not stereotypes that give rise to microaggressions.

Note that I mentioned the student was living at home with extended family. It would be tempting to assume this is because the client's family is low-income and so she cannot afford a dorm room and/or other family members would be financially strapped if they did not all crowd together in one place. Although this is certainly a possibility due to increased poverty among many racialized groups, this is a situation in which it would be important to understand different cultural values before making assumptions that could then become even more microaggressions. The therapist could simply ask the student why she lives at home and not in a dormitory. This might seem like a better option than making assumptions about the student's financial situation. However, embedded in that question is a racial microaggression. Can you identify it? There is a cultural assumption being made that the dormitory is a better option for students if they can afford it. This is rooted in a Eurocentric value system that normalizes more distant and fragmented family structures. Most people of color have collectivist cultures to varying degrees; as such, living at home, looking after siblings, and helping grandparents are normal and culturally adaptive ways of being that may or may not have anything to do with finances.

RECOGNIZING, ACCEPTING, AND REDUCING INTERRACIAL ANXIETIES

A key emotional process is intergroup anxiety, a regrettably normative, cross-situational anxiety response that in-group members have toward out-group members (and vice versa) when anticipating or engaging in intergroup interactions. For many individuals, during intergroup interactions, certain perceptual processes take over that focus attention on racial features and negative stereotypes, and as a result, intergroup anxieties are automatically elicited. Because our social context includes strong norms that it is unacceptable to display—and even privately experience—such racist tendencies, these processes result in what is called *experiential avoidance* (Kanter et al., 2019). Experiential avoidance has been defined as attempts to avoid thoughts, feelings, memories, sensations, and other internal experiences—even when doing so may cause harm in the long-run.

The predictable outcomes of interracial anxieties in an interracial interaction have been discussed previously. Dominant group members often react to racial conversations with shame, guilt, avoidance, defensiveness, and/or hostility.

Therapists may be told not to microaggress but are not given workable options for overriding automatic perceptual processes and stereotype activations that lead to microaggressions. In this context, it is not surprising that so many cross-racial interactions fail. As a result, the likelihood of microaggressions increases.

Most psychologists believe that they are adept at discussing cultural differences (Maxie, Arnold, & Stephenson, 2006), although White fragility and White privilege are major problems for many clinicians. Therapist trainees are likely to have difficulties with willingness to confront Whiteness and the fragility and privilege that typically come with it. These difficulties are pronounced for psychologists, who demonstrate less awareness and less willingness to address these issues compared to other mental health professionals, such as social workers and counselors. In general, White therapist trainees' reactions to efforts to increase their awareness of privilege are not much different than the general public, and may including anger and defensiveness, focusing on how they are exceptions to the rule, and other forms of denial. It is important for all clinicians to recognize they are not immune from the cultural forces that produce these difficulties for most White people (Kanter et al., 2019). The first step is awareness and recognition of the anxieties that generate counterproductive defensive behaviors.

MOVING OUT OF YOUR COMFORT ZONE AND EXERCISES

As cognitive–behavioral therapists, we know well that exposure will reduce anxieties and correct cognitive distortions. But when it comes to interracial anxieties, it seems we forget what we already know. Applying a cognitive–behavioral therapy model to reduce our own interracial anxieties surrounding racial and ethnic differences provides effective remedies for this common struggle. When we restrict our movements to worlds in which we are comfortable, privilege is difficult to see and cognitive distortions are never challenged. Growth requires that we immerse ourselves in different environments as a way of becoming aware of the privilege we enjoy and the dysfunctional scripts we have learned. For example, world travel is an indispensable strategy for cultivating a broader, multicultural perspective by getting out of those locations and contexts in which one may feel at home. World travel forces people to put privileged identities at risk by traveling to places where we often feel ill at ease or off-center and resist the temptation to retreat back to those places where we feel comfortable. In the process of traveling, our identities become clearer, scripts no longer work, and the luxury of retreating to a safe space is temporarily removed. Travel makes privilege visible, and we are provided a glimpse of how we are seen through the eyes of those whom we may have been taught to perceive as "others" or "less-than" (Bailey, 1998). Nonetheless, world travel by itself is not sufficient to fully understand differences when one is in a position of privilege due to finances or nationality.

An additional way to cultivate a multicultural perspective is through the use of thoughtfully planned exercises aimed at confronting differences to ultimately reduce anxiety, increase confidence, and reduce the propensity to microaggress. What follows are exercises I assign to my graduate students in clinical psychology as part of their culture and diversity training (Williams & Kanter, 2019). Each week, they do one experiential exercise, write about it, and then share their experience in class. They regularly tell me how helpful and impactful these exercises were for them. Like any good exposure, the exercises may seem daunting at first, but with practice they become easier. The exercises are as follows:

- Have a discussion with a colleague of a different race about race-related experiences. Share your experiences, and ask about theirs. Before doing the exercise, predict what you think will happen and then, after, reflect on what actually occurred. Do you feel closer or more distant from your partner after completing the conversation?
- Assess your own ethnic and racial identity and your stage of development, based on contemporary models of ethnic and racial identity development (Graham-LoPresti, Williams, & Rosen, 2019). Journal about any feelings of shame, embarrassment, stigma, and feelings of appreciation and pride. Share your journal with a supportive person in your life.
- Identify a stereotype or misconception you held about another ethnic group. Search the psychological literature to learn accurate information about the group. Reflect on the interpersonal implications of any misperceptions you held.
- Visit the Project Implicit website and take the IAT [Implicit Association Test] with a different ethnic or racial group. Explain your choice of groups and describe the findings. Reflect on your experience taking the test and the meaning of the result. The IAT is believed to access implicit attitudes about different groups. However, keep in mind that you are scored based on reaction times, which can be influenced by practice with the test, distractions, and motivation.
- Attend a service at a house of worship where everyone "looks different from you." Go by yourself, and experience what it's like to be a cultural outsider. Reflect on your anxieties and the experiences of others who are routinely marginalized due to differences in race, culture, or nationality.
- Attend a foreign language lecture, religious service, or event. Reflect on the experience of new immigrants to our country who don't speak English.
- Think about types of people you usually avoid based on appearance and stereotypes. Find 3 pictures on the internet that typify these types of individuals. Through a process of introspection, reflect on why you avoid them. In your real life, find someone that exemplifies each of the pictures and strike up a short conversation. This can be anywhere, at a grocery store, mall, or bus stop. Predict how you think it will go in advance, and then journal about what actually happened. Which of your predictions were accurate and which were inaccurate?

- Create a diagram of your friendship support network, which should feature the people that you would most readily call on if you needed help. On your map, indicate: 1) intimacy of relationship; 2) your friends' race; 3) ethnicity; 4) gender; 5) socioeconomic status; 6) sexual orientation; and 7) religion. Use artistic license to create your map (using words, symbols, and/or any organizing framework) that best works for you. Write about your experience creating the map, and your reflections on your friendship map regarding the dimensions of diversity represented and how this has informed your understanding of yourself and cultural differences.

CONNECTING WITH OTHERS WHO ARE DIFFERENT

The last exercise in the aforementioned list focused on peoples' friendship groups. Multicultural friendships are mutually supportive, congenial, and intimate relationships between two persons of different ethnic or racial backgrounds. You may wonder how the diversity of your friendship circle can impact your clinical practice. Research shows that multicultural friendships increase therapists' multicultural competence by providing alternative perspectives of race, racism, power, and privilege. Learning to acknowledge, address, and navigate power, privilege, and racism in cross-racial friendships may be similar to doing the same within a therapeutic relationship. These nonprofessional relationships will inform a therapist's personal and professional development, which means that nonprofessional relationships, like friendship, can be an important part of one's identity development. Such relationships may even be instrumental in the development of good cross-cultural skills, increasing self-confidence, personal responsibility, and successful practice (Okech & Champe, 2008).

However, 75% of White people have no friends of a different race (Cox, Navarro-Rivera, & Jones, 2016; Ingraham, 2014). Black people have 10 times as many Black friends as White friends. But White Americans have an astounding 91 times as many White friends as Black friends. The implication of these findings is that when we talk about race in our personal lives, we are primarily discussing it with people from our own ethnic group. Although troubling, this should not be surprising, given that most people lead very segregated lives. This starts in infancy when parents are choosing preschools for their children, and it progresses to choice of elementary schools, neighborhoods, churches, and social organizations. As a result, it may take a deliberate effort to diversity one's friendship network.

BEING AN ALLY

Allies are people who recognize the unearned privilege they receive from society's patterns of injustice and take responsibility for changing these patterns. For example, allies include White people who work to end racism, men who challenge sexism, heterosexual people who fight against heterosexism/homophobia, and non-indigenous people who actively engage in decolonizing processes. Part of becoming an ally is recognizing one's own experience of oppression. For example, a White woman can learn from her experience of sexism and apply it in becoming an ally to people of color, or someone from a low income community can learn from that experience how to respect others who may lack access due to living with a disability.

To be an ally, it is not enough to simply claim allyship or refrain from discrimination against others. Allyship is an active, ongoing, challenging process. Allies have a desire to proactively support social justice, to promote the rights of disempowered groups, and to eliminate social inequalities that may benefit allies. Furthermore, allies offer support by establishing meaningful relationships with people and communities where they wish to ally themselves, and they find ways to ensure accountability to those communities. Allyship is about supporting, not leading, and using the ally's power and privilege to change inequitable systems in communities where one is invested and accountable (Smith, Puckett, & Simon, 2015).

Unlike those who may unthinkingly enact racial schemas, the ally's task is to find ways to develop alternative approaches capable of disrupting the ubiquitous pro-White social bias. As noted by Bailey (1998), allies actively examine their "seat at the front of the bus" and find ways to be disloyal to systems that assign these seats. Some examples include choosing to pay attention to body language and patterns of avoidance and cultivating an awareness of how stereotypes shape (mis)perceptions of people of color. For example, telling, and permitting others to tell, racist jokes reinforces images about people of color that are harmful. The ally knows that it is appropriate to call attention to this behavior and stop it. Similarly, the woman who clutches her purse around dark-skinned men and steers her children away from Black friends and the person who acts uncomfortable or nervous in the presence of people of color send out a signal that members of these groups are to be feared. Allies point out and challenge these behaviors. White students who interrupt, ostracize, or dismiss the contributions of students of color in the classroom reinforce their invisibility by sending the message that these students' contributions are unimportant. Allies will interrupt this process and refocus attention on the contribution of the student of color. As allies rewrite common scripts in ways that do not reinforce subordinating behaviors, we can begin to visualize true equality.

One of the most important things to remember about allyship is that it is a continuous process and not a designation that one can earn and hold forever. It is not a diploma one can frame and hang on the wall—even if you have a CE certificate or "safe space" placard from a workshop you completed. Allies must continually engage in self-reflection and personal growth. They must keep working at being an ally toward people of color through learning, acting, and sustaining equitable relationships with people of color. One cannot be an ally without constantly casting a critical eye on oneself, considering how lifestyle and choices (directly or indirectly) are impacting others. Like cultural competence, allyship is a journey that one embarks upon, with the goal of "being an ally" never truly attainable because one can be seen as an ally in the eyes of one person of color but not another (Smith et al., 2015). Although would-be allies are well-intentioned, there will be times when they act in accordance with their goals of allyship and other times when they fail to act. Some have suggested doing away with the term ally entirely and replacing it with the term "active bystander" to acknowledge the choice that one has to be or not be an ally at any given moment (McKinnon, 2017).

For these reasons, it is not appropriate for any person to proclaim themselves an "ally" to another group. Allyship is something that is designated by those within the community with which one is aspiring to ally oneself. This is because it is only possible for people in a community to truly evaluate and ascertain the degree to which they think a person outside of that community is being their ally (Smith et al., 2015).

EXAMPLE OF MANAGING MICROAGGRESSIONS IN A COUPLES SESSION

Therapists can support clients experiencing microaggressions, act as allies, and help clients problem-solve around experiences of microaggressions. In this example, a husband and wife are attending therapy to resolve frequent conflicts surrounding finances. They are an interethnic couple, in which the wife is White and the husband is Hispanic American. They have been seeing the therapist for 2 months, with a focus on self-care for the wife and work challenges for the husband. The husband recently left a job as an administrative assistant for a new job as a research analyst at the local state university. Although he enjoyed his prior job and had good friends there, he and his wife agreed it did not provide them enough income and he was overqualified for that type of work.

CLIENT 1 (WIFE): Nice to see you.

THERAPIST: It's nice seeing you too. (*Turning to husband*) And what about you? How have you been?

CLIENT 2 (HUSBAND): Um, well, you know, it's been like four days since I started my new job.

THERAPIST: Yes! Congratulations.

CLIENT 2 (HUSBAND): Yes, thank you. (*Looks down*)

THERAPIST: Is it going well?

CLIENT 2 (HUSBAND): Um, yeah, I don't know. I liked my old job, but I'm getting better pay. It's closer and better hours, but I find it really hard to relate to the people working there. It's just—I don't know—seems like such a drastic change and everyone is just . . . it's hard to fit in with them.

THERAPIST: Hm, I'm sorry to hear that.

CLIENT 1 (WIFE): Don't worry you will get used to it, for sure, with time.

THERAPIST: And I'd like to hear a little bit more. What is it that makes you feel like you don't fit in or that it is difficult to fit in.

CLIENT 2 (HUSBAND): Well, you know it's like the guys are mostly a little bit older and really mostly predominantly men, not a lot of people from New York, and I don't have much relatability to the other guys, that are again mostly White. And, um, and I try talk to them, and I can't find anything in common, and you know they just said some things . . . One of them said something that rubbed me the wrong way.

THERAPIST: Okay, what was said that made you uncomfortable?

CLIENT 2 (HUSBAND): Yeah, well like during lunch I was sitting down with a couple of the other guys, and one of them started talking with me. He asked me where I am from, and I told him New York. I am from New York, and then he was like, "No, that's not what I meant. Where are you from, from." I was born and raised in New York, and then he was like, "No, you know, you look a little bit ethnic." And he tried guessing where I was from. He said a whole lot of different countries, and I just told him, "Hey, I am mixed race. I'm Latino and a lot of my family comes from Mexico." And then, he was just starting to say weird things like, "Oh, you don't really speak like a Mexican. You don't act like a Mexican, and you know this isn't a job that most people that are Latino get into."

CLIENT 1 (WIFE): I think you are just being a little too sensitive . . . and maybe a little overdramatic about this.

THERAPIST: Well, I think his feelings are important, and we should let him speak. Maybe we can just sit here and take a minute and work through this.

CLIENT 1 (WIFE): You're the therapist.

THERAPIST: Thank you. (*Turns to husband*) Okay, so it sounds like you had this encounter with these co-workers that made you feel uncomfortable because they assume that you are not qualified for the job based upon your ethnicity.

CLIENT 2 (HUSBAND): Yeah, I definitely got that vibe a little bit just because, you know, I applied and got more of a management type of job, so I am a little bit higher. But everyone else, that is my co-workers you know, they just assume that I am a diversity hire or initiative. I spent a lot of years in undergrad and even going to grad school for a bit. I love research, it is what I do, and you know, I was really happy to get the job, but now I don't know. I guess hearing that today brought me down a little made me feel like—am I not close with my culture? Do people see that, or is it like have I been white-washed over the years or something? It just makes me question a lot of things and makes me feel uncomfortable.

THERAPIST: Right, wow, sounds like you might be struggling with how you interpret your own identity based upon these kind of comments you have gotten from your co-workers. Sounds like they were pretty distressing comments as well, would you agree with that?

CLIENT 2 (HUSBAND): I mean I would say so, but I don't want to make it seem like it was super sensitive or anything. Like I understand guys just say things sometimes and just try to talk and get to know each other, but

I don't know. I didn't really feel comfortable there, and again I didn't really know this guy, so it just seemed like a weird situation for me.

THERAPIST: You know, I don't think it's an issue of sensitivity at all. Some of what you experienced is what we would call a microaggression. They really can cause serious distress and anxiety and tension in people of color when they experience microaggressions over and over. And so the fact that you dealt with several comments at once from co-workers in an environment you are going to be at every day—that has the potential to be very toxic for you. So it is important that you talk about these experiences, and I am really glad you brought it up today, because it is important. (*Turning to wife*) As his partner you know it is important for you to be willing to hear and understand his experience and try to be supportive. Have you ever experienced a racial microaggression?

CLIENT 1 (WIFE): I have not.

THERAPIST: Okay, and you could have experienced a gender microaggression, because you are a woman, and so many women do experience those kind of microaggressions. And there could be a number of other minority identities that you have that may not be physically visible. But because you haven't, it is really important to really try and listen and hear him, and be patient with him as he is explaining that this is happening to him. So, if he were to tell you that this is happening, and I weren't here, how would you respond?

CLIENT 1 (WIFE): Well, I thought he was being dramatic and sensitive. Because the job is so amazing and we need the money. I am really trying to look at it from this positive perspective, and I wish he would too.

THERAPIST: Sure, and I think that that is another skill right. It's important to have the ability to see the silver lining in situations, but you also don't want to look beyond this experience that he is having—of distress, frustration, anger, disappointment, or awkwardness. (*Turns to husband*) Right there are these are all things you mentioned that you have, so kind of finding ways to be positive and move forward but also work through how you are feeling, because if you try to ignore the fact that that happened what do you think will be the result?

CLIENT 2 (HUSBAND): I don't know, I think I would just let it happen at first, but I can see it escalating to hearing things about Mexico and jokes. . . . Which you know back in university I used to hear, "How did you get in this class?" or just stuff like that. At first it didn't really get to me, and I don't know, I just think and hoped that in a professional setting that it wouldn't have to be the case, but it very well could just be the same.

THERAPIST: It sounds like you have had a series of microaggressions in your life—during high school, college, and also graduate school.

CLIENT 2 (HUSBAND): Yeah, to some extent.

THERAPIST: And now, as a research analyst, I mean, that is a lot to carry with you every day. It can be dangerous, actually we have research that shows people with a minority identity are more prone to depression and anxiety, and so it is really important for you to be honest with yourself when you have these emotions, and we can kind of talk about helpful ways to deal with it. What I am a little worried about is you being in a context in which you are constantly experiencing microaggressions. Was this the first one at work this week?

CLIENT 2 (HUSBAND): I guess, I'd say so, probably.

THERAPIST: So we can probably think together about a good way to manage this, because I know you just got the job, and you are probably a little concerned about the fact you just got this job and you don't want to come in making demands or filing reports.

CLIENT 2 (HUSBAND): Yeah, I don't want to be like that person that, "Oh he's the only ethnic person and he wants to change everything," and I don't want to make it seem like I can't take a joke or something. I love laughing and having a joke, but it isn't the type of thing I want, and I don't want to be the type of person to report it to HR or anything.

THERAPIST: Right, I totally understand. There a number of things we can do, but in light of the fact that you just got the job, let's wait and see. Maybe that was a one-time thing. You can't make a report for every single time someone microaggresses against you, but I think that if this continues to happen this is a form of harassment at work and you could certainly write an email to your supervisor or write a report and send it to HR. Because that kind of behavior should not be tolerated. It is racist, it's harassment, it's distressing, it's so many things and you shouldn't have to experience that. So how, if this situation happens again, how do you think you will respond in that moment. Let's try and be proactive.

CLIENT 2 (HUSBAND): I don't know . . . I guess I can try and be upfront and tell them I don't like talking about this or try changing the subject maybe, so that way they can subtly get the message without trying to talk about this or it doesn't make me feel uncomfortable. But I think if it something outwardly discriminatory I will just have to go to HR and tell my boss, but also talk to the person upfront, and just be like, "I don't like that."

THERAPIST: I think that sounds like a fine plan. I think it will be important for you to find a way to express that it was hurtful or offensive or disrespectful or whatever it is you feel. Maybe not in front of the whole group, but maybe pulling the gentlemen to the side and just being honest upfront. You know, "Hey, that was a bit hurtful and offensive for me, and here is why," and hopefully that will be received by him, and if not the next step would certainly be to report it. That type of behavior, people commit microaggressions all the time and there aren't any penalties and don't recognize anything is wrong with it because they are never held accountable. If you get the opportunity again certainly tell him how you feel and if that doesn't work, things might have to escalate, professionally of course, and hopefully HR will be able to handle it professionally and put a stop to that kind of behavior because it is not fair to you to have to endure that.

CLIENT 2 (HUSBAND): I think I might.

THERAPIST: And, we also have to consider that HR might not do anything about it. They are supposed to, but they often don't. So we need a couple of strategies. If you were to tell this guy in the moment that that was hurtful or offensive, ideally, how would you like him to respond?

CLIENT 2 (HUSBAND): Ideally, he would apologize and understand, or apologize and then not do it again. That is the ideal. At the end of the day I do want to get to know people and not judge them the same way. But yeah, that's probably how I will handle that.

THERAPIST: Okay, I think that is a fair way to move forward. And I realized that just took up a good part of our session. But like I mentioned earlier I think it was really important for us to work through that. Would you both agree?

CLIENT 2 (HUSBAND): Yeah, definitely.

THERAPIST: (*Turning to wife*) He needs to feel comfortable sharing these things with you.

CLIENT 1 (WIFE): Yeah of course, and I'm sorry if I made you feel dismissed or uncomfortable.

CLIENT 2 (HUSBAND): Thank you.

Client 2, the husband, was struggling at his new job due to distress triggered by microaggressive statements that made him upset and also led to him even questioning his ethnic identity. The therapist helped by providing psychoeducation about microaggressions to help the client better conceptualize and discuss these difficulties in a safe space. She also interrupted the wife when she tried to dismiss the difficulties, modeling being an ally and underscoring the importance of validating the husband's racially challenging experiences. They ended with problem-solving, to help the husband be more prepared for future occurrences, and with a clear game plan if the situation got worse. By the end of the session, the wife recognized the importance of the discussion and better appreciated the difficulties that microaggressions at work were causing her husband.

SUPPORTIVE RACIAL STATEMENTS

Many therapists are so worried about being offensive that they completely avoid talking about race, ethnicity, and culture. The problem is interracial anxiety and avoidance which was discussed previously. It is important to engage clients around challenges and difficulties they may experience in connection with their stigmatized identities, but these identities are also an important source of belonging and pride in most people—difficulties notwithstanding. Positive statements about a person's culture can be an important means of helping them feel understood, appreciated, and supported. Unfortunately, many therapists miss opportunities to be supportive of a client's ethnicity out of fear of offending them.

In our own research focused on understanding the propensity of White students to commit microaggressions, in our initial battery of survey questions, we included non-microaggressive and supportive behaviors so that test-takers would not ascertain they should respond in the same manner to all items. But in examining our data more closely, we were surprised to discover that many of the items deemed supportive by our lab, diversity experts, and Black students alike were not regarded similarly by White students (Michaels, Gallagher, Crawford, Kanter, & Williams, 2018). Several items that would have made Black students feel supported were very unlikely for White students to do or say.

These discrepant items included asking an African American law student "What's it like for Black students in the law school?" at a casual get-together. They also included standing up for a Black friend at a party who objected to a karaoke song that contained the N-word, by either refusing to sing the song or beatboxing instead of singing. Another example that White students were very unlikely to endorse included a scenario in which a lost Black man was asking for directions to a nearby store, and the White student opts to walk with the lost Black man to the store because the student is going that way anyway. These findings suggest that White individuals' interracial anxieties and avoidance may result in hesitation to ask people of color about their racialized experiences, fail to provide assistance to people of color when the opportunity arises, and fail to assist when people of color are wanting allyship in the face of microaggressions. Analogous situations can also emerge within the therapeutic relationship; examples include failing to ask clients about racialized experiences, which has been discussed previously, changing the subject when cultural topics arise, or not providing support when clients share experiences of microaggressions.

Given that acts of omission and avoidance are counterproductive, what positive and affirming things can therapists say and do to show clients that they appreciate and respect their race, ethnicity, and culture? Table 7.1 presents six sample scenarios, based on our research surrounding the development of the Cultural Cognitions and Actions Scale and the input of mental health providers, that include both examples of microaggressions and racially supportive statements and behaviors.

Although the statements listed in Table 7.1 can be helpful, they should not necessarily be followed verbatim. Every client is different, and what may feel supportive for one person may not feel supportive to another, so some discretion is advised based on the particulars of your client and the therapeutic relationship.

After discussing racial issues with a client, a therapist can further process these themes by exploring racial differences in the therapeutic dyad. For example, the therapist can ask, "How was that to talk about painful things White people have said to you with another White person?" In this sort of scenario, we are working toward a culturally corrective experience; because the therapist modeled caring surrounding racial issues, the client can experience that not all White people are uncaring about racial issues and thereby prevent overgeneralizing racist attributes to all White people or all people in a single group (Miller et al., 2015).

Table 7.1 EXAMPLES OF MICROAGGRESSIONS AND RACIALLY SUPPORTIVE STATEMENTS IN THERAPY

Microaggressions	Scenario	Supportive Examples
"I have other Black clients."	**Black Law Student** A friend of yours has referred a client to you, saying they think you will like the person. You meet with this client for a consultation. He turns out to be a tall, fit-looking Black man who is a law student on a scholarship. He seems very smart and is interested in international law and global affairs. You like his personality.	"Many Black students have told me they don't get the support they need from their professional programs. How has that been for you?"
"Did you get into school through a minority scholarship?"		"The university was lucky to get a talented student like you."
"Have you seen (. . . a recent Black movie or TV show you have watched)?"		"Do you have to deal with much racism on campus?"
"Race doesn't matter. There is only one race— the human race."	**Group Therapy** You are providing group therapy for a racially diverse group of young adults. A woman of color in the group says that White people have an unfair advantage in most every area of American life due to "White privilege." A vigorous discussion about this begins.	"Too many people have a hard time talking about race, and that's a problem."
"Discrimination against White people has gotten as bad as discrimination against Blacks."		"Not everyone has the same opportunities in life, and race is one reason for that."
"Minorities can discriminate against other minorities."		"It's not fair, but I've gotten lots of advantages from being White."
"How long has your family been in the United States?"	**African-Style Client** You have a new client who is a 20-something-year-old African American female, wearing a traditional colorful African-style dress and has long hair with scores of tiny braids and golden beads woven into them. Her hair is rolled into a large twisted wrap.	"I would love to hear more about you, your friends, and your family."
"You speak English really well."		"I really like the colors you're wearing."
"Is your hair real?"		"Your hair looks fantastic. I love the gold beads."

(*continued*)

Table 7.1 CONTINUED

Microaggressions	Scenario	Supportive Examples
"Everyone suffers. Not just people of color."	Couples Counseling You are providing therapy for an interracial couple. They disagree on a number of racially charged political issues, including police brutality, affirmative action, unemployment, and education.	"I too am upset about the unfair treatment received by people of color."
"Everyone can succeed in this society, if they work hard enough."		"Racism is a major issue in our country."
"We shouldn't talk about race. It makes people uncomfortable."		"White nationalism needs to be addressed for our country to move forward."
"We need to support law enforcement because they put their lives on the line for all of us."	Police Violence in the Community Recently, an unarmed Black youth was shot by police after neighbors complained about a loud party. Drugs were found at the party. Your client of color is upset about the event and asks for your opinion.	"No law enforcement officer should ever shoot an unarmed person."
"He had to be doing something wrong to get shot by police."		"I'm sure race was a big factor in that shooting."
"Bad things happen when drugs are involved."		"I hope the police department investigates this and takes it very seriously.'"
"What are you, exactly?"	Racially Ambiguous Client You have a new client of color with long dark wavy hair, light brown skin, and green eyes. You cannot tell what racial or ethnic group she belongs to, but she speaks English without an accent. She wants help for problems she has had in dating relationships.	"Please let me know if you ever feel misunderstood or disrespected by me or anyone at our clinic."
"Where are your parents from?"		"I would love to learn more about you and your family."
"Do you date White guys or just other minorities?"		"Have you had any challenges around race or ethnicity in your dating life?"

As illustrated in Chapter 6, often clients have ingested so many negative ideas about themselves and their group that they exhibit psychopathology from an overwhelmingly toxic social environment. In these cases, an intensive "detox" is needed, which may include frequent affirming and positive statements about the client and their ethnic group to provide a counterperspective to the harmful negativity coming from all directions. These affirming comments must be genuine and not based on stereotypes. For example, "I like that Asian clients have strong families" could be viewed as latching onto a stereotype, thereby creating a microaggression. Think about specific attributes you see in your client that you genuinely admire. For example, a therapist could say,

> I love how your family makes a point to spend Easter together every year. I think so many people would be more resilient if they had those close-knit relationships and family traditions as an anchor for when times are tough.

Of course, such a statement would miss the mark if the client actually hates the family get-togethers, but if this is something mutually acknowledged as beneficial to the client, it could serve as a supportive and culturally detoxifying statement.

How can you be an effective source of cultural support and healing for your clients? Think about each of your clients of color, one by one. What have they shared with you about their cultures? What are cultural sources of strength for them? What facets of their culture do you admire? Write down 2-3 things for each client and look for opportunities to share these during sessions.

8

Issues and Controversies

ARE MICROAGGRESSIONS REALLY JUST PEOPLE BEING TOO SENSITIVE? THE ROLE OF NEGATIVE EMOTIONALITY

Not everyone agrees that microaggressions are a problem, and in fact, some view the increased social dialogue surrounding the harms of microaggressions as a sign of a threatening shift in cultural values. Attempts to address the problem have been branded by some sociologists as the product of a new "culture of victimhood," suggesting that victims of microaggressions are pathologically overly sensitive (Campbell & Manning, 2014). Indeed, Jonathan Haidt (2017), a business professor at New York University, referred to those complaining of microaggressions as "the most fragile and anxious students," who are now being socially trained to "react with pain and anger to ever-smaller specks that they learn to see in each other's eyes" (p. 177). Psychologist Scott Lilienfeld (2017) has questioned the connection between psychological harm and racial microaggressions, noting that the link may be better explained by the personality trait referred to as "neuroticism" or trait negative emotionality. People who are neurotic tend to be more anxious, overly sensitive, and are more likely to perceive and complain of victimization. He also notes that this trait is heritable, which seems to imply some genetic tendency for people of color to overreact to these experiences.

Unsurprisingly, negative emotionality is correlated to reports of both racial mistreatment and psychopathology, as negative emotionality is correlated to just about all mental health symptoms. Furthermore, to the extent that negative emotionality plays a role, it could very well be that the directionality is the opposite: Years of experiencing unchecked microaggressions could result in trait-like negative emotionality. There are a few other problems with Lilienfeld's (2017) line of reasoning surrounding negative emotionality. First, Lilienfeld employs a cultural deficit model to explain the relationship, which means he is searching for pathology in the target group without a genuine consideration of alternative explanations. For example, he overlooks the possibility that a unique set of talents, abilities, aptitudes, and training in some people may make them better detectors of microaggressions. In fact, a study conducted by Reid and Foels (2010) with a multiethnic sample demonstrated that the ability to identify subtle racism is a sign of greater attributional complexity—that is, a more sophisticated reasoning process about cause, effect, people, and situations. Attributional complexity is associated with intelligence, so it could be that higher intelligence is a predictor of greater recognition of microaggressions.

The second issue is that upon examining the literature, one finds that very little research has been conducted on ethnic differences in personality traits, and what little exists does not support Lilienfeld's (2017) notions about negative emotionality. For example, Consedine, Magai, Cohen, and Gillspie (2002) found that White study participants had significantly greater negative emotionality compared to Black participants. Furthermore, our own research found the same relationship between negative affectivity using the Positive and Negative Affectivity Scale (Watson, Clark, & Tellegen, 1988), with Black students showing significantly less trait negative affectivity compared to White students (Williams, Kanter, & Ching, 2018).

We then examined the relationships between frequency of experiencing microaggressions using the Racial Microaggressions Scale and measures of anxiety, stress, and trauma (the Beck Anxiety Inventory, the General Ethnic Discrimination Scale, and the Trauma Symptoms of Discrimination Scale). We found that trait negative affectivity in African Americans was related to some perceptions of the experience of discrimination but not all. Furthermore, a strong and significant relationship between racial mistreatment and symptoms of psychopathology was evident, even after controlling for negative affectivity. In other words, African Americans experience significant anxiety, stress, and trauma symptoms in connection with microaggressions that cannot be explained by negative affectivity or emotionality. Prospective studies have also provided similar findings. For example, a research study by Ong, Burrow, Fuller-Rowell, Ja, and Sue (2013) followed Asian American participants over a 2-week period and found that experiencing microaggressions predicted somatic symptoms and state negative affect, even after controlling for trait neuroticism.

ARE MICROAGGRESSIONS TRULY AGGRESSIVE?

In social psychology, aggression is most commonly defined as a behavior intended to harm another person who does not wish to be harmed, and violence is aggression that has extreme physical harm as its goal (Allen & Anderson, 2017; Bushman & Huesmann, 2010). Because microaggressions are believed to be often unintentional (or even well-intentioned) and harms are often small, under this definition they are not automatically considered a form of violence or aggression. However, there are many disciplines that have a broader conceptualization of these terms and consider all forms of racism to be violence and aggression.

In the journal *Aggression and Violent Behavior*, Lee (2015) provides a definition of violence, based on the one provided by the World Health Organization:

> The intentional reduction of life or thriving of life in human beings by human beings through physical, structural, or other means of force, that either

results in or has a high likelihood of resulting in depravation, maldevelopment, psychological harm, injury, death, or extinction of the species. (p. 202)

Racism can fit this definition because racism encompasses multifaceted behaviors by the dominant group forced upon subordinate racial groups, leading to many well-documented harms, as outlined in Chapter 3. Microaggressions also fit this definition because they are a form of racism that leads to negative mental and physical health outcomes. So, although this may not fit the most common social psychology definitions, the term would apply within many other academic disciplines, including peace and conflict studies, education, feminism, global health, racial/ethnic studies, and sociology. It is not that one discipline has a better definition or is more correct; rather, one discipline has a very specific definition and others are using such terms more broadly.

Furthermore, even within social psychology there is not complete agreement on this point. Because intentionality is a private event, Buss (1961) had argued that "intent is both awkward and unnecessary in the analysis on aggressive behavior; rather, the crucial issue is the nature of the reinforcing consequences that affect the occurrence and strength of aggressive responses" (p. 2). In all cases, microaggressions reinforce social hierarchies (consequences) and are racially offensive, conveniently explained away as valid, and distressing to victims (strength of response). Therefore, microaggressions need not be defined in terms of conscious intentionality to be aggressive.

Lilienfeld (2017) calls for more research to determine if the commission of microaggressions is correlated to aggressive tendencies in offenders. He suggests that the way to determine if microaggressions are correlated to conventional psychological conceptualizations of aggression is to administer measures of aggression along with measures of microaggression likelihood to potential offenders. If we accept that racism is a form of violence, then such a study is not necessary in order to classify racial microaggressions as a form of aggression. Given that most people seem to recognize that microaggressive behaviors are unacceptable, it would make sense that those who are more temperamentally aggressive would be less likely to suppress urges to microaggress. Mekawi and Todd (2018) examined this issue in their study of the acceptability of microaggressions (microinsults and microinvalidations, specifically) using the three-item subscales of the short version of the Buss–Perry Aggression Questionnaire (BPAQ; Buss & Perry, 1992). They did not find strong or consistent correlations between various types of microaggressions and verbal aggression or hostility. There were, however, some methodological weaknesses, such as mixing White students and students of color in the analyses. Furthermore, tendencies to be aggressive in one context (against out-group members) do not correlate to aggression in other contexts (against in-group members; e.g., Brewer, 1999), and measures such as the BPAQ may be inadequate for elucidating this link because they do not differentiate in terms of whether the targets of the aggressive acts are in-group or out-group members.

Furthermore, many common microaggressions already fit accepted definitions of aggression. One form of verbal aggression identified by Kinney (1994) is called "group membership attacks." These consist of messages that associate or place one into a negatively evaluated group in which one is a member—voluntarily or involuntarily. Kinney provides examples that include "He acts like such a male," "This is a very good paper for you being a football player. Who wrote it for you?" and "He's Japanese. He must be studying economics or engineering" (p. 192). These are very similar to microaggressions comprising the Negative Attitudes subscale on the Cultural Cognitions and Actions Scale measure of microaggression likelihood. Interestingly, such items were correlated with feeling annoyed, angry, surprised, and depressed.

We recently conducted a study to determine if microaggressions were correlated to other forms of aggression in a nationwide survey conducted through mTurk (Williams, Muir, Ching, & George, 2019). Measures included our 20-item version of the Cultural Cognitions and Actions Scale (CCAS), the Inventory of Hostility and Suspicious Thinking (HIS), the Overt-Covert Aggression Inventory (OCAI), and the full version of the Buss-Perry Aggression Questionnaire (BPAQ)—a gold-standard measure of aggressive tenencies. Examining the responses of White participants (N = 322), we found that tendencies to commit microaggressions as measured by the CCAS were robustly correlated to all three measures of aggression (OCAI r =.43, IHS r =.37, BPAQ r = .46, all p's < .001), providing evidence that microaggressions are to some degree aggressive in nature, even when aggression is defined more conservatively.

Finally, one must consider the aggression that often results when targets attempt to reject a microaggression, making targets afraid to confront offenders. Targets have learned that should they speak up, they risk suffering some degree of harm, such as invalidation (Sue et al., 2007), anger and defensiveness (DiAngelo, 2011), being called neurotic (Lilienfeld, 2017), or having one's character attacked (Haidt, 2017). This point is made doubly salient in the situation in which a person of color is microaggressed against in the form of an unjustified encounter with law enforcement, such as requests for identification, being searched, or being asked to leave a public place, because the target is powerless to object (Smith, Allen, & Danley, 2007). These responses are all forms of aggression.

SHOULDN'T WE JUST GIVE OFFENDERS THE BENEFIT OF THE DOUBT?

Some critics of microaggressions research have urged victims to give offenders the benefit of the doubt and simply choose not to be offended. Certainly, many people who encounter microaggressions do make a conscious choice to ignore them. However, it is also important to consider the dangers of ignoring microaggressions. Given that microaggressions are indicative of racial hostility, there could be damaging consequences for ignoring these subtle warning signs. A person of color might decide to trust someone who has microaggressed against them, only to find that that person subsequently behaves in a way that is hurtful, untrustworthy, or deceitful (Williams, 2020a).

Targets cannot simply assume everyone means well, as misinterpreting microaggressions can lead to real-life problems. As a Black woman in academia, I have experienced many subtle assaults to my intelligence, worthiness, work ethic, priorities, intentions, and abilities. If I had chosen to give all offenders the "benefit of the doubt," I would have arrived at some very unhelpful conclusions about myself and my work, and I would have quit the academy a long time ago. Unfortunately, many people of color do just that as they are worn down and de-moralized by these incessant small attacks (Williams & Kanter, 2019). This is why potential targets must learn to identify all forms of microaggressions—because they signal danger and taken at face value can lead to harmful consequences.

REDUCING MICROAGGRESSIONS ON CAMPUSES AND IN THE WORKPLACE

Students of color report that the day-to-day experience of campus life is weighted with a variety of different types of microaggressions (Smith et al., 2007; Smith, Mustaffa, Jones, Curry, & Allen, 2016). Some of these experiences are environ-mental, such as being the only student of color in a class, having no instructors or advisors from their ethnic group, campus buildings named after slave owners, or finding no realistic portrayals of people of color in textbooks. Much of the problem, however, is interpersonal, as a result of direct interactions between students of color and others on campus (Kanter et al., 2017). Qualitative studies of the campus life experiences of students of color, including a recent study of our own, show that such students experience interpersonal microaggressions and racist interpersonal interactions on a regular basis, not just from other students but also from faculty and others (Lewis, Chesler, & Forman, 2000; Smith et al., 2016; Solórzano, Ceja, & Yosso, 2000). These microaggressions range from slights that students experience so often they have habituated to them (e.g., being ignored by the cashier in the line at the cafeteria) to insults that shock and upset them for prolonged periods (e.g., a professor stating in a lecture on intelligence that re-search finds that Black people are inferior). As discussed previously, the accumu-lation of these experiences has deleterious effects on health.

Many higher education institutions throughout the nation have been making efforts to improve the racial climate. One typical product of such efforts is the provision of stand-alone or a series of workshops or dialogues for the larger campus community (faculty, staff, and students) that are intended to address the racist interpersonal interactions that students of color experience with regularity. Local diversity trainers may be hired to lead forums or dialogues, or in-house facilitators are used. Some research indicates that these dialogues are fraught with peril because many White people have been socialized to squelch and minimize the painful realities of inequality that are shared in these forums (Sue, Lin, et al., 2009). This process may generate, during the forums, the very microaggressions the forums intend to reduce. Overall, however, meta-analyses of the effects of di-versity trainings suggest that they produce small to moderate improvements on measures of White attitudes and bias, and these effects can be strengthened if the dialogue lasts longer or occurs in a series rather than stand-alone (Kalinoski et al., 2013).

Despite the dangers, it is important to provide these forums because they serve several important functions. In classrooms and pilot research that we have been developing using a contextual–behavioral science model, White students reported that they benefited from hearing about the negative experiences of their non-White peers; this can be an important means of raising awareness, promoting empathy, and exploring what it means to be White in a social racial hierarchy (Thurston-Rattue et al., 2015). The fact that a majority of White Americans (52%) believe that discrimination against their group has become as significant a problem as discrimination against people of color indicates widespread and massive misunderstandings regarding racial realities of our society (Jones, Cox, & Navarro-Rivera, 2014), and most people vastly underestimate racial disparities in income and wealth (Kraus, Rucker, & Richeson, 2017). So raising awareness of the extent of the problem is an important outcome in its own right.

A second important function of these dialogues is that they facilitate cross-group friendships and connections. Consistent with both intergroup contact theory and intergroup process theory (MacInnis & Page-Gould, 2015), research suggests that when cross-racial participants exchange personally vulnerable details of their lives with each other, interracial anxiety decreases and intimacy and friendship increase (Page-Gould, Mendoza-Denton, & Tropp, 2008). Thus, in our dialogues, White participants are encouraged to listen with empathy to the narratives of Black participants and also to reciprocally disclose vulnerable details from their own lives. Multiple participants from our dialogues have developed cross-racial friendships from this experience that have lasted beyond the workshop session (Thurston-Rattue et al., 2015).

One established example of how this work can be done is *intergroup dialogue*, studied extensively at the University of Michigan and subsequently utilized by many universities throughout the country (Gurin, Sorensen, Lopez, & Nagda, 2015). This is a group experience led by a facilitator that is designed to provide a safe and structured forum to explore attitudes about polarizing social issues. These dialogues have been shown to reduce bias and promote critical self-reflection and perspective taking. Most of these studies have been conducted in student samples, but one study conducted by Miller and Donner (2000) also noted positive outcomes among graduate students, faculty, and staff. Thus, intergroup dialogue can be one useful way to reduce racism by encouraging individuals to examine the socially constructed ideologies that guide or misguide their beliefs and improving interpersonal connection (Williams & Kanter, 2019).

THE RACIAL HARMONY WORKSHOP

As mental health professionals, we aim to not only help those who have been injured by microaggressions but also invest in the development of interventions to prevent microaggressions. Our research team developed an intervention specifically designed to reduce the commission of microaggressions: the Racial Harmony Workshop (RHW). It is a diversity workshop designed to be both educational and experiential, using the experiences and diversity of the participants to promote sharing and social connection. The RHW utilized two co-facilitators, one White and one person of color, to facilitate and model cross-racial interactions involving vulnerability and connection for the participants. In the first half of the workshop (Williams, 2019b), the facilitators gave a brief introduction, overview of the workshop, and set expectations. They then led a mindfulness exercise to encourage self-reflection and set an intention toward connection with others. Thereafter, the facilitators walked participants through instructional material and led discussion on topics including the definition of race, pathological stereotypes, racism, and automatic bias. The definition and examples of microaggressions were provided. Two important concepts that were taught were "away moves," feelings or behaviors that push others away, and "towards moves," feelings or behaviors that facilitate social connection.

The second half of the RHW was designed to promote social connectedness through small-group interracial interactions in which participants shared vulnerable details of their lives and responded empathically to each other's disclosures. For example, one exercise asked volunteers to share memories of personal disappointment or betrayal. The facilitators coached the participants while listening to the stories to use emotion coping strategies (e.g., acceptance) to manage their feelings of discomfort and to also engage in perspective taking and validation of the storyteller rather than problem-solving or advice giving. The workshop ended with participants developing a plan for the future, including values-driven behaviors they wanted to reduce, as well as behaviors they wanted to increase.

Participants were given pretest, post-test, and follow-up batteries to assess intergroup feelings and racial attitudes. Results indicated positive benefits for both Black and White participants, including significantly increased mood and positive feelings toward Black people for the White students, as well as increased racial identity for the Black students. White students in both conditions showed a decreased likelihood of committing microaggressions, and those in the RHW condition also showed a decreased likelihood of having microaggressive thoughts.

Components of this approach have also been integrated with other experiential exercises targeting bias in medical students to improve clinician emotional rapport in interracial encounters, with an emphasis on improved interactions with patients in racially challenging moments. Twenty-five medical students and recent graduates were randomized to the intervention or a wait list. Coders assessed video recordings of clinician rapport and responsiveness during simulated interracial patient encounters with standardized Black patients (actors) who presented specific racial challenges to clinicians. Improvements in emotional rapport and responsiveness, attitudes toward minorities, and working alliance with the Black standardized patients were observed by raters and reported by the clinicians who received the intervention (Kanter, Rosen, et al., 2020). Thus, research supports the usefulness of this approach as a potentially important and effective component of interventions to reduce microaggressions and bias and improve outcomes for people of color in domains of public health significance.

FUTURE DIRECTIONS

There is clear evidence demonstrating the mental health harms caused by microaggressions. As healing professionals, it is our duty to not only acknowledge these harms but to also help clients who are suffering as a result. African American psychiatrist Chester Pierce (1970) imagined a day when every Black child would be able to "recognize and defend promptly and adequately against every offensive microaggression. In this way, the toll that is registered after accumulation of such insults should be markedly reduced" (p. 280). To that end, therapeutic interventions should include helping every client learn how to identify, defend against, and stop microaggressions.

Funding this needed work should be a priority for our sponsors and funding agencies because microaggressions are a bona fide public health concern. There are still large gaps in our knowledge that require more study. Although some guidelines exist, more research is needed to operationalize how to best help people who are experiencing distress resulting from microaggressions. This book has described one-on-one interventions for working with clients within a cognitive–behavioral therapy framework. However, there may be other effective approaches as well. Group modalities may be equally or even better suited to help those who are suffering. Carlson, Endsley, Motley, Shawahin, and Williams (2018) developed a group intervention in the Veterans Administration (VA) hospital for veterans of color experiencing race-based stress and trauma. Having a safe space to speak freely and openly about racial stressors and triggers without fear of judgment may be a reparative experience. For the VA groups, the emotional validation that veterans felt in being able to share a racially distressing story and see other veterans nodding in solidarity with their experience and emotional reaction was very empowering and noted as a source of healing by many.

Furthermore, only limited literature exists to guide us on how targets should respond in the moment to microaggressions levied against them (Sue et al., 2019). Research is still needed to determine if and how certain responses can protect against the negative sequelae of experiencing a microaggression. Such responses would ideally educate rather than antagonize offenders, and given our social challenges in openly addressing racism, the best way to accomplish this goal is not always clear.

In addition, as a field, we could benefit from more research to better understand how different ethnic groups are affected by different types of microaggressions, based on their unique history and resulting pathological stereotypes, to better inform our interventions. This would also mean more study surrounding microaggressions based on intersectionalities of multiple stigmatized identities, and work in this area has been started but is by no means complete. It is hoped that this book will be an important step in bringing awareness to these and other related issues, advance treatment for those who are suffering, and stimulate research into healing the wounds caused by microaggressions for our diverse population.

DEMOGRAPHICS QI

We want to be able to best understand the clients we serve, and the following questions help us get a better sense of who you are. We know that many of these categories may not fully capture the complexities of your individual experience. You will have more opportunities to discuss these questions with your therapist.

1. Name: _____

2. Street Address: _____

   _____

3. City: _____ State: _____
   Postal Code: _____

4. Do you currently live in the United States?
   ☐ Yes   ☐ No (*specify country*): _____
   If not, how long have you been living outside of the U.S.? _____
   _____

5. What is your current age? (*please write in*) _____

6. What is your gender identity? (*check all that apply*)
   ☐ Male ☐ Female ☐ Transgender ☐ Nonbinary/gender fluid or queer
   ☐ Not listed (*please specify, if you choose*) _____

7. What is your sexual orientation?
   ☐ Heterosexual ☐ Bisexual ☐ Gay ☐ Lesbian ☐ Queer ☐ Asexual
   ☐ Not listed (*please specify, if you choose*) _____

8. With what religion or spiritual practice (if any) do you identify? _____

is the highest grade in school, year in college, or post-college gree work you have completed?

- [ ] 8th grade or less
- [ ] Some high school
- [ ] High school graduate or GED
- [ ] Some college or 2 year degree
- [ ] College graduate (4 year degree)
- [ ] Graduate degree

10. Are you currently a: [ ] Part-time student   [ ] Full-time student [ ] Not a student

11. Are you currently involved in paid work?

- [ ] Not at all
- [ ] Working 1–20 hours per week
- [ ] Working 21–30 hours per week
- [ ] Working 31–40 hours per week
- [ ] Working over 40 hours per week

Please write-in your occupation: _____

12. Currently, your total annual *household* income (all earners) is:

- [ ] $0 – $15,000
- [ ] $15,001 – $25,000
- [ ] $25,001 – $35,000
- [ ] $35,001 – $50,000
- [ ] $50,001 – $75,000
- [ ] $75,001 – $100,000
- [ ] $100,001 – $200,000
- [ ] More than $200,000

13. Were you financially supported by someone else over the past year?

[ ] Yes   [ ] No

14. What is the total number of people who depend on the household income listed above (including yourself)? _____

15. Currently, how would you describe the financial situation of your family?

- [ ] Routinely unable to purchase sufficient food or other basic necessities
- [ ] Occasionally unable to purchase sufficient food or other basic necessities
- [ ] Have enough money for the necessities
- [ ] Have more than enough money for necessities and some luxuries

16. What languages do you currently speak? (*check all that apply*)

☐ English   ☐ Spanish   ☐ Other(s) (*please specify*) _____

17. How fluent are you currently in English? (*circle one*)

Not at all fluent		*Moderately fluent*		*Completely fluent*
1	2	3	4	5

18. What language is currently used in your home most of the time?

☐ English   ☐ Spanish   ☐ Other (*please specify*) _____

RACIAL AND ETHNIC BACKGROUND

We're interested in getting a complete picture of your racial and ethnic background so that we can best serve you and ensure we are meeting our organizational goals of inclusivity. Because this information can be so complex, we are going to ask you several questions about your race and ethnicity in order to get as complete a picture as possible.

19. Racial categories are based on visible attributes (often skin or eye color and certain facial and bodily features) and self-identification. These groupings have social meanings that affect how people see themselves and are seen and treated by others. Race is not the same as ethnicity or culture. **In your own words, what is/are your racial identification(s)?** _____

_____

20. Although the categories listed below may not represent your full identity or use the language you prefer, for the purpose of this survey, please indicate which group(s) below best describes your **racial identification**? (*check all that apply*)

☐ Asian

☐ Black

☐ Native American/Alaskan, American Indian, Native/ Indigenous

☐ Pacific Islander, Native Hawaiian

☐ Middle Eastern, North African (Non-White)

☐ White

☐ Latinx/Hispanic (Non-White)

☐ Not listed (*please specify*):

_____

21. Multiracial people can identify in various ways, sometimes in relation to specific racial heritage, sometimes as "multiracial," or in other ways. Which of the following best captures how you primarily identify? Please choose one.

☐ Primarily Asian
☐ Primarily Black
☐ Primarily Native American/Alaskan, American Indian, Native/ Indigenous
☐ Primarily Pacific Islander, Native Hawaiian

☐ Primarily Middle Eastern, North African (Non-White)
☐ Primarily White
☐ Primarily Latinx/Hispanic (Non-White)
☐ Multiracial generally—without reference to any particular group
☐ Groups not listed (*please specify*): _____

22. How often do people perceive your race accurately? (*please circle one*)

Hardly ever perceived correctly		*Sometimes perceived correctly*		*Always perceived correctly*
1	2	3	4	5

23. If you indicated that people sometimes or frequently do not perceive you correctly (1, 2, or 3), please indicate the race that people most frequently perceive you to be: _____

_____

24. Ethnicity or ethnic culture refers to patterns of ideas and practices associated with a group of people sharing a common history, geographic background, and/or language, rather than their racial background. It might include things like values, patterns of interacting, food, dress, holidays, or ways of seeing the world, yourself, or other people. There are hundreds of different ethnic culture backgrounds within the people in the United States—such as Cuban American, Jamaican American, Filipino American, African American, European American, etc. You may have a Native American tribal affiliation that you identify with. We are interested in the ethnicity that reflects your daily experience, which may be the heritage of your ancestors, if you continue to practice and identify with that heritage, but it may also be a more pan-American or global/international ethnicity. **In your own words, with which ethnic group(s) do you most identify?** _____

_____

25. How much do you <u>embrace</u> the values in the *ethnic culture(s)* you identified above?

Not at all		*Somewhat*		*Very much*
1	2	3	4	5

FAMILY AND GENERAL BACKGROUND

26. Where were you born?

    ☐ In the United States (one of the 50 states)
    ☐ In a United States territory such as Puerto Rico, U.S. Virgin Islands, Guam, American Samoa, Northern Mariana Islands, etc. Please specify what territory: _____
    ☐ Outside the U.S. or its territories. Please specify what country: _____

27. If you were not born in the United States, how old were you when you came here? _____

28. What language(s) were primarily used in your home while you were growing up? (*check all that apply*)

    ☐ English   ☐ Spanish   ☐ Other (*please specify*) _____

29. If a language other than English was used in your home growing up, how fluent are you in that language currently?

Not at all fluent		*Moderately fluent*		*Completely fluent*
1	2	3	4	5

30. Was English the first language you learned? ☐ Yes   ☐ No

31. For most of the time growing up, my neighborhood was:

    ☐ Similar to both my race and ethnicity
    ☐ Similar to my race but of a different ethnicity
    ☐ Mostly different than my race and mostly people of color
    ☐ Mostly different than my race and mostly White European American
    ☐ Mixed White and people of color

32. Were you adopted?

    ☐ Yes   ☐ No   ☐ Other situation (*please describe*) _____
    _____

33. Growing up, how would you describe the financial situation of your family?

    ☐ Routinely unable to purchase sufficient food or other basic necessities
    ☐ Occasionally unable to purchase sufficient food or other basic necessities
    ☐ Have enough money for the necessities
    ☐ Have more than enough money for necessities and some luxuries

34. In what sort of community were you primarily raised?

    ☐ Farm/rural
    ☐ Small town
    ☐ Medium-sized town/suburb
    ☐ Small city/large suburb
    ☐ Urban

CURRENT CONTEXT

35. What is your current relationship status? (*check one*)

    ☐ Single   ☐ Married   ☐ Civil union   ☐ Cohabitating

    ☐ Separated   ☐ Divorced   ☐ Widowed

    ☐ Not listed (*please specify*): _____

If you are married or partnered, please answer the following questions about your partner/spouse:

36. What is the highest grade in school, year in college, or post-college degree work completed by your partner?

    ☐ 8th grade or less
    ☐ Some high school
    ☐ High school graduate or GED
    ☐ Some college or 2 year degree
    ☐ College graduate (4 year degree)
    ☐ Graduate degree

37. Is your partner currently a: ☐ Part-time student

    ☐ Full-time student   ☐ Not a student

38. Is your partner currently involved in paid work?

    ☐ Not at all
    ☐ Working 1–20 hours per week
    ☐ Working 21–30 hours per week
    ☐ Working 31–40 hours per week
    ☐ Working over 40 hours per week

    If working, please write in occupation: _____

DEMOGRAPHICS QUESTIONNAIRE (Canada)

We want to be able to best understand the clients we serve, and the following questions help us get a better sense of who you are. Please answer the questions to the best of your ability. We know that many of these categories may not fully capture the complexities of your individual experience. You will have more opportunities to discuss these questions with your therapist.

1. Name: _____

2. Street Address: _____

3. City/Town: _____ Province: _____
   Postal Code: _____

4. Do you currently live in Canada?

   ☐ Yes   ☐ No (*Specify country*): _____
   If not, how long have you been living outside of Canada? _____

5. What is your current age? (*please write in*) _____

6. What is your gender identity (*check all that apply*)?

   ☐ Male   ☐ Female   ☐ Transgender   ☐ Nonbinary/gender fluid or queer
   ☐ Not listed (*please specify, if you choose*) _____

7. What is your sexual orientation?

   ☐ Heterosexual ☐ Bisexual ☐ Gay ☐ Lesbian ☐ Queer ☐ Asexual
   ☐ Not listed (*please specify, if you choose*) _____

8. With what religion or spiritual practice (if any) do you identify? _____
   _____

9. What is the highest grade in school, year in college, or post-college degree work you have completed?

☐ 8th Grade or Less
☐ Some High School
☐ High School Graduate or GED
☐ College or 2-Year Degree
☐ University Graduate (3 or 4-year degree)
☐ Graduate Degree

10. Are you currently a: ☐ Part-time student   ☐ Full-time student
☐ Not a student

11. Are you currently involved in paid work?

☐ Not at all
☐ Working 1–20 hours per week
☐ Working 21–30 hours per week
☐ Working 31–40 hours per week
☐ Working over 40 hours per week
Please write-in your occupation: _____

12. Currently, your total annual *household* income (all earners) is:

☐ $0 - $15,000
☐ $15,001 – $25,000
☐ $25,001 – $35,000
☐ $35,001 - $50,000
☐ $50,001 - $75,000
☐ $75,001 - $100,000
☐ $100,001 - $200,000
☐ More than $200,000

13. Have you been financially supported by someone else over the past year?   ☐ Yes   ☐ No

14. What is the total number of people who depend on the household income listed above (including yourself)? _____

15. Currently, how would you describe the financial situation of your family?
☐ Routinely unable to purchase sufficient food or other basic necessities
☐ Occasionally unable to purchase sufficient food or other basic necessities
☐ Have enough money for the necessities
☐ Have more than enough money for necessities and some luxuries

16. What languages do you currently speak (*check all that apply*)?

☐ English   ☐ French   ☐ Other(s) (*please specify*)_____

17. How fluent are you currently in English? (*circle one*)

Not at all fluent   *Moderately fluent*   *Completely fluent*
          1   2   3   4   5

18. How fluent are you currently in French? *(circle one)*

Not at all fluent   *Moderately fluent*   *Completely fluent*

      1   2   3   4   5

19. What language is currently used in your home most of the time?

☐ English   ☐ French   ☐ Other (please specify)_____

RACIAL AND ETHNIC BACKGROUND

We're interested in getting a complete picture of your racial and ethnic background so that we can best serve you and ensure we are meeting our organizational goals of inclusivity. Because this information can be so complex, we are going to ask you several questions about your race and ethnicity in order to get as complete a picture as possible.

20. Racial categories are based on visible attributes (often skin or eye colour and certain facial and bodily features) and self-identification. These groupings have social meanings that affect how people see themselves and are seen and treated by others. Race is not the same as ethnicity or culture. **In your own words, what is/are your racial identification(s)?**

   _____

21. Although the categories listed below may not represent your full identity or use the language you prefer, for the purpose of this survey, please indicate which group(s) below best describes your **racial identification**? *(check all that apply).*

   ☐ Asian   ☐ Middle Eastern, North African
   ☐ Black   (Non-White)
   ☐ Indigenous/Aboriginal,   ☐ White
      Native in Canada (First   ☐ Latinx/Hispanic (Non-White)
      Nations, Inuit, Métis)   ☐ Not listed *(please specify):* _____

22. Multiracial people can identify in various ways, sometimes in relation to specific racial heritage, sometimes as "multiracial," or in other ways. Which of the following best captures how you primarily identify? *(Please choose one).*

   ☐ Primarily Asian   ☐ Primarily White
   ☐ Primarily Black   ☐ Primarily Latinx/Hispanic
   ☐ Primarily Indigenous/   (Non-White)
      Aboriginal, Native in Canada   ☐ Multiracial generally—without
      (First Nations, Inuit, Métis)   reference to any particular group
   ☐ Primarily Middle Eastern,   ☐ Groups not listed *(please
      North African (Non-White)   specify):* _____

23. How often do people perceive your race accurately? *(Please circle one)*[2]

Hardly ever perceived correctly		*Sometimes perceived correctly*		*Always perceived correctly*
1	2	3	4	5

24. If you indicated that people sometimes or frequently do not perceive you correctly (1, 2, or 3), please indicate the race that people most frequently perceive you to be: _____

25. Ethnicity or ethnic culture refers to patterns of ideas and practices associated with a group of people sharing a common history, geographic background, and/or language, rather than their racial background. It might include things like values, patterns of interacting, food, dress, holidays, or ways of seeing the world, yourself, or other people.

    There are hundreds of different ethnic culture backgrounds within Canada – such as Arab Canadian, Jamaican, Plains Cree, European Canadian, Singaporean Chinese, etc. We are interested in the ethnicity that reflects your daily experience, which may be the heritage of your ancestors, if you continue to practice and identify with that heritage, but it may also be a more general Canadian or global/international ethnicity. **In your own words, with which ethnic group(s) do you most identify?** _____

26. How much do you <u>embrace</u> the values in the *ethnic culture(s) you* identified above?

not at all		*somewhat*		*very much*
1	2	3	4	5

FAMILY AND GENERAL BACKGROUND

27. Where were you born?

    ☐ In Canada
    ☐ Outside of Canada. *Please specify what country*: _____

28. If you were not born in Canada, how old were you when you came here? _____

29. What language(s) were primarily used in your home while you were growing up *(check all that apply)*?

    ☐ English   ☐ French   ☐ Other *(please specify)* _____

30. If a language other than English or French was used in your home growing up, how fluent are you in that language currently?

Not at all fluent		*Moderately fluent*		*Completely fluent*
1	2	3	4	5

31. For most of the time growing up, my neighborhood was:
    ☐ Similar to both my race and ethnicity
    ☐ Similar to my race but of a different ethnicity
    ☐ Mostly different than my race and mostly people of colour
    ☐ Mostly different than my race and mostly White
    ☐ Mixed White and people of colour

32. Were you adopted?
    ☐ Yes   ☐ No ☐   Other situation *(please describe)* _____
    _____

33. Growing up, how would you describe the financial situation of your family?

    ☐ Routinely unable to purchase sufficient food or other basic necessities
    ☐ Occasionally unable to purchase sufficient food or other basic necessities
    ☐ Have enough money for the necessities
    ☐ Have more than enough money for necessities and some luxuries

34. In what sort of community were you primarily raised?
    ☐ Farm/rural
    ☐ Small town
    ☐ Medium-sized town/Suburb
    ☐ Small city/Large suburb
    ☐ Urban

CURRENT CONTEXT

35. What is your current relationship status? *(check one)*
    ☐ Single   ☐ Married   ☐ Civil Union   ☐ Cohabitating
    ☐ Separated ☐ Divorced ☐ Widowed
    ☐ Not listed *(please specify)*: _____

If you are married or partnered, please answer the following questions about your partner/spouse:

36. What is the highest grade in school, year in college, or post-college degree work completed by your partner?
    ☐ 8th Grade or Less
    ☐ Some High School
    ☐ High School Graduate or GED
    ☐ College or 2-Year Degree
    ☐ University Graduate (3 or 4-year degree)
    ☐ Graduate Degree

37. Is your partner currently a: ☐ Part-time student   ☐ Full-time student
    ☐ Not a student

38. Is your partner currently involved in paid work?
    ☐ Not at all
    ☐ Working 1-20 hours per week
    ☐ Working 21-30 hours per week
    ☐ Working 31-40 hours per week
    ☐ Working over 40 hours per week

    If working, please write-in occupation: _____

RESOURCES

The reading materials below are an excellent resource for learning more about microaggressions and the related topics covered in this book.

Bonilla-Silva, E. (2004). *Racism without racists: Color-blind racism and the persistence of racial inequality in the United States.* Lanham, MD: Rowman & Littlefield.

Claym, R. A. (2017, January). Did you really just say that? Here's advice on how to confront microaggressions, whether you're a target, bystander or perpetrator. *Monitor on Psychology, 48*(1), 46. Retrieved from https://www.apa.org/monitor/2017/01/microaggressions

DiAngelo, R. (2018). *White fragility: Why it's so hard for white people to talk about racism.* Boston, MA: Beacon.

Freeman, L., & Stewart, H. (2019). Microaggressions in clinical medicine. *Kennedy Institute of Ethics Journal, 28*, 411–449. doi:10.1353/ken.2018.0024

Guthrie, R. V. (2003). *Even the rat was white: A historical view of psychology.* Boston, MA: Pearson.

Miller, A., Williams, M. T., Wetterneck, C. T., Kanter, J., & Tsai, M. (2015). Using functional analytic psychotherapy to improve awareness and connection in racially diverse client–therapist dyads. *The Behavior Therapist, 38*(6), 150–156.

Nadal, K. L. (2018). *Microaggressions and traumatic stress: Theory, research, and clinical treatment.* Washington, DC: American Psychological Association.

Sue, D. W., Alsaidi, S., Awad, M. N., Glaeser, E., Calle, C. Z., & Mendez, N. (2019). Disarming racial microaggressions: Microintervention strategies for targets, White allies, and bystanders. *American Psychologist, 74*(1), 128–142.

Sue, D. W., Capodilupo, C. M., Torino, G. C., Bucceri, J. M., Holder, A. M., Nadal, K. L., & Esquilin, M. (2007). Racial microaggressions in everyday life: Implications for clinical practice. *American Psychologist, 62*(4), 271–286.

Sue, D. W., Sue, D., Neville, H., & Smith, L. (2019). *Counseling the culturally diverse: Theory and practice* (9th ed.). Hoboken, NJ: Wiley.

Terwilliger, J. M., Bach, N., Bryan, C., & Williams, M. T. (2013). Multicultural versus colorblind ideology: Implications for mental health and counseling. In A. Di Fabio (Ed.), *Psychology of counseling* (pp. 111–122). Hauppauge, NY: Nova Science. ISBN-13:978-1-62618-410-7

Wadsworth, L. P., Morgan L. P., Hayes-Skelton, S. A., Roemer, L., & Suyemoto, K. L. (2016). Ways to boost your research rigor through increasing your cultural competence. *The Behavior Therapist, 39*(3), 76–92.

Williams, M., & Halstead, M. (2019). Racial microaggressions as barriers to treatment in clinical care. *Directions in Psychiatry, 39*(4), 265–280.

Williams, M. T., Metzger, I., Leins, C., & DeLapp, C. (2018). Assessing racial trauma within a DSM-5 framework: The UConn Racial/Ethnic Stress & Trauma Survey. *Practice Innovations, 3*(4), 242–260. Instrument in English and Spanish available from http://www.mentalhealthdisparities.org/trauma-research.php

Williams, M. T., Rosen, D. C., & Kanter, J. W. (2019). *Eliminating race-based mental health disparities: Using contextual behavioral science to achieve equity and excellence across settings and communities.* New York, NY: New Harbinger. ISBN:978-1-68403-196-2

REFERENCES

Abrams, R., Hsu, T., & Eligon, J. (2018, May 29). Starbucks's tall order: Tackle systemic racism in 4 hours. *The New York Times*. Retrieved from https://www.nytimes.com/2018/05/29/business/starbucks-closing-racial-bias-training.html

Alabi, J. (2015). Racial microaggressions in academic libraries: Results of a survey of minority and non-minority librarians. *Journal of Academic Librarianship, 41*(1), 47–53.

Allen, J. J., & Anderson, C. A. (2017). Aggression and violence: Definitions and distinctions. In P. Sturmey (Ed.), *The Wiley handbook of violence and aggression*. New York, NY: Wiley. doi:10.1002/9781119057574.whbva001

Alvarez, A. N., & Juang, L. P. (2010). Filipino Americans and racism: A multiple mediation model of coping. *Journal of Counseling Psychology, 57*(2), 167–178. doi:10.1037/a0019091

American Psychiatric Association. (1994). *Diagnostic and statistical manual of mental disorders* (4th ed.). Washington, DC: Author.

American Psychiatric Association. (2013). *Diagnostic and statistical manual of mental disorders* (5th ed.). Arlington, VA: American Psychiatric Publishing.

Avery, D. R., Tonidandel, S., Thomas, K. M., Johnson, C. D., & Mack, D. A. (2007). Assessing the multigroup ethnic identity measure for measurement equivalence across racial and ethnic groups. *Educational and Psychological Measurement, 67*, 877–888.

Awad, G. H. (2010). The impact of acculturation and religious identification on perceived discrimination for Arab/Middle Eastern Americans. *Cultural Diversity and Ethnic Minority Psychology, 16*(1), 59–67. doi:10.1037/a0016675

Ayalon, L., & Gum, A. M. (2011). The relationships between major lifetime discrimination, everyday discrimination, and mental health in three racial and ethnic groups of older adults. *Aging & Mental Health, 15*, 587–594. doi:10.1080/13607863.2010.543664

Bailey, A. (1998). Locating traitorous identities: Toward a view of privilege-cognizant White character. *Hypatia, 13*(3), 27–42. doi:10.1111/j.1527-2001.1998.tb01368.x

Balsam, K. F., Molina, Y., Beadnell, B., Simoni, J., & Walters, K. (2011). Measuring multiple minority stress: The LGBT People of Color Microaggressions Scale. *Cultural Diversity and Ethnic Minority Psychology, 17*(2), 163–174.

Banks, K. H., Kohn-Wood, L. P., & Spencer, M. (2006). An examination of the African American experience of everyday discrimination and symptoms of psychological distress. *Community Mental Health Journal, 42*(6), 555–570. doi:10.1007/s10597-006-9052-9

Bartoli, E., & Pyati, A. (2009). Addressing clients' racism and racial prejudice in individual psychotherapy: Therapeutic considerations. *Psychotherapy: Theory, Research, Practice, Training, 46*(2), 145–157.

Baron, A. S., & Banaji, M. R. (2006). The Development of Implicit Attitudes Evidence of Race Evaluations From Ages 6 and 10 and Adulthood. *Psychological Science, 17*(1), 53–58.

Beatty Moody, D. L., Brown, C., Matthews, K. A., & Bromberger, J. T. (2014). Everyday discrimination prospectively predicts inflammation across 7-years in racially diverse midlife women: Study of women's health across the nation. *Journal of Social Issues, 70*, 298–314. doi:10.1111/josi.12061

Berger, M., & Sarnyai, Z. (2015). 'More than skin deep': Stress neurobiology and mental health consequences of racial discrimination. *Stress: The International Journal on the Biology of Stress*, 18(1), 1–10. doi:10.3109/10253890.2014.989204

Blume, A. W., Lovato, L. V., Thyken, B. N., & Denny, N. (2012). The relationship of microaggressions with alcohol use and anxiety among ethnic minority college students in a historically White institution. *Cultural Diversity and Ethnic Minority Psychology, 18*(1), 45–54. doi:10.1037/a0025457

Brewer, M. B. (1999). The psychology of prejudice: Ingroup love or outgroup hate? *Journal of Social Issues, 55*(3), 429–444. doi:10.1111/0022-4537.00126

Brown, D. L., & Tylka, T. L. (2010). Racial discrimination and resilience in African American young adults: Examining racial socialization as a moderator. *Journal of Black Psychology, 37*(3), 259–285.

Bushman, B. J., & Huesmann, L. R. (2010). Aggression. In S. T. Fiske, D. T. Gilbert, & G. Lindzey (Eds.), *Handbook of social psychology* (5th ed., pp. 833–863). New York, NY: Wiley.

Buss, A. H. (1961). *The psychology of aggression.* New York, NY: Wiley.

Buss, A. H., & Perry, M. (1992). The aggression questionnaire. *Journal of Personality and Social Psychology, 63*, 452–459.

Campbell, B., & Manning, J. (2014). Microaggression and moral cultures. *Comparative Sociology, 13*(6), 692–726.

Canel-Çınarbaş, D., & Yohani, S. (2018). Indigenous Canadian university students' experiences of microaggressions. *International Journal for the Advancement of Counselling, 41*(2), 1–20. doi:10.1007/s10447-018-9345-z

Carlson, M. D., Endsley, M., Motley, D., Shawahin, L. N., & Williams, M. T. (2018). Addressing the impact of racism on veterans of color: A race-based stress and trauma group. *Psychology of Violence, 8*(6), 748–762. doi:10.1037/vio0000221

Chou, T., Asnaani, A., & Hofmann, S. G. (2012). Perception of racial discrimination and psychopathology across three U.S. ethnic minority groups. *Cultural Diversity and Ethnic Minority Psychology, 18*(1), 74–81.

Clark, D. A., Kleiman, S., Spanierman, L. B., Isaac, P., & Poolokasingham, G. (2014). "Do you live in a teepee?" Aboriginal students' experiences with racial microaggressions in Canada. *Journal of Diversity in Higher Education, 7*(2), 112–125. doi:10.1037/a0036573

Clark, R., Anderson, N. B., Clark, V. R., & Williams, D. R. (1999). Racism as a Stressor for African Americans: A Biopsychosocial Model. *American Psychologist, 54*(10), 805–816.

Clark, T. T., Salas-Wright, C. P., Vaughn, M. G., & Whitfield, K. E. (2015). Everyday discrimination and mood and substance use disorders: A latent profile analysis with African Americans and Caribbean Blacks. *Addictive Behaviors, 40*, 119–125. doi:10.1016/j.addbeh.2014.08.006

Cheng, H., Wang, C., McDermott, R. C., Kridel, M., & Rislin, J. L. (2018). Self-stigma, mental health literacy, and attitudes toward seeking psychological help. *Journal of Counseling & Development, 96*(1), 64–74. doi:10.1002/jcad.12178

Cokley, K., Hall-Clark, B., & Hicks, D. (2011). Ethnic minority–majority status and mental health: The mediating role of perceived discrimination. *Journal of Mental Health Counseling, 33*(3), 243–263.

Colen, C. G., Ramey, D. M., Cooksey, E. C., & Williams, D. R. (2018). Racial disparities in health among nonpoor African Americans and Hispanics: The role of acute and chronic discrimination. *Social Science & Medicine, 199*, 167–180.

Consedine, N. S., Magai, C., Cohen, C. I., & Gillspie, M. (2002). Ethnic variation in the impact of negative affect and emotion inhibition on the health of older adults. *Journal of Gerontology: Psychological Sciences, 57B*, 396–408.

Constantine, M. G. (2007). Racial microaggressions against African American clients in cross-racial counseling relationships. *Journal of Counseling Psychology, 54*, 1–16.

Constantine, M. G., & Sue, D. W. (2007). Perceptions of racial microaggressions among Black supervisees in cross-racial dyads. *Journal of Counseling Psychology, 54*, 142–153. doi:10.1037/0022-0167.54.2.142

Cooper, C. (2017, August 17). To the therapist who called me a "strong Black woman." *The Mighty*. Retrieved from https://themighty.com/2017/08/therapy-racial-bias-strong-black-woman

Cooper, L. A., Roter, D. L., Carson, K. A., Beach, M. C., Sabin, J. A., Greenwald, A. G., & Inui, T. S. (2012). The Associations of Clinicians' Implicit Attitudes About Race With Medical Visit Communication and Patient Ratings of Interpersonal Care. *American Journal of Public Health, 102*, 979–987. doi: doi.org/10.2105/AJPH.2011.300558

Crowe, C. (2018, September 14). What Happened When One University Moved a Confederate Statue to a Museum. *Chronicle of Higher Education*, p. 1.

Cox, D., Navarro-Rivera, J., & Jones, R. P. (2016, August 3). *Race, religion, and political affiliation of Americans' core social networks*. Public Religion Research Institute. Retrieved from https://www.prri.org/research/poll-race-religion-politics-americans-social-networks

Dailey, D. E. (2009). Social stressors and strengths as predictors of infant birth weight in low-income African American women. *Nursing Research, 58*(5), 340–347. doi:10.1097/NNR.0b013e3181ac1599

Dale, S. K., & Safren, S. A. (2019). Gendered racial microaggressions predict posttraumatic stress disorder symptoms and cognitions among Black women living with HIV. *Psychological Trauma: Theory, Research, Practice, and Policy*. doi:10.1037/tra0000467.supp

Davis, P. (1989). Law as microaggression. *Yale Law Journal, 98*, 1559–1577.

DeLapp, R. C. T., & Williams, M. T. (2015). Professional challenges facing African American psychologists: The presence and impact of racial microaggressions. *The Behavior Therapist, 38*(4), 101–105.

DeLapp, R. C. T., & Williams, M. (2016, July 19). Proactively coping with racism. *Psychology Today*. Retrieved from https://www.psychologytoday.com/ca/blog/culturally-speaking/201607/proactively-coping-racism

DeLapp, R. C. T., & Williams, M. T. (2019). Preparing for racial discrimination and moving beyond reactive coping: A systematic review. *Current Psychiatry Reviews, 15*(1), 58–71. doi:10.2174/1573400515666190211114709

Desai, S. R., & Abeita, A. (2017). Institutional Microaggressions at a Hispanic Serving Institution: A Diné (Navajo) Woman Utilizing Tribal Critical Race Theory through Student Activism. *Equity & Excellence in Education, 50*(3), 275–289. doi:10.1080/10665684.2017.1336498

DeSilva, R., Aggarwal, N. K., & Lewis-Fernández, R. (2015, June 30). The DSM-5 cultural formulation interview and the evolution of cultural assessment in psychiatry. *Psychiatric Times, 32*(6). Retrieved from http://www.psychiatrictimes.com/special-reports/dsm-5-cultural-formulation-interview-and-evolution-cultural-assessment-psychiatry/page/0/1

DiAngelo, R. (2011). White fragility. *International Journal of Critical Pedagogy, 3*(3), 54–70.

Dovidio, J. F., Kawakami, K., & Gaertner, S. E. (2002). Implicit and explicit prejudice and interracial interaction. *Journal of Personality and Social Psychology, 82*(1), 62–68.

Dovidio, J.F., Gaertner, S.L., Kawakami, K., & Hodson, G. (2002). Why can't we just get along? Interpersonal biases and interracial distrust. *Cultural Diversity & Ethnic Minority Psychology, 8,* 88–102.

Durhams, S. (2013, December 30). Remember when UW Photoshopped a Black student onto an admissions brochure? *Milwaukee-Wisconsin Journal Sentinel.* Retrieved from http://archive.jsonline.com/newswatch/237991911.html

Endo, R. (2015). How Asian American female teachers experience racial microaggressions from pre-service preparation to their professional careers. *The Urban Review, 47*(4), 601–625.

Ennis, S. R., Ríos-Vargas, M., & Albert, N. G. (2011, May). The Hispanic Population: 2010. 2010 Census Briefs. U.S. Census Bureau. https://www.census.gov/prod/cen2010/briefs/c2010br-04.pdf

Essed, P. (1991). *Understanding everyday racism.* Newbury Park, CA: Sage.

Faber, S. C., Williams, M. T., & Terwilliger, P. R. (2019, July). Implicit racial bias across ethnic groups and cross-nationally: Mental health implications. In M. Williams & N. Buchanan (discussants), Racial issues in the assessment of mental health and delivery of cognitive behavioral therapies. Paper presented at the World Congress of Behavioral and Cognitive Therapies, Berlin, Germany.

Farzan, A. (2019, July 26). Ole Miss frat brothers brought guns to an Emmett Till memorial: They're not the first. *The Washington Post.* Retrieved from https://www.washingtonpost.com/nation/2019/07/26/ole-miss-emmitt-till-guns-kappa-alpha-fraternity

Forman, T. A., Williams, D. R., & Jackson, J. S. (1997). Race, place, and discrimination. In C. Gardner (Ed.), *Perspectives on social problems* (pp. 231–261). Greenwich, CT: JAI Press.

Forrest-Bank, S. S., & Jenson, J. M. (2015a). The relationship among childhood risk and protective factors, racial microaggression and ethnic identity, and academic self-efficacy and antisocial behavior in young adulthood. *Children and Youth Services Review, 50,* 64–74. doi:10.1016/j.childyouth.2015.01.005

Forrest-Bank, S. S., & Jenson, J. M. (2015b). Differences in experiences of racial and ethnic microaggression among Asian, Latino/Hispanic, Black, and White young adults. *Journal of Sociology & Social Welfare, 42*(1), 141–161.

Gaertner, S. L., & Dovidio, J. F. (2005). Understanding and addressing contemporary racism: From aversive racism to the common ingroup identity model. *Journal of Social Issues, 61*(3), 615–639.

Gaztambide, D. J. (2012). Addressing cultural impasses with rupture resolution strategies: A proposal and recommendations. *Professional Psychology: Research and Practice, 43*(3), 183–189. doi:10.1037/a0026911

Gee, G. C., Spencer, M. S., Chen, J., & Takeuchi, D. (2007). A nationwide study of discrimination and chronic health conditions among Asian Americans. *American Journal of Public Health, 97*(7), 1275–1282. doi:10.2105/AJPH.2006.091827

Gerrard, M., Stock, M. L., Roberts, M. E., Gibbons, F. X., O'Hara, R. E., Weng, C., & Wills, T. A. (2012). Coping with racial discrimination: The role of substance use. *Psychology of Addictive Behaviors, 26*(3), 550–560. doi:10.1037/a0027711

Graham-LoPresti, J., Williams, M. T., & Rosen, D. C. (2019). Culturally responsive assessment and diagnosis for clients of color. In M. T. Williams, D. C. Rosen, & J. W. Kanter (Eds.), *Eliminating Race-Based Mental Health Disparities: Promoting Equity and Culturally Responsive Care Across Settings* (pp. 169–185). Oakland, CA: New Harbinger Books.

Greenwald, A. G., McGhee, D. E., & Schwartz, J. L. K. (1998). Measuring individual differences in implicit cognition: The implicit association test. Journal of *Personality and Social Psychology, 74*(6), 1464–1480. https://doi.org/10.1037/0022-3514.74.6.1464

Gurin, P., Sorensen, N., Lopez, G. E., & Nagda, B. A. (2015). Intergroup dialogue: Race still matters. In R. Bangs, L. E. Davis, R. Bangs, L. E. Davis (Eds.), *Race and social problems: Restructuring inequality* (pp. 39–60). New York, NY, US: Springer Science + Business Media. doi:10.1007/978-1-4939-0863-9_3

Haidt, J. (2017). The unwisest idea on campus: Commentary on Lilienfeld (2017). *Perspectives on Psychological Science, 12*(1), 176–177.

Harding, R. (2005). The media, aboriginal people and common sense. *Canadian Journal of Native Studies, 25*(1), 311–333.

Harwood, S. A., Huntt, M. B., Mendenhall, R., & Lewis, J. A. (2012). Racial microaggressions in the residence halls: Experiences of students of color at a predominantly White university. *Journal of Diversity in Higher Education, 5*(3), 159–173.

Hernandez, P., Carranza, M., & Almeida, R. (2010). Mental health professionals' adaptive responses to racial microaggressions: An exploratory study. *Professional Psychology: Research and Practice, 41*(3), 202–209.

Hoffman, K. M., Trawalter, S., Axt, J. R., & Oliver, M. N. (2016). Racial bias in pain assessment and treatment recommendations, and false beliefs about biological differences between Blacks and Whites. *Proceedings of the National Academy of Sciences of the USA, 113*(16), 4296–4301. doi:10.1073/pnas.1516047113

Hollingsworth, D. W., Cole, A. B., O'Keefe, V. M., Tucker, R. P., Story, C. R., & Wingate, L. R. (2017). Experiencing racial microaggressions influences suicide ideation through perceived burdensomeness in African Americans. *Journal of Counseling Psychology, 64*(1), 104–111. doi:10.1037/cou0000177

Hook, J. N., Farrell, J. E., Davis, D. E., DeBlaere, C., Van Tongeren, D. R., & Utsey, S. O. (2016). Cultural humility and racial microaggressions in counseling. *Journal of Counseling Psychology, 63*(3), 269–277. doi:10.1037/cou0000114

Hudson, D. L., Bullard, K. M., Neighbors, H. W., Geronimus, A. T., Yang, J., & Jackson, J. S. (2012). Are benefits conferred with greater socioeconomic position undermined by racial discrimination among African American men? *Journal of Men's Health, 9*(2), 127–136. doi:10.1016/j.jomh.2012.03.006

Hughes, D., Rodriguez, J., Smith, E. P., Johnson, D. J., Stevenson, H. C., & Spicer, P. (2006). Parents' ethnic–racial socialization practices: A review of research and directions for future study. *Developmental Psychology, 42*(5), 747–770. doi:10.1037/0012-1649.42.5.747

Huynh, V. W. (2012). Ethnic microaggressions and the depressive and somatic symptoms of Latino and Asian American adolescents. *Journal of Youth and Adolescence, 41*(7), 831–846. doi:10.1007/s10964-012-9756-9

Hyers, L. L. (2006). Myths used to legitimize the exploitation of animals: An application of social dominance theory. *Anthrozoos, 19*(3), 194–210. doi:10.2752/089279306785415538

Ingraham, C. (2014, August 25). Three quarters of Whites don't have any non-White friends. *The Washington Post.* Retrieved from https://www.washingtonpost.com/news/wonk/wp/2014/08/25/three-quarters-of-whites-dont-have-any-non-white-friends

Jagannathan, M. (2019, March 8). "Nice skirt!" How to respond to microaggressions at work. MarketWatch. Retrieved from https://www.marketwatch.com/story/nice-skirt-where-did-you-learn-english-how-to-respond-to-microaggressions-at-work-2019-02-21

Johnston, M. P., & Nadal, K. L. (2010). Multiracial microaggressions: Exposing monoracism in everyday life and clinical practice. In D. W. Sue (Ed.), *Microaggressions and Marginality: Manifestation, Dynamics, and Impact* (pp. 123–144). New York: Wiley & Sons.

Jones, M. L., & Galliher, R. V. (2015). Daily racial microaggressions and ethnic identification among Native American young adults. *Cultural Diversity and Ethnic Minority Psychology, 21*(1), 1–9. doi:10.1037/a0037537

Jones, R. P., Cox, D., & Navarro-Rivera, J. (2014). *Economic insecurity, rising inequality, and doubts about the future: Findings from the 2014 American Values Survey.* Washington, DC: Public Religion Research Institute.

Johnston, M. P., & Nadal, K. L. (2010). Multiracial microaggressions: Exposing monoracism in everyday life and clinical practice. In D. W. Sue (Ed.), *Microaggressions and Marginality: Manifestation, Dynamics, and Impact* (pp. 123–144). New York: Wiley & Sons.

Kalinoski, Z. T., Steele-Johnson, D., Peyton, E. J., Leas, K. A., Steinke, J., & Bowling, N. A. (2013). A meta-analytic evaluation of diversity training outcomes. *Journal of Organizational Behavior, 34*(8), 1076–1104.

Kanter, J. W., Rosen, D. C., Manbeck, K., Branstetter, H., Kuczynski, A., Corey, M., . . . Williams, M. T. (2020). Improving provider responsiveness and emotional rapport in racially charged interactions: A preliminary randomized trial. *BMC Medical Education, 20*(88), 1–14. doi:10.1186/s12909-020-02004-9.

Kanter, J. W., Rosen, D. C., Manbeck, K. E., Kuczynski, A. M., Corey, M. D., & Branstetter, H. M. L. (2019). Using contextual–behavioral science to understand racism and bias. In M. T. Williams, D. C. Rosen, & J. W. Kanter (Eds.), *Eliminating race-based mental health disparities: Promoting equity and culturally responsive care across settings* (pp. 99–125). Oakland, CA: New Harbinger.

Kanter, J. W., Williams, M. T., Kuczynski, A. M., Manbeck, K., Debreaux, M., & Rosen, D. (2017). A preliminary report on the relationship between microaggressions against Blacks and racism among White college students. *Race and Social Problems, 9*(4), 291–299. doi:10.1007/s12552-017-9214-0

Kay, J. (2014, July 11). Jonathan Kay: Stop calling people "racialized minorities": It's silly and cynical. *National Post.* Retrieved from http://nationalpost.com/opinion/jonathan-kay-stop-calling-people-racialized-minorities-its-silly-and-cynical

Keith, V. M., Nguyen, A. W., Taylor, R. J., Chatters, L. M., & Mouzon, D. M. (2017). Microaggressions, discrimination, and phenotype among African Americans: A latent class analysis of the impact of skin tone and BMI. *Sociological Inquiry, 87*(2), 233–255.

Keum, B. T., Brady, J. L., Sharma, R., Lu, Y., Kim, Y. H., & Thai, C. J. (2018). Gendered Racial Microaggressions Scale for Asian American Women: Development and initial validation. *Journal of Counseling Psychology, 65*(5), 571–585. http://dx.doi.org/10.1037/cou0000305.

Kinney, T. A. (1994). An inductively derived typology of verbal aggression and its association to distress. *Human Communication Research, 21*(2), 183–222. doi:10.1111/j.1468-2958.1994.tb00345.x

Kraus, M. W., Rucker, J. M., & Richeson, J. A. (2017). Americans misperceive racial economic equality. *Proceedings of the National Academy of Sciences of the USA, 114*(39), 10324–10331. doi:10.1073/pnas.1707719114

Kugelmass, H. (2016). "Sorry, I'm not accepting new patients": An audit study of access to mental health care. *Journal of Health and Social Behavior, 57*(2), 168–183. doi:10.1177/0022146516647098

LaFromboise, T. D., Coleman, H. L., & Hernandez, A. (1991). Development and factor structure of the Cross-Cultural Counseling Inventory–Revised. *Professional Psychology: Research and Practice, 22*(5), 380–388. doi:10.1037/0735-7028.22.5.380

Landrine, H., & Klonoff, E. A. (1996). A measure of racial discrimination and a study of its negative physical and mental health consequences. *Journal of Black Psychology, 22*, 144–168.

Landrine, H., Klonoff, E. A., Corral, I., Fernandez, S., & Roesch, S. (2006). Conceptualizing and measuring ethnic discrimination in health research. *Journal of Behavioral Medicine, 29*(1), 79–94.

Lee, B. X. (2015). Causes and cures I: Toward a new definition. *Aggression & Violent Behavior, 25*, 199–203. doi:10.1016/j.avb.2015.10.004

Lee, S., Wong, N. A., & Alvarez, A. N. (2009). The model minority and perpetual foreigner: Stereotypes of Asian Americans. In N. Tewari & A. N. Alvarez (Eds.), *Asian American psychology: Current perspectives* (pp. 69–84). New York, NY: Psychology Press.

Lewis, A. E., Chesler, M., & Forman, T. A. (2000). The impact of "colorblind" ideologies on students of color: Intergroup relations at a predominantly White university. *Journal of Negro Education, 69*, 74–91.

Lilienfeld, S. O. (2017). Microaggressions: Strong claims, inadequate evidence. *Perspectives on Psychological Science, 12*(1), 138–169. doi:10.1177/1745691616659391

Lin, A. I. (2010). Racial microaggressions directed at Asian Americans: Modern forms of prejudice and discrimination. In D. W. Sue (Ed.), *Microaggressions and marginality: Manifestation, dynamics, and impact* (pp. 85–103). John Wiley & Sons Inc.

Lorenzo-Blanco, E. I., Unger, J. B., Ritt-Olson, A., Soto, D., & Baezconde-Garbanati, L. (2013). A longitudinal analysis of Hispanic youth acculturation and cigarette smoking: The roles of gender, culture, family, and discrimination. *Nicotine Tobacco Research, 15*(5), 957–968. doi:10.1093/ntr/nts204

Lorenzo-Hernandez, J., & Ouellette, S. C. (1998). Ethnic identity, self-esteem, and values in Dominicans, Puerto Ricans, and African Americans. *Journal of Applied Social Psychology, 28*, 2007–2024.

Lowery, W., & Stankiewicz, K. (2016, February 15). "My demons won today": Ohio activist's suicide spotlights depression among Black Lives Matter leader. *The Washington Post.*

Luo, Y., Xu, J., Granberg, E., & Wentworth, W. M. (2012). A longitudinal study of social status, perceived discrimination, and physical and emotional health among older adults. *Research on Aging, 34*(3), 275–301. doi:10.1177/0164027511426151

MacInnis, C. C., & Page-Gould, E. (2015). How can intergroup interaction be bad if intergroup con-tact is good? Exploring and reconciling an apparent paradox in the science of intergroup rela-tions. *Perspectives on Psychological Science, 10*(3), 307–327.

Maxie, A. C., Arnold, D. H., & Stephenson, M. (2006). Do therapists address ethnic and racial differences in cross-cultural psychotherapy? *Psychotherapy: Theory, Research, Practice, Training, 43*(1), 85. doi:10.1037/0033-3204.43.1.85

McCracken, L. M. (2005). *Contextual Cognitive-Behavioral Therapy for Chronic Pain* (Progress in Pain Research and Management, Volume 33). IASP Press: Seattle.

McKinnon, R. (2017). Allies behaving badly: Gaslighting as epistemic injustice. In I. J. Kidd, J. Medina, & G. Pohlhaus (Eds.), *The Routledge handbook on epistemic injustice* (pp. 167–174). New York, NY: Routledge. ISBN-13:978-1138828254

Mekawi, Y., & Todd, N. R. (2018). Okay to say? Initial validation of the Acceptability of Racial Microaggressions Scale. *Cultural Diversity and Ethnic Minority Psychology, 24*(3), 346–362. http://dx.doi.org/10.1037/cdp0000201

Mercer, S. H., Zeigler-Hill, V., Wallace, M., & Hayes, D. M. (2011). Development and initial validation of the Inventory of Microaggressions Against Black Individuals. *Journal of Counseling Psychology, 58*(4), 457–469. doi:10.1037/a0024937

Michaels, T. I., Gallagher, N., Crawford, M., Kanter, J. W., & Williams, M. T. (2018). Racial differences in the appraisal of microaggressions through cultural consensus modeling. *The Behavior Therapist, 41*(7), 314–321.

Miller, J., & Donner, S. (2000). More Than Just Talk: The Use of Racial Dialogues to Combat Racism. *Social Work with Groups, 23*(1), 31–53.

Miller, A., Williams, M. T., Wetterneck, C. T., Kanter, J., & Tsai, M. (2015). Using functional analytic psychotherapy to improve awareness and connection in racially diverse client-therapist dyads. *The Behavior Therapist, 38*(6), 150–156.

Mouzon, D. M., Taylor, R. J., Keith, V. M., Nicklett, E. J., & Chatters, L. M. (2017). Discrimination and psychiatric disorders among older African Americans. *International Journal of Geriatric Psychiatry, 32*(2), 175–182. doi:10.1002/gps.4454

Murty, K. S., & Vyas, A. G. (2017). African American Students' Reactions to the Confederate Flag: A Social-Psychological Approach to Integrate Post Traumatic Slave Syndrome and Microaggression Theory. *Race, Gender & Class, 24*(1/2), 133–159.

Nadal, K. L. (2011). The Racial and Ethnic Microaggressions Scale (REMS): Construction, reliability, and validity. *Journal of Counseling Psychology, 58,* 470–480.

Nadal, K. L. (2014). A guide to responding to microaggressions. *CUNY Forum 2*(1), 71–76.

Nadal, K. L. (2018). *Microaggressions and traumatic stress: Theory, research, and clinical treatment.* Washington, DC: American Psychological Association.

Nadal, K. L., Griffin, K. E., Wong, Y., Hamit, S., & Rasmus, M. (2014). The impact of racial microaggressions on mental health: Counseling implications for clients of color. *Journal of Counseling & Development, 92*(1), 57–66. doi:10.1002/j.1556-6676.2014.00130.x

Nadal, K. L., Sriken, J., Davidoff, K. C., Wong, Y., & McLean, K. (2013). Microaggressions within families: Experiences of multiracial people. *Family Relations, 62*(1), 190–201. doi:10.1111/j.1741-3729.2012.00752.x

Nadal, K. L., Vigilia Escobar, K. M., Prado, G. T., David, E. J. R., & Haynes, K. (2012). Racial microaggressions and the Filipino American experience: Recommendations for counseling and development. *Journal of Multicultural Counseling and Development, 40*(3), 156–173.

Nadal, K. L., Wong, Y., Griffin, K. E., Davidoff, K., & Sriken, J. (2014). The adverse impact of racial microaggressions on college students' self-esteem. *Journal of College Student Development, 55*(5), 461–474. doi:10.1353/csd.2014.0051

Niemann, Y. F. (1999). The Making of a Token: A Case Study of Stereotype Threat, Stigma, Racism, and Tokenism in Academe. Latina/Chicana Leadership. *Frontiers: A Journal of Women Studies, 20*(1), 111–134. doi:10.2307/3346994

Okech, J. E. A., & Champe, J. (2008). Informing culturally competent practice through cross-racial friendships. *International Journal for the Advancement of Counselling, 30,* 104–115.

O'Keefe, V. M., Wingate, L. R., Cole, A. B., Hollingsworth, D. W., & Tucker, R. P. (2015). Seemingly harmless racial communications are not so harmless: Racial microaggressions lead to suicidal ideation by way of depression symptoms. *Suicide & Life-Threatening Behavior, 45*(5), 567–576. doi:10.1111/sltb.12150

Oklahoma Commission to Study the Tulsa Race Riot of 1921. (2001). *Tulsa race riot.* Retrieved from http://www.okhistory.org/research/forms/freport.pdf

Ong, A. D., Burrow, A. L., Fuller-Rowell, T. E., Ja, N. M., & Sue, D. W. (2013). Racial microaggressions and daily well-being among Asian Americans. *Journal of Counseling Psychology, 60,* 188–199.

Oshin, L., Ching, T. H. W., & West, L. M. (2019). Supervising therapist trainees of color. In M. T. Williams, D. C. Rosen, & J. W. Kanter (Eds.), *Eliminating race-based mental health disparities: Promoting equity and culturally responsive care across settings* (pp. 188–201). Oakland, CA: New Harbinger.

Owen, J., Tao, K. W., Imel, Z. E., Wampold, B. E., & Rodolfa, E. (2014). Addressing racial and ethnic microaggressions in therapy. *Professional Psychology: Research and Practice, 45*(4), 283–290.

Pahlke, E., Bigler, R. S., & Suizzo, M. (2012). Relations between colorblind socialization and children's racial bias: Evidence from European American mothers and their preschool children. *Child Development, 83*(4), 1164–1179.

Page-Gould, E., Mendoza-Denton, & Tropp, L. R. (2008). With a little help from my cross-group friend: Reducing anxiety in intergroup contexts through cross-group friendship. *Journal of Personality and Social Psychology, 95*(5), 1080–1094.

Parker, K., Horowitz, J. M., Morin, R., & Lopez, M. H. (2015, June 11). Multiracial in America: Proud, Diverse and Growing in Numbers. Pew Research Center. Retrieved from https://www.pewsocialtrends.org/2015/06/11/multiracial-in-america/

Parigoris, R., Kuczynski, A. M., Carey, C. M., Corey, M. D., Williams, M. T., & Kanter, J. W. (2018, July). Measuring microaggressions in White individuals I: Self-reported microaggressions predict prejudice and racism. In A. M. Kuczynski (Chair), Discrimination and microaggressions: CBS research findings and a call to action. Symposium presentation at ACBS World Conference 16, Montréal, Québec, Canada.

Penner, L. A., Blair, I. V., Albrecht, T. L., & Dovidio, J. F. (2014). Reducing racial health care disparities: A social psychological analysis. *Health and Well-Being, 1*(1), 204–212.

Phillips, L. T., & Lowery, B. S. (2018). Herd Invisibility: The Psychology of Racial Privilege. *Current Directions in Psychological Science, 27*(3), 156–162.

Pierce, C. (1970). Offensive mechanisms. In F. Barbour (Ed.), *In the Black seventies* (pp. 265–282). Boston, MA: Porter Sargent.

Pierce, C. M. (1974). Psychiatric problems of the Black minority. In S. Arieti (Ed.), *American handbook of psychiatry* (pp. 512–523). New York, NY: Basic Books. ISBN:9780465001477

Pittman, C. T. (2011). Getting mad but ending up sad: The mental health consequences for African Americans using anger to cope with racism. *Journal of Black Studies, 42*(7), 1106–1124. doi:10.1177/0021934711401737

Plant, E. A., & Butz, D. A. (2006). The causes and consequences of an avoidance-focus for interracial interactions. *Personality and Social Psychology Bulletin, 32*(6), 833–846. doi:10.1177/0146167206287182

Poolokasingham, G., Spanierman, L. B., Kleiman, S., & Houshmand, S. (2014). 'Fresh off the boat?' racial microaggressions that Target South Asian Canadian students. *Journal of Diversity in Higher Education, 7*(3), 194–210. doi:10.1037/a0037285

Pratto, F. (1999). The puzzle of continuing group inequality: Piecing together psychological, social, and cultural forces in social dominance theory. *Advances in Experimental Social Psychology, 31*, 191–263.

Priest, N., Walton, J., White, F., Kowal, E., Baker, A., & Paradies, Y. (2014). Understanding the complexities of ethnic–racial socialization processes for both minority and majority groups: A 30-year systematic review. *International Journal of Intercultural Relations, 43*(Part B), 139–155.

Purdie-Vaughns, V., Steele, C. M., Davies, P. G., Ditlmann, R., & Crosby, J. R. (2008). Social identity contingencies: How diversity cues signal threat or safety for African Americans in mainstream institutions. *Journal of Personality and Social Psychology, 94*(4), 615–630. http://dx.doi.org/10.1037/0022-3514.94.4.615

Reed, S. (2019, January 10). *The damage of White feminism: An anecdote*. Chacruna. Retrieved from https://chacruna.net/the-damage-of-white-feminism-an-anecdote

Reid, L. D., & Foels, R. (2010). Cognitive complexity and the perception of subtle racism. *Basic and Applied Social Psychology, 32*(4), 291–301. doi:10.1080/01973533.2010.519217

Ríos, M., Romero, F., & Ramírez, R. (2014, March). Race Reporting Among Hispanics: 2010. Working Paper No. 102. Population Division. Washington DC: U.S. Census Bureau. Retrieved from https://www.census.gov/content/dam/Census/library/working-papers/2014/demo/shedding-light-on-race-reporting-among-hispanics/POP-twps0102.pdf

Rivas-Drake, D., Seaton, E. K., Markstrom, C., Quintana, S., Syed, M., Lee, R. M., . . . Yip, T. (2014). Ethnic and racial identity in adolescence: Implications for psychosocial, academic, and health outcomes. *Child Development, 85*, 40–57. doi:10.1111/cdev.12200

Roberts, R. E., Phinney, J. S., Masse, L. C., Chen, Y. R., Roberts, C. R., & Romero, A. (1999). The structure of ethnic identity of young adults from diverse ethnocultural groups. *Journal of Early Adolescence, 19*, 301–322.

Ryan, A. (2016). *At mama's knee: Mothers and race in Black and White*. Lanham, MD: Rowman & Littlefield. ISBN-13:978-1442265639. (As cited in https://www.washingtonexaminer.com/book-michelle-obama-invisible-because-shes-black)

Sabin, J. A., & Greenwald, A. G. (2012). The influence of implicit bias on treatment recommendations for 4 common pediatric conditions: Pain, urinary tract infection, attention deficit hyperactivity disorder, and asthma. *American Journal of Public Health, 102*(5), 988–995. doi:10.2105/AJPH.2011.300621

Saleem, F. T., Anderson, R. E., & Williams, M. T. (2020). Addressing the "myth" of racial trauma: Developmental and ecological considerations for youth of color. *Clinical Child and Family Psychology Review, 23*(1), 1–14. doi:10.1007/s10567-019-00304-1

Salter, P. S., Adams, G., & Perez, M. J. (2018). Racism in the structure of everyday worlds: A cultural–psychological perspective. *Current Directions in Psychological Science, 27,* 150–155.

Shin, R. Q., Smith, L. C., Welch, J. C., & Ezeofor, I. (2016). Is Allison more likely than Lakisha to receive a callback from counseling professionals? A racism audit study. *The Counseling Psychologist, 44*(8), 1187–1211. doi:10.1177/0011000016668814

Sidanius, J., & Pratto, F. (2012). Social dominance theory. In P. M. Van Lange, A. W. Kruglanski, E. T. Higgins, P. M. Van Lange, A. W. Kruglanski, & E. T. Higgins (Eds.), *Handbook of theories of social psychology* (pp. 418–438). Thousand Oaks, CA: Sage. doi:10.4135/9781446249222.n4

Sidanius, J., Pratto, F., & Devereux, E. (1992). A comparison of symbolic racism theory and social dominance theory as explanations for racial policy attitudes. *Journal of Social Psychology, 132*(3), 377–395.

Smith, W. A., Allen, W. R., & Danley, L. L. (2007). "Assume the position . . . you fit the description": Psychosocial experiences and racial battle fatigue among African American male college students. *American Behavioral Scientist, 51*(4), 551–578.

Smith, W. A., Mustaffa, J. B., Jones, C. M., Curry, T. J., & Allen, W. R. (2016). "You make me wanna holler and throw up both my hands!" Campus culture, Black misandric microaggressions, and racial battle fatigue. *International Journal of Qualitative Studies in Education, 29*(9), 1189–1209.

Smith, J., Puckett, C., & Simon W. (2015). *Indigenous Allyship: An Overview.* Office of Aboriginal Initiatives, Wilfrid Laurier University.

Solórzano, D., Ceja, M., & Yosso, T. (2000). Critical race theory, racial microaggressions, and campus racial climate: The experiences of African American college students. *Journal of Negro Education, 69,* 60–73.

Spatz. (2004, November 22). Soul searching on values [blog]. Community Section. *Daily Kos.* Retrieved from https://www.dailykos.com/stories/2004/11/22/75439/-Soul-Searching-on-values

Steele, C. M. (2010). *Whistling Vivaldi and other clues how stereotypes affect us.* New York, NY: Norton.

Stevenson, H. J. (1994). Racial socialization in African American families: The art of balancing intolerance and survival. *The Family Journal, 2*(3), 190–198. doi:10.1177/1066480794023002

Sue, D. W., Alsaidi, S., Awad, M. N., Glaeser, E., Calle, C. Z., & Mendez, N. (2019). Disarming racial microaggressions: Microintervention strategies for targets, White allies, and bystanders. *American Psychologist, 74*(1), 128–142.

Sue, D. W., Capodilupo, C. M., Torino, G. C., Bucceri, J. M., Holder, A. M., Nadal, K. L., . . . Esquilin, M. E. (2007). Racial microaggressions in everyday life: Implications for counseling. *American Psychologist, 62,* 271–286.

Sue, D. W., Lin, A. I., Torino, G. C., Capodilupo, C. M., & Rivera, D. P. (2009). Racial microaggressions and difficult dialogues on race in the classroom. *Cultural Diversity and Ethnic Minority Psychology, 15,* 183–190. doi:10.1037/a0014191

Sue, D. W., & Sue, D. (2016). Racial/cultural identity development in people of color: Therapeutic implications. In D. W. Sue & D. Sue (Eds.), *Counseling the culturally diverse: Theory and practice* (7th ed., pp. 355–388). Hoboken, NJ: Wiley.

Suleiman, M. W. (1988). *Arabs in the mind of America*. Brattleboro, VT: Amana Books.

Thai, C. J., Lyons, H. Z., Lee, M. R., & Iwasaki, M. (2017). Microaggressions and self-esteem in emerging Asian American adults: The moderating role of racial socialization. *Asian American Journal of Psychology, 8*(2), 83–93. doi:10.1037/aap0000079

Thompson, B. (2018, February 18). The racial wealth gap: Addressing America's most pressing epidemic. *Forbes*. Retrieved from https://www.forbes.com/sites/brianthompson1/2018/02/18/the-racial-wealth-gap-addressing-americas-most-pressing-epidemic/#526ba2497a48

Torres, L., Driscoll, M. W., & Burrow, A. L. (2010). Racial microaggressions and psychological functioning among highly achieving African-Americans: A mixed-methods approach. *Journal of Social and Clinical Psychology, 29*(10), 1074–1099. doi:10.1521/jscp.2010.29.10.1074

Torres, L., & Taknint, J. T. (2015). Ethnic microaggressions, traumatic stress symptoms, and Latino depression: A moderated mediational model. *Journal of Counseling Psychology, 62*(3), 393–401. doi:10.1037/cou0000077

Torres-Harding, S., Torres, L., & Yeo, E. (2020). Depression and perceived stress as mediators between racial microaggressions and somatic symptoms in college students of color. *American Journal of Orthopsychiatry, 90*(1), 125–135. doi:10.1037/ort0000408

Torres-Harding, S. R., Andrade, A. J., & Romero Diaz, C. E. (2012). The Racial Microaggressions Scale (RMAS): A new scale to measure experiences of racial microaggressions in people of color. *Cultural Diversity and Ethnic Minority Psychology, 18*(2), 153–164.

Thurston-Rattue, M., Kanter, J. W., Hakki, F., Kuczynski, A. M., Santos, M. M., Tsai, M., & Kohlenberg, R. J. (2015, July). Increasing racially diverse social connections through contextual behavioral science. Presented at the Association for Contextual Behavioral Science Conference, Berlin, Germany.

Utsey, S. O., Giesbrecht, N., Hook, J., & Stanard, P. M. (2008). Cultural, sociofamilial, and psychological resources that inhibit psychological distress in African Americans exposed to stressful life events and race-related stress. *Journal of Counseling Psychology, 55*(1), 49–62.

Van Ryn, M., Hardeman, R., Phelan, S. M., Burgess, D. J., Dovidio, J. F., Herrin, J., . . . Przedworski, J. M. (2015). Medical school experiences associated with change in implicit racial bias among 3547 students: A medical student CHANGES study report. *Journal of General Internal Medicine, 30*(12), 1748–1756. doi:10.1007/s11606-015-3447-7

Vandenberghe, L. (2008). Culture-sensitive Functional Analytic Psychotherapy. *The Behavior Analyst, 31*(1), 67–79.

Wadsworth, L. P., Morgan L. P., Hayes-Skelton, S. A., Roemer, L., & Suyemoto, K. L. (2016). Ways to boost your research rigor through increasing your cultural competence. *The Behavior Therapist, 39*(3), 76–92.

Walls, M. L., Gonzalez, J., Gladney, T., & Onello, E. (2015). Unconscious biases: Racial microaggressions in American Indian health care. *Journal of the American Board of Family Medicine, 28*(2), 231–239. doi:10.3122/jabfm.2015.02.140194

Watson, D., Clark, L. A., & Tellegen, A. (1988). Development and validation of brief measures of positive and negative affect: The PANAS scales. *Journal of Personality and Social Psychology, 54*, 1063–1070.

Williams, D. R., Yu, Y., Jackson, J. S., & Anderson, N. B. (1997). Racial differences in physical and mental health: Socio-economic status, stress and discrimination. *Journal of Health Psychology, 2*(3), 335–351. doi:10.1177/135910539700200305

Williams, M. T. (2014, February 2). Culturally incompetent therapy: When therapists do harm. *Psychology Today*. Retrieved from https://www.psychologytoday.com/us/blog/culturally-speaking/201402/culturally-incompetent-therapy-when-therapists-do-harm

Williams, M. T. (2019a). Adverse racial climates in academia: Conceptualization, interventions, and call to action. *New Ideas in Psychology, 55*, 58–67. doi:10.1016/j.newideapsych.2019.05.002

Williams, M. T. (2019b). Cultural competence 101: Teaching about race and racism. In M. T. Williams, D. C. Rosen, & J. W. Kanter (Eds.), *Eliminating race-based mental health disparities: Promoting equity and culturally responsive care across settings* (pp. 129–146). Oakland, CA: New Harbinger.

Williams, M. T. (2019c, September 1). Responding to microaggressions: Safety first. *Psychology Today*. Retrieved from https://www.psychologytoday.com/ca/blog/culturally-speaking/201909/responding-microaggressions-safety-first

Williams, M. T. (2020a). Microaggressions: Clarification, evidence, and impact. *Perspectives on Psychological Science, 15*(1), 3–26. doi:10.1177/1745691619827499

Williams, M. T. (2020b). Psychology cannot afford to ignore the many harms caused by microaggressions. *Perspectives on Psychological Science, 15*(1), 38–43.

Williams, M. T., Beckmann-Mendez, D., & Turkheimer, E. (2013). Cultural Barriers to African American Participation in Anxiety Disorders Research. *Journal of the National Medical Association, 105*(1), 33–41.

Williams, M. T., Chapman, L. K., Buckner, E., & Durrett, E. (2016). Cognitive behavioral therapy. In A. Breland-Noble, C. S. Al-Mateen, & N. N. Singh (Eds.), *Handbook of mental health in African American youth* (pp. 63–78). New York, NY: Springer. ISBN:978-3-319-25501-9

Williams, M. T., Chapman, L. K., Wong, J., & Turkheimer, E. (2012). The role of ethnic identity in symptoms of anxiety and depression in African Americans. *Psychiatry Research, 199*(1), 31–36. doi:10.1016/j.psychres.2012.03.049

Williams, M. T., Duque, G., Chapman, L. K., Wetterneck, C. T., & DeLapp, R. C. T. (2018). Ethnic identity and regional differences in mental health in a national sample of African American young adults. *Journal of Racial and Ethnic Health Disparities, 5*(2), 312–321. doi:10.1007/s40615-017-0372-y

Williams, M. T., Duque, G., & Wetterneck, C. T. (2015, November). Ethnic identity and regional differences as buffers against anxiety and depression in a national sample of African American young adults. In B. A. Feinstein & T. A. Hart (Chairs), The role of resilience in the health and well-being of minority populations. Symposium conducted at the Association of Behavioral and Cognitive Therapies, Chicago, IL.

Williams, M. T., Gooden, A. M., & Davis, D. (2012). African Americans, European Americans, and pathological stereotypes: An African-centered perspective. In G. R. Hayes & M. H. Bryant (Eds.), *Psychology of culture* (pp. 25–46). Hauppauge, NY: Nova Science. ISBN-13:978-1-62257-274-8

Williams, M. T., & Kanter, J. W. (2019). Promoting diversity and inclusion on college campuses. In M. T. Williams, D. C. Rosen, & J. W. Kanter (Eds.), *Eliminating race-based mental health disparities: Using contextual behavioral science to achieve equity and excellence across settings and communities* (pp. 243–276). Oakland, CA: New Harbinger.

Williams, M. T., Kanter, J. W., & Ching, T. H. W. (2018). Anxiety, stress, and trauma symptoms in African Americans: Negative affectivity does not explain the relationship between microaggressions and psychopathology. *Journal of Racial and Ethnic Health Disparities, 5*(5), 919–927. doi:10.1007/s40615-017-0440-3

Williams, M. T., Kanter, J. W., & Debreaux, M. (2017, November). Psychometric properties of the Anxiety Symptoms of Discrimination Scale in Black and White students. Poster session at the 51st Annual Convention of the Association of Behavioral and Cognitive Therapies, San Diego, CA.

Williams, M. T., Kanter, J. W., Peña, A., Ching, T. W. C., & Oshin, L. (2020). Reducing microaggressions and promoting interracial connection: The Racial Harmony Workshop. *Journal of Contextual and Behavioral Science, 16,* 153–161. doi:10.1016/j.jcbs.2020.04.008

Williams, M. T., Metzger, I., Leins, C., & DeLapp, C. (2018). Assessing racial trauma within a DSM-5 framework: The UConn Racial/Ethnic Stress & Trauma Survey. *Practice Innovations, 3*(4), 242–260. doi:10.1037/pri0000076

Williams, M. T., Mier-Chairez, J., & Peña, A. (2017). Tools for treating obsessive–compulsive disorder among Latinos. In L. T. Benuto (Ed.), *Toolkit for counseling Spanish-speaking clients* (pp. 139–172). New York, NY: Springer. ISBN:978-3-319-64880-4

Williams, M. T., Muir, R., Ching, T., & George, J. (2019, November 22). Racial microaggressions are socially unacceptable and aggressive. Paper presented at the Association of Behavioral and Cognitive Therapies, Atlanta, GA.

Williams, M. T., Printz, D., Ching, T., & Wetterneck, C. T. (2018). Assessing PTSD in ethnic and racial minorities: Trauma and racial trauma. *Directions in Psychiatry, 38*(3), 179–196.

Williams, M. T., Printz, D., & DeLapp, R. C. T. (2018). Assessing racial trauma with the Trauma Symptoms of Discrimination Scale. *Psychology of Violence, 8*(6), 735–747. doi:10.1037/vio0000212

Williams, M. T., Reed, S., & Aggarwal, R. (2020). Culturally-informed research design issues in a study for MDMA-assisted psychotherapy for posttraumatic stress disorder. *Journal of Psychedelic Studies, 4*(1), 40–50. doi:10.1556/2054.2019.016

Williams, M. T., Taylor, R. J., Mouzon, D. M., Oshin, L. A., Himle, J. A., & Chatters, L. M. (2017). Discrimination and symptoms of obsessive–compulsive disorder among African Americans. *American Journal of Orthopsychiatry, 87*(6), 636–645. doi:10.1037/ort0000285

Wong, G., Derthick, A. O., David, E. R., Saw, A., & Okazaki, S. (2014). The what, the why, and the how: A review of racial microaggressions research in psychology. *Race and Social Problems, 6*(2), 181–200. doi:10.1007/s12552-013-9107-9

Wood, P. H. (2015, May 19). The birth of race-based slavery. *Slate.* Excerpted from *Strange New Land: Africans in Colonial America* by Peter H. Wood. Published by Oxford University Press. Retrieved from http://www.slate.com/articles/life/the_history_of_american_slavery/2015/05/why_america_adopted_race_based_slavery.html

Yosso, T. J., Smith, W. A., Ceja, M., & Solórzano, D. G. (2009). Critical race theory, racial microaggressions, and campus racial climate for Latina/o undergraduates. *Harvard Educational Review, 79*(4), 659–690.

Zahodne, L. B., Kraal, A. Z., Sharifian, N., Zaheed, A. B., & Sol, K. (2019). Inflammatory mechanisms underlying the effects of everyday discrimination on age-related memory decline. *Brain, Behavior, and Immunity, 75,* 149–154. doi:10.1016/j.bbi.2018.10.002

INDEX

Tables and figures are indicated by *t* and *f* following the page number

For the benefit of digital users, indexed terms that span two pages (e.g., 52–53) may, on occasion, appear on only one of those pages.

Made in the USA
Las Vegas, NV
12 May 2023